Praise for Laur

Play Money
"A savvy insider's vastly entertaining line on aspects of the money game."
—*Kirkus Reviews* (starred review)

Beginner's Luck
"Funny, sweet-natured, and well-crafted...Pedersen has created a wonderful assemblage of...whimsical characters and charm."
—*Kirkus Reviews*

"A fresh and funny look at not fitting in."
—*Seventeen*

Going Away Party
"Pedersen shows off her verbal buoyancy. Their quips are witty and so are Pedersen's amusing characterizations of the eccentric MacGuires. Sentence by sentence, Pedersen's debut can certainly entertain."
—*Publishers Weekly*

Last Call
"Pedersen writes vividly of characters so interesting, so funny and warm that they defy staying on the page."
—*Hartford Courant*

Heart's Desire
"Funny, tender, and poignant, *Heart's Desire* should appeal to a wide range of readers."
—*Booklist*

The Big Shuffle
"Be prepared to fall in love with a story as wise as it is witty."
—*Compulsive Reader*

Deschutes
Public Library

Also by Laura Pedersen

Nonfiction
Play Money

Fiction
Going Away Party
Beginner's Luck
Last Call
Heart's Desire
The Sweetest Hours
The Big Shuffle

www.laurapedersenbooks.com

C.1

Buffalo Gal

a Memoir

Laura Pedersen

FULCRUM
GOLDEN, COLORADO

© 2008 Laura Pedersen

All rights reserved. No part of this book may be reproduced, stored in a
retrieval system, or transmitted in any form or by any means, electronic, mechanical,
photocopying, recording, or otherwise, without written permission from the publisher.

Library of Congress Cataloging-in-Publication Data

Pedersen, Laura.
  Buffalo gal : a memoir / Laura Pedersen.
    p. cm.
  ISBN 978-1-55591-692-3 (pbk.)
  1. Pedersen, Laura--Childhood and youth. 2. Pedersen, Laura--Homes and haunts--New
York (State)--Buffalo. 3. Novelists, American--20st century--Biography. 4. Novelists,
American--21st century--Biography. 5. Floor traders (Finance)--United States--Biography. I.
Title.
  PS3566.E2564Z46 2008
  813'.54--dc22
  [B]
                              2008026025

Printed on recycled paper in Canada by Friesens Corp.
0 9 8 7 6 5 4 3 2

Cover and design by Jack Lenzo
Cover images © Shutterstock

Fulcrum Publishing
4690 Table Mountain Drive, Suite 100
Golden, Colorado 80403
800-992-2908 • 303-277-1623
www.fulcrumbooks.com

Making friends is like investing in stocks;
find a few good ones and hold for the long term.

For Mary, Debbie, Heather, and Karen:
thanks for four decades of friendship.

And to my teachers Pete, Russ, Linda, and Kathy,
who made learning fun.

It is impossible for a man who is warm to fully understand one who is cold.

—Aleksandr Solzhenitsyn

Contents

Preface 1

One: God's Frozen People 3

Two: The First Event Leading Up to My Death 13

Three: American Buffalo...The King of Cool
 and Demon Rum 19

Four: He'd Always Have Paris...Trading Up...
 Danish for Beginners: 27

Five: Getting Up Your Irish...Family Diversity...
 Three's a Mob 36

Six: When Johnny Comes Typing Home...
 Wedding-Bell Blues 44

Seven: Onward Catholic Soldiers...Everything's
 Good in the Hood...The Sinusitis Capital 50

Eight: Buffalo Runs Riot 70

Nine: A Full House 76

Ten: Egg Salad Days...Beads of Paradise 85

Eleven: The Tundra Years 97

Twelve: Mary Tyler Moore for President...Hit
 Parade...The Americans with No Abilities Act 105

Thirteen: Born in the UUA...Keeping Kosher 121

Fourteen: Water Hazard...Is That Your Child? 134

Fifteen: Will Joke for Food...It's a Mad,
 Mad House...How I Learned to Cook 138

Sixteen: The Birth of an Entrepreneur...
 From Socks to Stocks...The Wizard of Odds 151

Seventeen: Everyone Was Groovy...Stardate 1965 163

Eighteen: Sleet Happens: The Blizzard of '77 170

Nineteen: Taking a Turn for the Nurse.. 175

Twenty: Bus Stop 182

Twenty-One: Enter, Stage Left...O.B. (Order Big)...
    A Decent Docent Doesn't Doze 189

Twenty-Two: Down on the Farm...
    Doing Time...Beat It.. 198

Twenty-Three: Real World 101 214

Twenty-Four: Earl and Me...The Sewing
    Circle Turns Square..220

Twenty-Five: Will Work for AC...
    Mom Turns Pro...The Mosquito Coast 226

Twenty-Six: Home at Sweet Home...
    Class Clown...Dressing Down.. 237

Twenty-Seven: Can't We All Get a Lawn?...
    Pedersen v. Pedersen...Telling It to the Judge...
    The Play within the Play..249

Twenty-Eight: Disappearing Act...
    The Walkway Less Traveled..260

Twenty-Nine: Are Red and Green Making You Blue? 268

Thirty: In All Probability 271

Thirty-One: Home Alone 275

Thirty-Two: It Could Be Worse.. 281

Thirty-Three: The (Sweet) Home Stretch...Faking It 286

Thirty-Four: When the Chips Are Down,
    the Buffalo's Empty... 298

Epilogue: The People's Republic of Buffalo..302

About the Author..*307*

Preface

I was fourteen years old when I first stepped onto the trading floor of the American Stock Exchange in downtown Manhattan. A retired stockbroker who happened to catch me studying data banks in *The Wall Street Journal* had kindly organized a tour. Since I was unaware that shorts and a tank top were not part of the official stock-exchange dress code, the security guard provided an extra-large men's trading jacket that hung down, dresslike, to my knees. On Wall Street less than an hour, and I was already taking part in a cover-up.

Moments later, I was standing at the pulsating heart of capitalism, inside a noisy, cavernous building six stories high that covered almost a full New York City block. Like the interior of a giant casino, there were bells ringing, wild shouts, and no natural light. You couldn't tell if it was night or day, summer or winter. However, unlike a casino, there were clocks everywhere and, high overhead, an electronic ticker tape with feverish green neon digits racing from left to right.

Throngs of middle-aged men hurtled past me while hollering and furiously waving their arms, using extended hands and fingers to throw signals toward clerks up in balconies. Every few seconds a burst of staccato yelling erupted from another area of the trading floor like a round of machine-gun fire and a rush of brokers sprinted past, heading in the direction of the cacophony. If the stock exchange didn't already exist, Stephen King would've created it.

Toward noontime, not everyone was as frantically busy. Traders munched on sandwiches like horses that feed while standing in the front of their stalls, able to gaze out and remain alert while chewing.

Others leaned against counters, talking and laughing and checking lottery tickets.

Suddenly a broker wearing a bright yellow jacket and black trousers came barreling around the corner, slipped on the mess of paper that littered the floor like large squares of confetti and landed flat on his back, giving the appearance of a giant bumblebee that had crash-landed. Five guys standing at the post nearest to where he went down casually removed signs that they apparently stored within arm's reach for just such occasions. The men proceeded to line up and solemnly raise numbers from one to ten, scoring the broker's fall as if he were an Olympian and they were the judges. Then, something happened with one of the stocks they were in charge of trading, a roar went up, and the action suddenly shifted to this area of the floor. Goofing-around time was over.

I was standing in the way, mesmerized by the pandemonium, and my tour guide swiftly ushered me to safety so I wouldn't end up as floorkill. Whatever they were doing, I wanted to do it too. Vowing to someday return, I went back to Buffalo to finish high school.

What I didn't know at the time was how well my unusual upbringing had prepared me for working in this strange and exciting place. It was Darwinian, or possibly Jungian. The spoils went to the quick and, it appeared to me, the crazy. When I did return, three and a half years later, I would become the youngest person ever to have a seat on the stock exchange.

One

God's Frozen People

Buffalo, New York, probably turns out more priests and nuns than any other city, except perhaps Rome. Not just because there's a large Catholic population to begin with, but because big blizzards can make you a believer. They can also make you a serious doubter—of weathermen.

I can't recall the weatherpersons predicting many of the really spectacular storms that swept in off Lake Erie, the kind that fill a person with an odd combination of terror and exhilaration that's better described as a spiritual awakening, or perhaps psychosis. Growing up in the Frost Belt, you learn to regard meteorologists as frustrated novelists—folks who wanted to study creative writing, but whose parents wouldn't pay for something so frivolous, and so they had to study meteorology. Weather forecasters were consulted for fashion more than anything else: Will the toupee blow off without a hat today? Are platform shoes really a sensible choice in an ice storm?

Our climatic soothsayers usually played it safe by predicting a "wintry mix," which covered everything from rain to hail to sleet to a full-fledged blizzard. Over the years I noticed there wasn't any springy mix, or autumny mix, or even a summery mix of sunshine, birdsong, and gentle zephyrs.

However, it was difficult to determine whether or not it was snowing simply by looking out the window. That's because nine months of the year our windows were shrouded in plastic to keep the wind from blowing the plates off the table and snowdrifts from accumulating behind the couch. Seen through these heavy-gauge tarps, the neighborhood appeared to be a gigantic blur that may as well have been McMurdo Station in Antarctica. You were on the other side of the looking glass and summer was just a rumor from there.

Buffalo usually receives the second largest annual snowfall of any city in the state, with flakes beginning in October and finally tapering off sometime around April, like a bad chest cold. The city itself gets around 85 inches, the suburbs 120 inches, and the towns slightly to the south about 160 inches per year. And that's the last you'll hear about inches, because a true Buffalonian measures snow in feet. Syracuse, 150 miles to the east, is considered slightly snowier, depending on the winter and whom you choose to believe. However, Buffalo retains the distinction of being on the receiving end of the truly dramatic storms that make national news. Said snow is accompanied by a face-numbing wind howling off Lake Erie, shivering thermometers with mercury registering three clapboards below the bulb, and icicles that, if they were to break off the eaves and hurtle to earth, could easily harpoon a child or split a grown man's head in two.

Lake-effect snow occurs when cold air passes over the relatively warm water of a large lake, picks up moisture and heat, and upon reaching the downwind shore is forced to drop the moisture in the form of snowflakes that can chip your teeth. The accompanying winds will not just turn your umbrella inside out, but carry it directly to Neptune, right along with anyone dumb enough to hang on.

And this is how Buffalo can have worse weather than neighboring Toronto, Canada. On the bright side, in summertime the lake acts as a massive air conditioner.

Early on I became used to hearing my mother describe me as a "blond-haired, blue-eared child." My first full sentence was most likely, "Turn the wheel into a skid." Ask anyone raised in Buffalo during the 1970s' energy crisis to complete the following sentences: If you're cold… (put on a sweater). Close the front door…(are we heating the entire neighborhood?). Shut the refrigerator door…(is there a movie playing in there?). Ninety percent of your body heat is lost if…(you don't wear a hat). Don't complain about the rain because…(it could be snow). There's no such thing as bad weather…(just the wrong clothing).

What Dylan Thomas called "useful presents" in his classic short story "A Child's Christmas in Wales" seemed to be the overriding theme when it came to gift giving. Christmas and Hanukkah weren't complete without the ritual exchanges of jumper cables, flashlights, sweaters, flannel bathrobes, hats, scarves, gloves, electric socks, and quilted slippers. Nothing says "Happy Holidays" quite like a woolen face mask!

Nowadays people dress lightly in winter on the theory that they only have to make it to the car and then into an office building or the mall. But those clunky automobile heaters of the seventies were slow to get rolling, and the inside of the vehicle was just beginning to thaw out by the time you arrived at your destination. Whereas people down South worry about their milk spoiling if left in the car, we were trying to prevent our fresh vegetables from becoming flash frozen.

A white car, like a long white coat, was NOT a good idea. If you were parallel parked in the street, the plow would heave the vehicle over the curb right along with the snow. A black car wasn't such a great idea either because of treacherous driving conditions on a dark night. The "be alert, don't get hurt" families opted for fire-engine red. Even then, it was best to put some identifying mark such as a Wonder Woman bobblehead on the dashboard so you didn't accidentally spend a lot of time scraping off someone *else's* red car. After a big snowstorm and a few plow runs, the street doesn't look anything like it did when you parked. You may as well be in *The Twilight Zone* creator Rod Serling's hometown of Binghamton, New York.

By the end of October, the Norse gods pulled the trigger on the starter pistol and winter was officially on. Some years it had already snowed and the temperature dipped below freezing by then. As a kid, you knew that your Halloween costume had better somehow incorporate a down parka, wool hat, mittens, and possibly boots. A ghost was a good idea; simply throw a sheet over your coat. A hobo worked well too: a little burnt cork on the face and a stick with a satchel made from a red bandanna over the shoulder. And you could never go wrong as the Abominable Snowman.

Growing up in a cold climate you don't realize how it is such a big part of your life until you leave. Upon moving to New York City shortly after my eighteenth birthday, I threw off my hat the way Mary Tyler Moore did in the opening of her show. Then I tossed out the heavy scarf, gloves, and boots like an ailing pilgrim reaching the promised land. Though only 450 miles away, Manhattan is usually ten to thirty degrees warmer than Buffalo and has about one-fiftieth the snowfall.

While working on the floor of the stock exchange in Manhattan that first winter, I was shocked when all the traders, clerks, and brokers dashed off the trading floor one day in early January. With so much money at stake, people often won't even leave during bomb scares or to use the bathroom, never mind to see a doctor or have lunch. There was so much paper scattered around that I thought a fire had broken out. Then a multimillionaire partner in a trading firm came skipping past and giddily announced, "It's snowing!" New York City may be only seven hours away from Buffalo by car, but it truly feels like one has crossed into a more temperate zone.

Another strange thing that New Yorkers do is open their windows in the middle of winter as a way of adjusting the temperature indoors. When Buffalonians raised during the energy crisis see an open window in winter, we practically faint, while hearing the distant voice of an irate father shouting, "Who is going to pay for that?!" It's the upstate New Yorker's version of recovered-memory therapy.

Manhattan gets a good snowstorm every few years, the kind that Buffalo kindergartners would think nothing of walking to school in. And it's hit by the occasional nor'easter, a gale-force rainstorm that leaves in its wake a mass graveyard of take-out menus and commuter-sized umbrellas. When a storm is predicted, even one with only a few inches of snow that will last a day at most, New Yorkers stampede their neighborhood delis and grocery stores, purchasing enough batteries and food to be trapped inside their apartments for a month. And not just your storm staples like milk, bread, and eggs, but pimentos, papayas, and taco shells, as if terrified by the thought of not being able to have an omelet with Gruyère cheese, capers, pearl onions, and shiitake mushrooms for eight hours.

The only weather system truly indigenous to Manhattan is the trash twister. This microtornado of pedestrian refuse—discarded wrappers, unwanted subpoenas, parking tickets, takeout menus, newspapers, and plastic bags—hovers between skyscrapers for an hour or so prior to settling back down on the pavement or blowing out to sea.

While New York City kids are taught how to ride the subways, in Buffalo I learned the correct way to pull on double mittens and wrap a scarf around my head, face, and neck mummy-style, so only my eyes showed through. My first driving lesson was how to rock the car back and forth in order to get unstuck in the snow. Next, I learned how to pump the brakes when skidding on ice (this was before antilock brakes). After a certain amount of practice we developed the fine art of banging frozen windshield wipers against the glass hard enough to chip off the ice, but not so hard that they snap in two.

Outdoor parades between October and April could be a problem, with only the hale and hearty participating in the high school marching band. Picture the mouthpiece of a metal instrument as the equivalent of a flagpole or pump handle, or anything else you really don't want to lick in the cold. The paramedics were called upon to deal with tongues frozen to flutes almost as often as they were for hypothermia.

It's only logical that a snowblower society like Buffalo is going to produce more gender confusion than the Bikini Belt, and perhaps for this reason it's a hub of lesbian folk-rock music and the potential staging ground for a bisexual revolution. Snowshoeing around town semiclad was a handwritten invitation to frostbite. Buffalo is no place to show a little leg, or even a little nose, for that matter. When it came to outerwear, we didn't care if it was from the men's or the women's department, as long as it was warm and waterproof. And menswear often claimed superiority in this area, antediluvian manufacturers assuming that only the menfolk were outside starting cars, while women in spike heels and pillbox hats warmed hot cocoa in the kitchen. Result: The Sasquatch Sisters. Darn, that would have been a good name for a band.

We wore fluffy down parkas that made a size-four woman resemble the Pillsbury doughboy. Snorkel jackets lined with neon orange and a gray ring of fur around the face suggested deranged bounty hunters and offered no peripheral vision. Add moon boots, ski gloves with the circumference of oven mitts, caps with earflaps that made you look like Piglet, electric socks, wool sweaters, bank-robber-style face masks with cutout eye- and mouth holes, a Buffalo Sabres scarf to top it all off, and you had a winter carnival at the psych center. Astronauts appeared to be dressing pretty lightly from where we were standing.

Mitten strings and mitten clips were forced upon children. (The mittens hang from opposite ends of a piece of yarn that goes through the coat sleeves, making mittens *theoretically* impossible to lose. Or clips attach to the wrist of each sleeve for the same purpose.) Then there's my dad, who is legally without memory the way some people are legally blind and became so tired of losing his gloves that he wore mitten clips until he was fifty-seven. He only retired them because he moved to New Mexico, where he now regularly misplaces his cap.

The good news is that in subzero temperatures, fashion mutations are understandably forgiven. Winter maxim: The warmer you feel, the dumber you look. It's a place where down jackets, quilted flannel shirts, and turtlenecks will never go out of style. An entire city clomping around like mushers in search of the Iditarod, we sported the layered look long before stores like Gap and Banana Republic mass-marketed it as a fashion statement. When onetime Buffalo resident Mark Twain said that naked people have little influence on society, he didn't have to worry about us. In fact, with almost nine months of chilly weather, Buffalonians needn't worry about storing bulky winter clothes and coats. We didn't even bother to move them to the back of the closet.

It's safe to say there aren't a lot of naturalists raised in Buffalo. However, we do know our types of snow, road salt, and tires. If it's true that Eskimos have fifty words for snow, then Buffalonians have fifty-one. We've added *Sisters snow*, a storm that leaves a sheet of ice on which your grandma slips and breaks a hip, and winds up in Sisters Hospital.

If any out-of-work war correspondent wants to do a book on Buffalo blizzards called *What They Carried*, let me get you started. First are the fifty-pound sacks of kitty litter that serve double duty. They sit in the trunk and provide ballast while navigating slippery turns, but if you get stuck on ice, simply break open a bag and scatter it under the wheels for traction. Somewhere in every car there's a blanket tucked away so you don't freeze to death if caught in a storm. There's also a first-aid kit. This is slightly mysterious because getting stranded in a blizzard doesn't usually pose a health threat aside from the aforementioned freezing to death. But women knew that the plastic container housing Band-Aids and surgical tape also made a good place to pee if you were stuck in the car for hours on end. Finally, the roll of paper towels and bottle of Windex. Cars are made better now, but back then road salt corroded the windshield washer–fluid dispenser, and the slushy salt spraying up from the street turned the glass a milky gray every two or three blocks, making it impossible to see. So at every stoplight, people hopped out to swab the windshield.

After a single winter, a car showed more rust than paint, especially if you didn't have a garage. When the salt corroded the bottom of an automobile so much that it was possible to see the pavement, cardboard was pasted over the holes and it was referred to as a Fred Flintstone car. Our shoes and boots had wavy white salt stains along the sides and over the tops, making them look as if the ocean had washed up to our laces before receding.

When we were stuck in our cars on the highway, we'd leave the heat on for a while and then, to conserve gas, turn the engine off until our faces began to go numb. If the blizzard was still raging when the motor finally conked out, we tried to get into the cars in front of or behind us. Eventually everyone would be packed into the few automobiles that could still run their heaters, like circus clowns crammed into a Volkswagen.

Every Buffalonian has a story about being stranded with strangers and the human chain stretching from a barn in search of firewood, or else being saved by the warmth of an animal, or the milk of a cow, or a clothesline leading back to the house. Women in Buffalo take Lock De-Icer wherever they go, the way folks in New York City carry around emergency Valium and Mace. Men can always unfreeze a lock by peeing into it.

For some reason known only to thermodynamic engineers, in the seventies the way-back window of a station wagon was always the last to freeze shut. Therefore, in the grocery-store parking lot you could usually spot some poor housewife rolling down the back window, squeezing through, and then climbing over the seats to open a front door using the inside handle.

The first naked people I saw were Canadians. And we weren't on a date together. The Canadian loonie was flying high, and so the Frostbacks would slip over the border to take advantage of cheaper prices and avoid higher taxes back home. After shopping, they'd change in the mall parking lot, ripping off old clothes along with the price tags on their new ones. I'm convinced that the majority of Buffalo's homeless population was outfitted in these Canadian castoffs, all conveniently located in and around mall parking lots. The other way to pick out Canadians, when they weren't undressing in the mall parking lot, was to catch them in the act of pouring vinegar on their fish and french fries.

When a storm blew in, all sorts of public service announcements came over the radio—what roads and bridges were dangerous or closed; what schools, churches, and community centers were canceling classes and events. Kids would call radio stations and impersonate their principals and superintendents in an attempt to close their own schools. Unfortunately, a special code was needed. In an effort to get the superintendent to make the call, high school students with cars would drive over to his house early in the morning, purposely slam on the brakes, and do doughnuts out front in order to make the roads appear treacherous. They were hoping he'd glance out the window and make up his mind at that very moment.

Most organizations didn't need passwords to announce cancellations, and so kids would call in the names of bogus groups just to see if they could get them announced on the radio—a meeting of the Rutabagas Recipe Exchange Club in the basement of Saint Benedict's, or Saint Jim Bob's Apple Bobbing Competition for the Left-handed. As the area was predominantly Catholic, we were pretty safe so long as we stuck the word *saint* in there somewhere. The downside was that the preponderance of schools and organizations beginning with *saint* resulted in a very long wait for those of us hoping to hear Sweet Home, the name of my school district. *Saint Mary* was good for about a dozen listings all on its own. The closings were followed by the usual litany of ads for plow services, tow-truck operators, and collision shops.

The other big entertainment when the snow filled the streets faster than the plows could remove it was pogeying, also known as bumper sledding. This entailed hiding behind a tree or newspaper box until a car went by, and then hitching onto the back bumper and being pulled along, your boots skating atop the icy slush. Drivers (especially those who were once Buffalo kids themselves) would be on the lookout for devotees of this treacherous sport, so you had to be ready to run if one stopped the car and jumped out to yell about how dangerous it was. Some drivers used the more Darwinian teaching technique of braking fast so that we'd slide underneath the back of the car, right between the wheels.

Oftentimes a ban on driving was issued, with the exception of emergency vehicles, including anyone involved in snow removal, police, fire, and medical services. So if I wanted to go someplace, it was necessary to sneak into my mom's closet and cadge her student-nurse cap (she'd since graduated to the real thing). Mom worked evening or zombie shifts and slept during the day. Her car was a stadium-sized yellow Oldsmobile Custom Cruiser station wagon with simulated wood paneling that was crashed in on the left side from bow to stern. It regularly needed jump-starting, the "heater" blew arctic blasts, the gearshift was dubious, the shock absorbers indifferent, and the brakes unpredictable, at best. It's doubtful the Joads would have taken it as a trade-in for their dust-bowl jalopy. The vehicle was, to quote the British writer Saki, "The one they call 'The Envy of Sisyphus,' because it goes quite nicely uphill if you push it."

However, during a snowstorm the rules of the road drastically change to favor the most battered wrecks. Lights and stop signs no longer matter, because if you brake you're likely to go into a hard-nosed skid. Thus, folks with cars in good condition must wait while the junkers briefly reign over icy streets. On the bright side, all the gargantuan potholes made by the plows and salt trucks are filled in for a few days and, for a change, you don't have to worry about dropping your transmission.

Rarely does anyone fall asleep while driving in Buffalo. When you take into account that Catholics usually have only one hand on the wheel, since the other is being used to bless themselves, it's just too darn exciting, like a ride at an amusement park. From a kid's point of view, the weather was a lot like God's will—everybody talked about it, but nobody could do anything about it.

Two

The First Event Leading Up to My Death

Unlike Chicago, which is named after an Indian word meaning "bad smell," and Toronto, called so after the Huron tribal word for "meeting place," how the city of Buffalo came upon its name has been much disputed. Some historians speculate that buffalo may have roamed the area centuries ago, much as repo men and antiabortionists do today. Or possibly the name was borrowed from a local creek whose Indian name meaning "beaver" was mistranslated, since the area is indeed rife with beaver.

Others say the name comes from the French, since the region was visited by French explorers in the 1700s. *Beau fleuve* means "beautiful river," referring to the nearby scenic Niagara River, which flows thirty-six miles from Lake Erie to Lake Ontario. Obviously this hypothetical Frenchman passed through in July or August, otherwise he would have instead opted for the more appropriate *beaucoup neige*, meaning "much snow."

I was born in Buffalo on October 8, 1965, under the dark architectural cloud of urban renewal, at the height of The Great Folk Music Scare. Although the chart-topping "California Dreamin'" had just been released by a newly formed group called the Mamas and the Papas, my fair complexion suggested Scandinavia, not Santa Barbara, as my latitudinal sister.

It was three in the afternoon on a Friday, exactly when school lets out. In my imagination the first words I heard were those of the obstetrician seeing this unruly mop of hair emerge and shouting, "Nurse, get

13

me a scrunchy!" But scrunchies had not yet been invented, and so the doctor probably called for a rubber band, hairnet, or, more likely, an electric hedge trimmer.

After locating an eight-pound infant under the tangle of strawberry blond curls, the attending nurse wrote "Pumpkin" on my birth card and possibly ordered a 1500-watt hair dryer for the maternity ward. It was a stroke of luck that I ended up in the newborn nursery and not the nearby farmers market. Perhaps during my mother's pregnancy a Buffalo Zoo poster had terrified her.

I was later informed by my parents that my birth was not an accident. However, the fact that I'm an only child was no accident either. Immediately following the delivery, my mother ensured that I was the end of the line. What did she know and when did she know it? A month earlier, the Beatles' newly released song "Help" had quickly shot up to number one on the pop charts.

As for my father, he probably didn't know much of anything since he was off chain-smoking Lucky Strike cigarettes in the waiting room. I was a southpaw born of two solid righties, and so perhaps there was talk of witchcraft.

Meantime, 450 miles away, in my nation's capital, Lyndon B. Johnson was serving his first elected term as president following the assassination of John F. Kennedy. An escalation of troops in Vietnam had brought the number up to almost 200,000, and the war became more controversial with every body bag that appeared on the evening news. Ironically, the nightly broadcast contained the refrain "Do you know where your children are?"

Demonstrators carried daffodils and chanted "flower power," a term coined by the Beat poet Allen Ginsberg to describe his nonviolent strategy of political action. Protestors held up placards that said Stop the Bombing and No Vietnamese Ever Called Me a Nigger. The term *politically correct* had not yet been invented.

Less than a month after my birth, the Quaker pacifist Norman Morrison set himself on fire and died outside Secretary of Defense Robert McNamara's Pentagon office in Washington, DC. McNamara, who witnessed the immolation, is reported to have vomited.

The early part of 1965 was also filled with unrest that could not be categorized as war related. Malcolm X had been assassinated in February, purportedly by black Muslims. The thirty-nine-year-old Black Nationalist was delivering a speech calling for a more militant prescription to furthering civil rights than Reverend Dr. Martin Luther King Jr.'s strategy of passive resistance. Likewise, the newly formed, beret-wearing Black Panthers were advocating armed combat in order to gain power over the existing establishment.

The following month, some six hundred black Americans marched the fifty-four miles of US Route 80 from Selma to Alabama's state capital of Montgomery in search of liberty and justice for all. Primary on their agenda was the right to vote, which was legal but often impossible because blacks were regularly kept from the polls. Only 65 of 15,100 local blacks were registered. A white Unitarian minister named James Reeb traveled south to support the march and was bludgeoned to death by white demonstrators.

In Los Angeles that August, riots erupted in the district known as Watts following the arrest of an African American on DWI charges and subsequent allegations of police brutality. Marvin Jackson coined the phrase "Burn, baby, burn" during five days of looting and fires that involved fifteen thousand National Guardsmen. This offered a preview of the racially charged urban uprisings to come in the latter half of the sixties. It's still hard to believe that it took until 1967 for the Supreme Court to finally strike down bans on interracial marriages.

Despite what one saw on the nightly news, it wasn't all riots, sit-ins, lie-ins, teach-ins, and bed-ins. Social reformer Betty Friedan had sold 3 million copies of *The Feminine Mystique*, thereby kick-starting the modern women's movement. Her book highlighted the frustration of housewives who'd supposedly done everything right by marrying well and moving to the suburbs, and it outlined the gap between what women supposedly had versus the reality of what they were experiencing. Harvard University had no women MBA candidates in 1965, and most medical schools capped admissions for women at 5 percent.

On television, Barbara Walters was only permitted to interview women and cover the four Fs—food, family, fashion, and furnishings.

In Delano, California, the grape pickers had gone out on strike and were joined by César Chávez, the cofounder of the National Farm Workers Association. These migrant laborers stood out as probably the most exploited group in the country, living and working in horrible conditions, and being paid a pittance, without job security or any other benefits.

Native Americans were also organizing and protesting. The United States government had signed more than four hundred treaties with them over the years and violated practically every one. In 1965, five Native American activists landed on Alcatraz Island, off the California coast near San Francisco, which had until 1963 been used as a maximum security prison. They claimed Alcatraz as rightfully theirs, citing an 1868 treaty between the United States and the Sioux Indians stating that any surplus land would be turned over to Indians. When federal marshals arrived, the activists left willingly. However, these types of Red Power protests would continue, and many would not end as peacefully. The American Indian Movement was organized in 1968 to fight for sovereignty and the protection of rights granted by treaties, laws, and the United States Constitution.

The sixties weren't a time of discontent only among minorities. Young people were searching for more freedom of expression and, thus, the counterculture was born. The *San Francisco Chronicle* first observed the beginnings of the hippie movement by noting that the Haight-Ashbury section had become "a hip hangout" for beatniks. If that wasn't evidence enough, 1965 is the year that the lava lamp was launched in the United States, The Who recorded "My Generation," and a rock band called the Grateful Dead formed in San Francisco.

Harvard professor and drug prophet Timothy Leary, famous for popularizing "Turn on, tune in, drop out," penned an essay called "Politics of Ecstasy," which advocated exploring LSD and other mind-bending hallucinogenic drugs to see how they altered consciousness. Participants in the psychedelic side of the sixties like to say that if you can remember it, then you weren't there.

The infamous motorcycle gang Hells Angels, along with Ken Kesey's communal hippie family, the Merry Pranksters, were at the height of their notoriety. When radical reformer Abbie Hoffman wasn't levitating the Pentagon, penning *Steal This Book,* or staging human be-ins where you went to just "be," he was tossing dollar bills from the New York Stock Exchange's visitors' gallery to watch the capitalists fight over them (in case you were wondering why there's now a Plexiglas partition).

With their espousal of free love, the counterculture was more accepting of homosexuality, which was still widely classified as a disease and shunned in polite society. Gay liberation symbolically began in Manhattan's Greenwich Village when, in June of 1969, homosexuals assaulted police officers raiding the Stonewall Inn, a gay bar. The following year people gathered for the first gay-pride parade.

For young men, the sixties centered on rejecting traditional bourgeois goals. This required growing long hair and pork-chop sideburns, donning fringed suede vests over wide-collared shirts open to the navel and flared trousers worn above the leather ankle boots of a tango dancer, and applying Hai Karate Oriental Lime cologne in large doses. When it came to women, the birth control pill had recently arrived on the mass-market contraceptive scene, thereby giving females a new sexual liberty, especially when combined with micro-miniskirts and thigh-high white go-go boots. Or as comedian Lily Tomlin said about the sixties, "the only thing we didn't pull out of was Vietnam." Though, no matter how many conquests any hippie worth his or her hip-hugger jeans was able to claim, it's doubtful they could compete with what had constituted the secret sex life of President John F. Kennedy.

In 1965, a loaf of bread cost twenty-one cents, a half gallon of milk fifty-three cents (delivered), and a five-pound bag of sugar was fifty-nine cents. Stamps were a nickel, the average price of a new home $21,500, and gas cost thirty-one cents for a regular gallon. *The Sound of Music* hit theaters on Memorial Day weekend, and admission was a quarter. In order to vote you had to be at least twenty-one, but to drink and be drafted you only had to be eighteen. Soon the hills were alive with the Vietnam cry of "Old enough to fight, old enough to vote," which helped lower the voting age, while increased concerns about drunk driving eventually raised the legal age to drink.

Three

American Buffalo...
The King of Cool and Demon Rum

Around the time I was born, Buffalo was the picture of an industrial city in decline, much like Cleveland, Detroit, Milwaukee, and Pittsburgh—all part of that mid-twentieth-century constellation of decay known as the Rust Belt. However, this had not always been the case.

Located on the western edge of New York State and along the eastern shore of Lake Erie, arguably the least great of the Great Lakes, the area that includes Buffalo was "purchased" from the Seneca Indians. This was accomplished through a series of slippery treaties and, one assumes, while looking down the barrel of a gun. The Indians believed the world was created on the back of a giant turtle, as opposed to the Christian Genesis story. Thus, it's safe to say the original inhabitants probably had slightly different views on land ownership. For example, that the earth should be shared by everyone, and that treaties are long-term agreements.

Much like today's planned communities that take their names from native trees and birds, like Oakwood and Meadowlark (after removing most of the aforementioned oaks, meadows, and larks for the development), Indian names were kept for the newly established English towns and villages—Tonawanda ("swift running water"), Cheektowaga ("place of the crabapple tree"), Lackawanna ("the meeting of two streams")—while the Natives were sent packing. Same with Buffalo's downtown streets called Huron, Mohawk, Pawnee, Tuscarora, Shoshone, and Scajaquada. Even Lake Erie takes its name from the tribe of Iroquois who once lived on the south shore. Their totem animal was the bobcat or puma, and they wore its tail as a ceremonial headdress. *Erie* means "long-tailed."

The Holland Land Company paid ten thousand dollars for a large parcel of land in 1797, which had the Genesee River to the east, Lake Ontario to the north, the Niagara River and Lake Erie to the west, and Pennsylvania to the south. In 1803, Joseph Ellicott, an agent for the company, laid out an elegant grid pattern with curves to accommodate Lake Erie, making Buffalo one of the first planned cities in America. He modeled it after Washington, DC, where he'd worked with his brother, civil engineer Major Andrew Ellicott, who was an assistant to Pierre L'Enfant, architect of the new nation's capital.

Buffalo was incorporated in 1816 and began to thrive when the Erie Canal was completed in 1825. This 363-mile-long artificial waterway from Buffalo to Albany and then down along the Hudson River to New York City made Buffalo the transfer point between canal boats and Great Lakes vessels. The first iron foundry went up in 1826, and the first steam engine plant in 1829. By 1845, the city also had a stove factory, bell foundry, nail factory, cabinet factory, and dozens of other plants turning out products such as mirrors, bathtubs, and picture frames.

In the meantime, the fertile soil of the Midwest had turned the Plains states into the breadbasket of America. While visiting Buffalo in October of 1861, the English author Anthony Trollope wrote, "I went down to the granaries and climbed up into the elevators. I saw the wheat running in rivers from one vessel into another, and from the railroad vans up into the huge bins on the top stores of the warehouses—for these rivers of food run up hill as easily as they do down."

Trollope failed to mention that when it came to nightlife, Buffalo was an early version of Las Vegas. The city, with its sailor-rich environment, was perhaps the most notorious port on the Great Lakes in the 1870s and 1880s, according to historian Frederick Stonehouse.

Back then, 60 percent of the buildings on Canal Street in the infamous waterfront area known as The Flats were bordellos, and 30 percent were taverns. A popular hangout in the 1880s and 1890s was Boney's Concert Hall, where the bar was almost seventy feet long and staffed by a dozen bartenders and thirty or so prostitutes with rooms upstairs. "A trip to America wasn't complete without including The Flats on the itinerary," writes Stonehouse.

By 1900, Buffalo was the eighth largest city in the country in terms of population, about to overtake Chicago for the number seven slot. The rapid development of railroads had turned it into a major grain and livestock market. In fact, Buffalo is where the grain elevator was developed. As the Northeast turned increasingly industrial, the Midwest provided its food supply.

The railroads allowed for large-scale steel production by linking Buffalo to the coalfields of Pennsylvania and utilizing iron ore from Minnesota that could be easily transported across the Great Lakes by massive cargo ships. The *Edmund Fitzgerald* was such a vessel; it sank in 1975 and became immortalized in a song by Gordon Lightfoot.

Just twenty miles north, the city of Niagara Falls was fast becoming the Silicon Valley of the new century, attracting the nation's best scientists and inventors with the possibilities of hydroelectric power. And now that reliable transportation was available to connect it with other major cities, the magnificence of the falls attracted travelers, artists, and famous writers. It became renowned as the honeymoon capital of the world. (Or "a bride's second biggest disappointment," according to Oscar Wilde.)

From an Indian word meaning "thundering water," Niagara is a remnant of the last ice age, when melting glaciers sent torrents of water down the Niagara River. With an almost ever-present rainbow arched above the mist, the falls are truly one of the most spectacular sights in the world. They provided the breathtaking scenery for the popular 1953 movie *Niagara*, a thriller starring blond bombshell Marilyn Monroe, as well as a nail-biting rescue scene from 1978's *Superman*, featuring Christopher Reeve as the man of steel.

The falls are actually two separate waterfalls. On the American side is the cleverly named American Falls, which is 1,060 feet wide and 167 feet high. Just opposite, but on the Canadian side, is Horseshoe Falls, which is 2,600 feet wide and 158 feet high. Unfortunately for Americans, the Canadians got the slightly better-looking falls. Fortunately for Americans, many people say the best view of it is from the American side.

The transcontinental railroad, completed in 1869, was the final piece making it possible to transport large amounts of raw materials, supplies, and finished merchandise from one end of the country to the other. With the Erie Canal and a major railway hub, Buffalo was now a significant link between the old country and the new frontier, with goods moving from Europe and the Southeast to New York City, up to Buffalo on the canal, and then across to Chicago and the fast-developing Plains, Rockies, and California.

In 1901, Buffalo boasted sixty millionaires, more per capita than any other city in the United States. This new wealth, created by entrepreneurial titans of business and industry, allowed Buffalo's leaders to build a culturally and architecturally grand city with the latest and greatest in commercial and governmental buildings, public parks, and elegant mansions. Spare-no-expense commissions attracted such famous architects as Stanford White, Louis Sullivan, H. H. Richardson, and Frank Lloyd Wright. The park system, planned by renowned landscape architect Frederick Law Olmstead, became a splendid sanctuary for people seeking to escape the mills and factories and enjoy nature, much like Central Park in Manhattan, which Olmstead had designed a decade earlier.

The residents of Buffalo proudly sent two sons to the White House—Millard Fillmore (usually ranked as one of the worst presidents) and Grover Cleveland (ranked slightly better than the worst presidents). Prior to heading to Washington, Cleveland was mayor of Buffalo and, before that, sheriff of Erie County. In his capacity as sheriff, he put an end to public hangings by installing a screen in front of the proceedings. Furthermore, he saved the citizens the ten dollars typically paid to the hangman by pulling the gallows lever himself.

Buffalo was a center of social activism that hosted the first NAACP conference in 1905 and had famously helped slaves along the Underground Railroad; once across the Niagara River, fugitive slaves were free. But before we start reminiscing about how Negro spirituals used to communicate information about the journey north, let's make it clear that there was also a branch of the Ku Klux Klan operating in the area.

Buffalonians were satisfied to have their city chosen as the site of the 1901 World's Fair (known as the Pan-American Exposition), a six-month-long national event recognizing the industrial and cultural achievements of the United States, also aimed at promoting trade and friendship among the States, Canada, and Latin America. It showcased the new technological breakthrough known as electricity at America's first hydroelectric power plant in nearby Niagara Falls. As a result, Buffalo was one of the first cities in North America to be electrified.

Unfortunately, the 1901 World's Fair in Buffalo would become better known as the place where President William McKinley was assassinated by the anarchist Leon Czolgosz. Vice President Theodore Roosevelt was sworn in at the Wilcox Mansion up the street. His inauguration in September of 1901 occurred at the height of the city's grandeur. It was wealthy, thriving, and self-confident. Gracious mansions with wide terraces and elaborate gardens lined Delaware Avenue. On the periphery were dozens of factories and warehouses. Grain elevators and steel mills that exhaled flames like fire-breathing dragons towered over the waterfront. The enormous, smoke-belching steel plants in Lackawanna coated the area in a layer of orange dust that resembled fluorescent pollen when it settled on windowpanes.

You'll often hear people talk about downtown Buffalo. Prosperity didn't last long enough to have an uptown.

Perhaps the ultimate irony is that frigid Buffalo is the place where air-conditioning was invented. While working in the drafting department of the Buffalo Forge Company in the early 1900s, Willis Carrier received a

United States patent on an "apparatus for treating air." This engineer from the Snowbelt would pave the way for the creation of the Sunbelt boom. "And think of the difference he's made," columnist Molly Ivins wrote about the King of Cool. "As anyone who has ever suffered through a brutal summer can tell you, if it weren't for Carrier's having made human beings more comfortable, the rates of drunkenness, divorce, brutality, and murder would be Lord knows how much higher. Productivity rates would plunge 40 percent over the world; the deep-sea fishing industry would be deep-sixed; Michelangelo's frescoes in the Sistine Chapel would deteriorate; rare books and manuscripts would fall apart; deep mining for gold, silver, and other metals would be impossible; the world's largest telescope wouldn't work; many of our children wouldn't be able to learn; and in Silicon Valley, the computer industry would crash."

Being home to the invention that would spark the industrial South marked the start of an unusual pattern that continued throughout the century: Buffalo often acted as its own worst enemy—every move made in the name of innovation and increased productivity seemed not to result in the desired progress, but in just the opposite, providing local citizens with another reason to leave.

Prohibition (1920–1933) was perhaps the exception, since Buffalonians regarded the national alcohol ban as more of an opportunity than an encumbrance. Much of the fuel that made the twenties roar was ethanol, better known as rotgut, firewater, hooch, bathtub gin, and moonshine. The "noble experiment," as it was called by President Hoover, served to make the Great Lakes a headquarters for rumrunners between the United States and Canada, which had loophole-ridden Prohibition laws. Although the province of Ontario outlawed the retail sale of liquor, the Canadian government approved and licensed distilleries and breweries for its manufacture, distribution, and export.

In the meantime, there was no shortage of bays, coves, inlets, and other hiding places to prevent the heartland from experiencing an alcohol drought. Secondary fuel tanks, false floorboards, steamer trunks with fake bottoms, and even coffins were used to hoodwink police, the Coast Guard, and customs officials. Hundreds of boats hauled millions of gallons of illicit booze across the lakes, while bullets occasionally whizzed past as bootleggers and government agents did battle. One trick of the trade was to dump the containers overboard and return for them later, which often resulted in delighted fishermen and beach-combers harvesting divine gifts from the sea. If patrol boats came too close before the bootleggers could unload, they'd oftentimes set fire to their vessels in order to destroy the evidence.

Local thirst was easily slaked by the home-brewing operations of immigrants, and literally hundreds of speakeasies popped up overnight. Even Buffalo mayor Francis Xavier Schwab, part owner of a local brewery, was charged with manufacturing and selling beer, in 1922. He pleaded no contest and promptly paid a five-hundred-dollar fine.

Another happy-hour option was the booze cruise, a short ferry-boat ride from Buffalo to Fort Erie, Canada. Bootleggers also made profitable use of this narrow stretch of the Niagara River, which served as a rather ungovernable border between the two countries.

That the city of Buffalo was heavily Catholic enabled it to take full advantage of the exemptions from the Prohibition laws that applied to alcoholic beverages used for sacramental purposes. Interestingly, the demand for sacramental wine increased by 800,000 gallons between 1922 and 1924, according to a report by the Department of Research and Education of the Federal Council of the Churches of Christ. Obviously so much clean living was creating lots of converts.

Back in the twenties, Buffalo was not only lively with commerce and cocktails, but it was also recognized as one of the most beautiful cities in the world, especially Delaware Avenue, with its majestic canopy of Dutch elm trees. In 1929, just before the stock market plunged the economy into crisis, the New York Central Railroad built its palatial new terminal in Buffalo, a symbol of the bustling energy of this transportation giant.

The city prospered until midcentury, when its population peaked at 580,000 (twice what it is today). People came from surrounding towns and even Canada to shop at the large downtown department stores like AM&A's and Kleinhan's, and to see nationally known big bands play at local nightclubs.

But the Central could not hold. A perfect storm had begun, only this time it wasn't a blizzard. With the birth of jet engines and the building of an interstate highway system in the forties, railroads were eclipsed as the transportation of choice. In the fifties, the Saint Lawrence Seaway began siphoning business away from Buffalo. The city was unable to reinvent itself as manufacturing jobs moved abroad. In Mexico, plant workers earned one-tenth of what Bethlehem Steel employees made. As a result, local factories were shuttered one by one, year after year.

Dutch elm disease destroyed most of the trees lining stately Delaware Avenue and other streets, while highways ruined much of the rest of downtown. What was once known as the City of Light had by the seventies become the City of Blight. Strong unions, which had done so much to support the rights of the workers, were making demands that the steel companies could not meet and still remain profitable against competition from overseas.

Buffalo had always been hailed as a solid union town and viewed this as a source of economic strength, not the mark of death. In fact, the national longshoremen's union started at the Swannie house near the Buffalo waterfront. And Buffalo was the only place in the country that could boast a grain-scoopers union. When I was growing up, a popular joke was, "How many people work at Bethlehem Steel?" The answer: "About one-third." Others dubbed the city "Mistake on the Lake." (This moniker is shared by Cleveland, Ohio.)

Economic decline was exacerbated by Mother Nature. The blizzard of 1977, with its twenty-foot snowdrifts that buried cars and homes, generated a run of one-liners by Johnny Carson, and Buffalo became once and for all a national joke synonymous with snow. Even today you'd be hard pressed to get a local citizen to turn out for a conference on global warming. It's tough to be all that concerned about the environment when it's so busy trying to kill you.

Make fun of the blizzards all you want. Buffalonians are quick to tell you that they're quite happy not having to worry about earthquakes, volcanoes, monsoons, and tsunamis.

Four

He'd Always Have Paris...
Trading Up...Danish for Beginners

My father, John Anders Pedersen, moved to Buffalo in 1955 to take a job as a court reporter. He was born in Manhattan in 1931, shortly after the start of the Great Depression, and named after John the Baptist—not the apostle John, a pope John, John Donne, or even Johnnie Walker. I assume this was because John the Baptist was also an only child of older parents.

My father's folks were both immigrants from Denmark, a tiny Scandinavian country on a peninsula north of Germany that had only 3 million people back in the early 1900s, with almost a quarter of them settled near the capital, the port city of Copenhagen. Denmark is probably best known for being the home of famous fairy-tale author Hans Christian Andersen, who viewed himself as the original ugly duckling. His friends didn't exactly rush to dissuade him from this notion, nor the local women to declare themselves. One friend described Andersen as a "long, thin, fleshless, boneless man, wriggling and bending like a lizard with a lantern-jawed cadaverous visage." Once again, great angst becomes great art.

Dad's mother, Betty Nora Andersen, was born in Jutland, the largest of the three main islands that make up the country of Denmark. In the early 1920s, she was working as a shampoo girl at a Copenhagen barbershop owned by Grandpa's father, and that's where they met.

My grandfather, Peder Hjalmar Ingerman Pedersen, was born in

Copenhagen in 1902. Like my father and me, he was also an only child, but this was a result of his four older sisters' deaths during infancy. As to being Peder Pedersen, that's a popular joke that Scandinavians play on their kids—Nils Nilsson, Lars Larson, John Johnson. The *son* or *sen* at the end of the last name means "son of."

As was the custom in most Danish working-class families at the time, Grandpa left school upon completing the eighth grade. At age twelve, he took a job as a baggage boy in the Copenhagen railroad station. The "war to end all wars" (we weren't yet savvy or cynical enough to start numbering them) was under way, and Denmark, which remained neutral, was a hub of wartime activity. Grandpa earned so much money in tips that he planned to retire by the age of twenty.

However, World War I came to a close when he was sixteen, the rail station fell silent in postwar hard times, and Grandpa took a job as a waiter in a local restaurant. A waiters' union existed in most European countries back then, and his was soon called to go on strike when an establishment in Copenhagen gave two women jobs serving tables (oh, horrors!).

After being unemployed for several months, and uninterested in working at the barbershop, Grandpa headed down to the docks and took a waiter position aboard a steamship. He was dating my grandmother, so they had to curtail their romance while she stayed behind in the hair salon and he went off to seek his fortune.

The ship took Grandpa to Paris, where he found work in the kitchen of a hotel restaurant. He didn't speak a word of French, but was a hearty young man about six feet tall, with so much wavy brown hair on top that it balanced out a somewhat overly large nose on an otherwise handsome face.

On the first day at his new job, Grandpa was given the task of delivering a room-service tray. He was surprised to find two young, nubile French women lying naked atop their beds. They giggled at his embarrassment, tipped generously, and said to return when he was off duty. After a typical Scandinavian upbringing (to call it conservative would be like saying that pickled herring is slightly fishy), Grandpa decided he was going to like France very much. However, that after-noon, when the dumbwaiter came up and the chef shouted *"Chaud!"* (hot), Grandpa picked up the tray and promptly dropped it back down the chute and onto the chef's head. So ended Paris. Grandpa was sent packing and returned to the shipyard looking for work.

A steamer was bound for Cuba, where the crew would take on enormous sea turtles and lash them to the deck for the purpose of being made into ladies shoes and handbags back in the States. It was the beginning of the Jazz Age, and Americans who craved exotic food and fashion from all over the world were willing to pay dearly to get it. One of Grandpa's jobs was to pour buckets of water over the turtles to keep them alive during the long voyage. He particularly liked the port of Havana because you could roll up a dollar, tie it with string, and lower it over the side of the ship, whereupon a rowboat would magically appear and a boy would replace the bill with a bottle of rum.

When Grandpa's ship docked in Hoboken, New Jersey, he hopped off and lit out for the smorgasbord tables of Manhattan. From an immi-gration standpoint, his timing was perfect. The economy was going gangbusters, and America welcomed industrious newcomers, especially from Europe. An immigrant was able to wash ashore and apply for first papers, which almost guaranteed citizenship.

It was 1923 and horses and buggies were still as prevalent on New York City streets as automobiles. Not that Grandpa could afford either a carriage or a Model T, since he started life in the United States with only five dollars in his pocket.

Telephones, elevators, and central heating, all still relatively new, were found only in the mansions of the wealthy, such as those owned by industrialists like the Carnegies, Astors, and Vanderbilts. These robber barons turned blue bloods had been clever enough to make their mil-lions before the advent of income tax in 1913.

The poor were less fortunate, especially when one considered the circumstances in which most lived and worked. On March 25, 1911, the Triangle Shirtwaist Factory fire in the heart of Manhattan (now the area known as Greenwich Village) resulted in the deaths of 146 workers, mostly young women, because doors were kept locked by management to control the labor force. Probably one of the worst workplace disasters since the start of the Industrial Revolution, this tragedy brought national attention to labor exploitation, particularly the treatment and compensation of women toiling away in sweatshops. As a result, workers organized into powerful unions that would protect their rights and promote safe working conditions.

Women were also agitating to participate in their so-called democracy. After substantial groundwork, begun most notably by Elizabeth Cady Stanton back in the 1840s and taken up by Susan B. Anthony, women were finally granted the right to vote in 1919 with the passage of the Nineteenth Amendment. (Neither suffragette lived to see her dream become a reality.) Some cities instituted a rule that voters had to state their age to enter the polls, with the hope that vanity would keep women at home. No such luck.

Once settled in Manhattan, Grandpa took jobs in Scandinavian restaurants, the precursors to the all-you-can-eat buffet. Only instead of shrimp and roast beef, the specialties were Norwegian yellow-pea soup, Havarti and Jarlsberg on pumpernickel, smoked eel and mackerel, *medisterpølse* (Danish pork sausage), reindeer meatballs, and *forloren skildpadde* (mock turtle stew), all washed down with a strong, clear liquor called aquavit. For dessert there was lingonberry pie, almond fingers, raisin meringue, and gingered apple ring.

Between waiter jobs, Grandpa lived on bunches of bananas and went to the movies all day since both cost only a nickel. In 1990, when he saw the book *New York on $25 a Day*, he laughed and said that he'd often done New York on less than twenty-five cents a day. In 1930, Grandpa would get lunch at the Automat and then stand on the corner of Thirty-Third Street and Sixth Avenue watching the Empire State Building rise above the skyline. Mohawk Indians known as "skywalkers" worked fearlessly along narrow steel beams fifty stories in the air. For the most part, times were good, and Grandpa eventually saved enough to marry his sweetheart back in Denmark.

Immigration laws continued to tighten in the late twenties, and Grandma wasn't able to enter the United States for another year. When she finally arrived in Manhattan, Grandma perfected her English by copying songs from church hymnals. Like so many Scandinavians, they were Lutheran, which is still the official religion of Denmark.

In appearance, Grandma was slender and quick-moving, like a bird. She was the same age as the Swedish-born film star Greta Garbo and bore an amazing resemblance to the stunning screen actress. People constantly stopped her on the Manhattan subway, mistaking her for Garbo, who was by then famous for such movies as *Queen Christina* and *Camille*. Though one wonders if passengers didn't think it odd that the great Garbo would be slumming as a straphanger on the A train.

During the thirties, Grandma began investing in the stock market—companies like IBM, Pepsi-Cola, General Motors, American Tobacco, and AT&T. It was the Depression, and prices were low compared to their recent heyday in the twenties. Ledger entries show her buying shares at five-eighths and selling them a week later at seven-eighths, or buying at fourteen and one-quarter and selling a month later at eighteen. There were losses, but they were systematically cut and only about one-eighth the size of her gains.

Grandma was a day trader by 1930s' housewife standards. Armed with only the newspaper, she bought and sold like a professional, letting profits run and cutting losses short. Though this sounds easy and commonsensical, it's actually rather difficult, as any trader knows, because the practice goes against every natural instinct, like trying not to break a fall by outstretching your hands.

Grandma remained in the United States as a resident alien throughout her life and had to bicycle down to the post office and register every year. It's a good thing that Denmark never declared war on the United States or she probably would've been sent to an internment camp and forced to design chairs. Worse, Americans might have been without Legos, purple-haired troll dolls, and butter cookies.

31

Speaking of war, the only fact about Denmark that still manages to make American high school history books is the phenomenal organization and heroic efforts of its resistance movement throughout World War II. Though the Nazis easily occupied this tiny country adjacent to Germany, the powerful Danish underground managed to save about 7,200 of their 7,800 resident Jews from extermination by smuggling them out of the country, mostly by using small boats that carried them to neutral Sweden. There was little time to prepare, and participants were without the benefit of blogs, e-mail, or cell phones that play customized ringtones.

For the past two centuries, the Danes have been viewed as a peaceful and progressive people—the first to prohibit slavery and make schooling compulsory and free. Like the wolves in Yellowstone National Park, they have no known natural predators that I'm aware of. However, the 2006 "cartoon scandal"—in which a Danish paper printed cartoons lampooning Islam—possibly altered that legacy.

Then there is the sedate Little Mermaid statue in the harbor, a symbol of Copenhagen drawn from a Hans Christian Andersen fairy tale. It has endured two beheadings, lost a right arm, been painted red, draped in a protest burka, and even blasted off the perch with dynamite.

✽ ✽ ✽

Grandpa learned English by listening to people talk in restaurants and kitchens, and he never lost his Danish accent (think of Danish comedian/pianist Victor Borge). Whenever I suggested that Grandpa teach me some Danish he'd say, "Why do you want to learn Danish? It's a troat disease." He eventually developed an unusual Danish-Brooklyn dialect that bore a remarkable resemblance to the last bit of bath-water going down the drain. Like many European immigrants, Grandpa couldn't pronounce the "th" sound, thereby giving us words like *tick* instead of *thick*, *tree* instead of *three*, and *turd* instead of *third*. Or as Victor Borge liked to say about the matter, "To pronounce 'th' you need to stick your tongue out. Denmark is a cold country and you don't want to stick out anything you can't be sure you'll get back in again."

Unable to say the "j" sound very well, a "y" was slid in as a soft substitute. From speaking with Grandpa as a child I picked up some unusual pronunciations that were unwittingly carried into adulthood, such as *yetty* for *jetty*, *yaywalking* for *jaywalking*, and a person who couldn't take criticism was said to be *tin-skinned*.

Grandpa only went back once to visit his parents in Denmark. He walked in the front door and scared his mother so badly with this surprise appearance that she said, "Don't ever do that again." He never did. Years later he heard that his father was in a nursing home in Copenhagen, blind and fond of starting happy hour at 5:00 AM instead of the more traditional 5:00 PM. One afternoon, following a liquid lunch, my great-grandfather wandered outside and was killed by a streetcar.

Grandpa worked as a waiter into his eighties and only stopped temporarily when Grandma had a stroke and needed full-time care at home. Whereas she had always been miserable, even when healthy, throughout his long life Grandpa was easygoing and fun loving; he would twirl plates in the air like a circus juggler, spin teacups on saucers so they appeared on the brink of crashing to the floor, and make doves and skyscrapers out of napkins as if trained in Japanese origami.

Working as a waiter for sixty years had paid the bills, but nothing more. So, in retirement he was left with a modest Social Security income. However, Grandma's stock investments had grown substantially from that initial outlay of $757.50 for one hundred shares of a small company called Radio Corporation, which later became RCA. And when she died in her early sixties, Grandma left Grandpa a nice portfolio.

Other than a bronze Camaro and his apartment, Grandpa didn't purchase anything after Grandma died—quite the opposite. He threw away everything except the furniture and a place setting for one. Out went the linens, dishes, bric-a-brac, and anything else nonessential to daily life, thereby developing a new school of design best described as Danish monastic. When I lived with Grandpa while searching for an apartment in Manhattan, he was forced to borrow an extra plate and glass from a friend.

Grandpa was charming. Waitresses were forever giving him extra scoops of ice cream, and widows were always trying to get his phone number and sit next to him. He had twinkling blue eyes and a mane of thick white hair that women wanted to run their fingers through. As he grew older, the number of women pursuing him only increased, since there were fewer available men around. Even his optometrist, an attractive Danish woman, continued passing him on eye exams so that he could renew his driver's license, right up until he died. Truth be told, on the DMV version of the eye exam, he'd only have received credit for identifying the building.

In his eighties, Grandpa once left the apartment at nine in the evening with a bottle of Cutty Sark tucked under his arm, saying he was off to assist a woman who'd asked him to translate a few letters written in Danish. Sometime after midnight I went to bed and Grandpa still wasn't home.

The next morning I asked, "So, how were the letters?"

He smiled impishly and said, "There weren't any letters."

When Grandpa was eighty-eight years old, he went to the doctor and the man's stethoscope practically fell off his neck; the office hadn't heard from Grandpa in over ten years. That long-ago visit had been handled by the doctor's father, who'd diagnosed Grandpa with lung cancer and then promptly passed away himself. After a certain length of time the office had closed Grandpa's file.

"Do you smoke?" asked the stunned physician.

"No, I quit," replied Grandpa.

"Excellent," the doctor replied and wrote something on his chart. "How long did you smoke?"

Grandpa had to think for a moment and do some math. "Seventy years," he finally answered.

Several months later, Grandpa enacted a typically Scandinavian death. One morning shortly before his eighty-ninth birthday he said, "Take me to the hospital. I'm done."

He seemed okay to me. Maybe he meant that he was done with breakfast. "Done with what?" I asked.

"I did everything I wanted to do. The leaves to the dining room table are in the closet, my tax returns are in the desk drawer, and the keys to the car are on the TV."

I took him to the hospital where the admissions person laughed in my face to hear his name was Peder Pedersen. No faker, Grandpa climbed in bed, closed his eyes, and refused everything but water. I said, "I'll call Dad," who was now living in New Mexico.

"No. I don't want to bother him," replied Grandpa.

"He's retired. It's not that big a bother."

Dad arrived. Grandpa said hello and that he shouldn't have bothered. Dad said it was no bother, and Grandpa died.

Five

Getting Up Your Irish...
Family Diversity...Three's a Mob

While my father is 100 percent Danish, my mother's ancestors hail from the British Isles—a maltlike blend of Irish, Scottish, and English. In the great oral tradition of the Celts, even those with little schooling were able to recite epic poems, often in Greek or Latin. Certainly the damp and dark climate of industrial upstate New York continued to foster this custom. Though we have no heath or bog in Buffalo, over 50 percent of the days are gray. Following in the footsteps of their gifted literary ancestors, many of Mom's forebears became men of letters; more specifically, they became letter carriers employed by the post office.

My mother, Ellen Elizabeth Watson, was born January 2, 1937, and given the names of her two grandmothers. She has a brother, James Eugene Watson, who is ten months younger, commonly known as an Irish twin in Buffalo, and a sister, Sarah Frances, three years her junior.

Whereas Uncle Jim and Aunt Sue look more typically Irish, with wavy light hair and pink skin like their mother, Mary Frances Costello, Mom is black Irish in appearance, with dark curly hair, hazel eyes, and glass-of-milk skin. To see her as a young girl, pick up any copy of Anne Frank's diary and consult the author photo on the cover. As an adult, her uncanny resemblance to England's Queen Elizabeth I has been commented on by many people.

The most distinguishing feature about Mom is her natural Afro. She traces it back to the Spanish Armada, when part of the fleet was wrecked off the coast of Ireland. Once, when a gas pump malfunctioned and seven gallons of fuel sprayed her, the station attendant looked alarmed upon seeing Mom's hair standing on end, thinking it was a result of the accident rather than her normal coiffure. Otherwise, she's the only person I know with skin paler than mine and who can get burned by the moon on a cloudy night.

My maternal grandfather, Alexander Baker Watson, was a native of Buffalo but worked as an itinerant newspaperman. He certainly wasn't constantly on the move because he had any difficulty finding stories. No, the trouble was that more often than not back in the phone-booth and fedora days, the truly good stories were *about* him rather than *by* him. Grandpa Watson was by all accounts a talented drinker with a writing problem, and this led to an endless round of hirings and firings.

"Aleck worked the night beat and could be seen most days trolling and casting in the river from a small rowboat," wrote his colleague Anne McIlhenney Matthews. "He knew where the best fish haunts were and seldom came home without a sizable catch. Often he brought presents of the fish to headquarters. He would forget what desk drawer he put them in, with the obvious result. Being a cub and eager to please it was usually my job to clean up. Aleck worked on most newspapers in Buffalo at one time or another, got fired every time, either for nonappearance or for insulting the city editor, who quite often hired him back. After a bit of bourbon to get the creative juices flowing he was known to heave every typewriter in the pressroom out the window. Luckily it faced out onto the old Terrace tracks so the shower of metal didn't kill anyone below."

Grandpa Watson's newspaper cronies would get up to such tricks as installing drugstore-style pay phones in the pressroom to avoid being scooped by one another. Of course, it wouldn't be long before someone borrowed a stethoscope from a doctor friend to hear every word being said.

When the Polish boy-wonder chess-expert Samuel Reshevsky arrived in Buffalo to play thirty games with local experts, the nine-year-old prevailed in every match but one. Grandpa beat him. And though Reshevsky was young at the time, he'd go on to become a world grand master.

When he was at home, Grandpa would shave in the bathroom while calling out his chess moves to my uncle Jim, who then moved the pieces across the chess board in the living room. Grandpa followed the positions of all the pieces in his head and almost always won.

In his free time, Grandpa could usually be found at a local watering hole, Tommy Martin's speakeasy, performing all twenty or so verses of the World War I song "Sing Me to Sleep." According to eyewitnesses, the proprietor was not pleased when the barroom bard began to declaim, as it had the effect of dispersing his clientele.

Grandpa Watson also regularly recited "In Flanders Fields," by Lieutenant Colonel John McCrae. Like the poem's author, Grandpa fought with Canada in World War I. He enlisted on August 4, 1914, the day after Canada declared war on Germany. Canada was joining the effort with Great Britain, which in turn was coming to the aid of France against the Germans. The United States simultaneously declared neutrality, and President Wilson didn't ask Congress for a declaration of war until April 2, 1917.

Grandpa spent the next thirty-seven months as an infantry scout with the Canadian Expeditionary Forces in the trenches of France and Belgium, and he fought in the famous Battle of Ypres. He was decorated for bravery in the Battle of Amiens and received a military medal for bravery in the field from the Prince of Wales (who later became King Edward VIII and abdicated the throne to marry the American divorcée Wallis Simpson). They'd meet again at the opening of the Peace Bridge between the United States and Canada in 1927. Grandpa kept these medals in a small gold box given to him by Queen Mary when she visited the troops one Christmas day during the early years of the war.

Grandpa was among those who led the first tanks into the initial Battle of the Somme. For his efforts he received a bullet in the back that was never removed, and it's probably a good thing he didn't have to deal with airport metal detectors. He returned from the Great War and got back to business as usual. When not hot after a story or gone fishing or rescuing a little girl from an oncoming trolley, he could be found at the racetrack betting on the nags. My aunt once watched him lose two thousand dollars on a horse without blinking an eye, knowing full well that he probably didn't have two dollars in his pocket to get through the remainder of the week.

The rest of his time was spent in gin mills. Grandpa drank his way out of so many jobs that in his forties the only work he could get was picking tomatoes for Campbell's Soup, which paid twenty-five cents a day. A monk found him in a ditch and brought him to Alcoholics Anonymous. Grandpa eventually became the head of AA in New Jersey, occasionally visiting Buffalo and lecturing his old bar buddies on the evils of demon rum. One friend remarked, "I preferred his performance of 'Far, Far from Ypres.'"

As it turned out, Grandpa Watson's finest hours may not have been during the war; over the last seventeen years of his life, he helped many people become sober, and the hundreds who turned up at his funeral spoke to the family through heartfelt tears about all he'd done for them.

Just before he died of lung cancer at the age of seventy-three, Grandpa's old friend Anne McIthenney Matthews wrote in the *Buffalo Courier-Express*, "He worked the police beat in the Roaring 20s and his was one of the loudest roars, with antics to match anything in Chicago, New York, and the heyday of the no holds-barred cops and robbers rat-race of prohibition."

From what I've heard about the funeral, had Damon Runyon still been around, he'd have picked up a few more characters for his famous underworld stories that eventually became the framework for the musical *Guys and Dolls*.

Having been at the dedication of the Peace Bridge, Grandpa Watson wanted his ashes scattered from that spot into the Niagara River, where he'd enjoyed so many hours of fishing in his rowboat. My uncle and aunt fulfilled his wish while Mom waited in the car, fearful they'd be arrested.

Grandpa Watson had some lively brothers and sisters, which possibly accounts for Grandma's favorite warning: Never put the Yorkshire pudding in the oven until you see the whites of your company's eyes. When I was eleven, my mother announced that we were going to visit her father's sister Catherine who was in a mental institution.

Despite being ninety-three years old, Aunt Kate didn't seem like any nutter to me. She was sweet, partially lucid, and excellent at rhyming words and recalling song lyrics. It transpired that in the twenties, Kate's mother had plans for her daughter to be an opera singer. Though talented, Kate had fallen in love with a young man whom she desperately wanted to marry. Back then a gal couldn't do both. So she attempted suicide by leaping from the bridge in Delaware Park and at the age of twenty was institutionalized for the rest of her life. As we left Aunt Kate, my mother the psychiatric nurse said, "Nowadays if you take a lover's leap they rarely even keep you for a couple days, just send you home with some medication and counseling twice a week."

Mom also had an uncle who was an architect and dabbled in magic, specifically, making himself disappear for several days at a time.

However, my favorite relative to hear about was Mom's aunt Gertrude, another of her father's sisters. Gertrude was a concert violinist and one of the first female Spiritualist ministers in the community of Lily Dale, located an hour south of Buffalo and better known as the Transylvania of upstate New York. Spiritualists are members of a religious group that combines a belief in "the God of your own understanding" with the idea that it's possible to live and communicate with the dead. Today in Lily Dale one can still find over fifty registered mediums, regular clairvoyant conferences, "development circles" that send and receive messages from the departed, hypnotherapy, past-life regression, future-life progression, and sessions in natural healing. "Lily Dale is to Spiritualism as Rome is to Catholicism," according to local historian Ron Nagy.

Back in the 1800s, western and central New York State became known as the Burned-Over District, as it was roiled by the religious fervor of not only Spiritualists, but seers, Mormons, mystics, Millerites, the Chautauqua Movement, and other freethinkers. The Shakers first had a village outside Albany, where they practiced communal living and celibacy while crafting unornamented, functional, finely made furniture. It's difficult to grow a commune while practicing celibacy, so they eventually died out, but not before inventing the clothespin.

The Oneida Community, established near Syracuse, was populated by self-described "perfectionist vegetarian Bible communists." These utopian visionaries, who practiced free love, are better remembered for incorporating themselves as the makers of quality flatware and having Charles Guiteau, who would go on to assassinate President James Garfield in 1881, as a member.

One had to listen quietly and carefully in order to patch together the family tree. Furthermore, it could only be done late at night, usually when cards were being dealt. During the daytime, recollections dimmed, becoming what seemed purposefully vague, and the information one did unearth was considerably less interesting.

❋ ❋ ❋

My mother and her brother and sister grew up in Buffalo during the forties, in a freewheeling household where the three high-spirited children outmatched the adults. The Second World War was on and this meant shortages and rationing of everything from meat, milk, and sugar to clothing, gas, oil, and coal. Forget about having any hosiery or butter. The only good thing was that with so many of the men off fighting, there wasn't a shortage of employment for women.

Their mother worked as an aide at a nearby hospital. Back then, hospitals were also repositories for mental patients, and Grandma would often be kicked and scratched so that by the end of a shift she was covered with bruises and sometimes blood. Having attended the prestigious Nardin Academy for girls in Buffalo, Grandma had been trained to write neatly, set a proper table, and have good posture. Her parents had at one time been solidly middle class, but their finances were wiped out by the stock market crash in 1929.

Meantime, back at the family home, if their ambidextrous paternal grandmother Jessie wasn't in the kitchen ironing with one hand and writing a letter with the other, it probably meant the ponies were running that day and she was off to the racetrack. To be sure, you could check the teapot in the kitchen cupboard and see if she'd taken her bankroll. My mom remembers her grandmother as a formidable opponent who moved down the street like a ship under full sail. She was one of the first women in the neighborhood to wear pants, she kept a bottle of Old Overholt Canadian rye above the sink, and she suggested that the children should go to an orphanage.

In Great-Grandma's defense, at times the youthful inmates truly took over the asylum. Wooden slats meant for weighing down the window shades were employed as swords in epic battles, after which the broken pieces were shoved back into their cloth coverings. Parquet floors in the long hallway were ruined by roller-skating, and oftentimes a table lamp or knickknack paid the price.

Allegiances quickly shifted and when the two girls needed to retaliate against their brother, they utilized Camp Fire Girl creativity. One such escapade involved flooding the floor outside his door with water, placing a hundred tacks pointy side up, and yelling *"Fire!"* The girls first made sure that he was barefoot.

In the kitchen you could find Ichabod, a chicken that lived under the table. The yard was where the Watson trio invented games and played catch with snakes. They were usually flanked by a pack of hunting dogs—dogs hunting for a place to lie down, most notably the ABC mutts: Archie, Banjo, and Corky.

Without a television, the children easily amused themselves. When not trying to kill one another, they played guessing games such as twenty questions or a ship came into the harbor. If conversation lagged, their mother taught them the Gaelic she'd learned from her Irish father, Eugene Costello. Though all my mother can remember of this is how to make the sign of the cross and say "kiss my ass."

Times were tough, with shortages during and after the war, and the month was always considerably longer than the money. Rarely was there enough food or clothing, and they were regularly without utilities. My mother has always threatened that she's going to die young as a result of poor childhood nutrition, but now that she's reached age seventy in fighting form, I'm no longer convinced.

Growing up in reduced circumstances was something my mother would never forget, particularly banging the broom against the stairwell to scare away the rats before going down to fetch the coal, if they were fortunate enough to have any. Mom later said the only good thing about having a small bathroom is that when you are sick and unsure of where the most activity is going to take place, you can sit on the toilet while leaning over to vomit in the tub.

Six

When Johnny Comes Typing Home...
Wedding-Bell Blues

My father's childhood was lived slightly above the poverty line. And it was much more sober, in every sense of the word. He was born on the Upper West Side of Manhattan, near the George Washington Bridge, on May 20, 1931, and remained there throughout the Depression. When Dad was five years old, his mother took him by ship to Denmark to meet his relatives. A New York neighbor recalls him returning six months later yammering away in Danish and confused that old friends could no longer understand him. Shortly thereafter he was speaking English again and can't remember a word of Danish to this day. It didn't help that he wasn't allowed to speak Danish in his home.

The European immigrants who arrived at the beginning of the last century were not always interested in preserving their culture. They'd left for a reason, whether to escape religious and political persecution, family expectations, or poverty, and they were fixed on becoming full-fledged, freedom-loving, flag-waving Americans. That meant taking American names, speaking English, and eating hamburgers, though sometimes kosher burgers or ones drenched in Limburger.

By 1941, Grandpa Pedersen had saved enough money to pursue his dream of starting a Scandinavian smorgasbord restaurant. The Scandia Arms opened in Mamaroneck, twenty miles north of Manhattan, with Grandpa as proprietor and Grandma as hostess. The first night was a huge success, except for the two goldfish swimming in a bowl on the buffet table, meant to be a decorative touch. Grandpa put a candle underneath the fish bowl, and they were accidentally boiled.

As bad luck would have it, the United States entered World War II a few months later and gas shortages sent the business the way of the goldfish. People couldn't afford to take their cars out, and energy use was rationed.

In debt, Grandpa moved the family to Huntington, Long Island, to work at a restaurant owned by his Danish friend Peter Nielsen. The pressing need to pay off creditors and support his family through the difficult postwar period kept Grandpa from ever again opening his own establishment. He'd work as a waiter for the rest of his life. And although Grandma was bright and ambitious, she was a woman of her time, which was not all that great a time to be a woman, and would remain a housewife. Dad and Grandpa always said that if Grandma had been born fifty years later she'd have run a large corporation, as opposed to just investing in them.

Growing up, my father was tall, skinny, and fast—six foot two inches tall, 150 pounds, and all legs. He claims to have taken up table tennis in high school to avoid getting pulverized, reasoning that when the bullies came looking for trouble, one would recognize him and say, "Hey, that's John. He's the Ping-Pong champion of Long Island." The strategy worked.

After high school, Dad went to junior college and studied office machines, accounting, bookkeeping, and English. Upon graduating in 1951 he received job offers from Shell, Mobil, and IBM. However, the offer he couldn't refuse came from Uncle Sam, full time and all expenses paid. Drafted into the United States Army for the job of fighting the Korean War, he found the bullets a bit too widespread and effective to call it a police action. Or a conflict, as some politicians referred to it, as in "We are at conflict!" And though it would later be called The Forgotten War, Dad remembers Korea all too well.

Following basic training, he was shipped to the front line where, despite his two years spent learning office skills (Dad can type faster than you can drive), he was made a forward observer. This entailed darting around enemy territory and then telling the fellows with the heavy artillery where to shoot. The position carried with it the kind of stress level that encouraged Dad to make full use of his cigarette ration, and thus began a beautiful friendship with nicotine.

After Dad spent several months dodging cross fire, digging fox-holes, and sharing tents with poisonous snakes, Uncle Sam realized a mistake had been made and recalled him for a clerical job in Seoul. They'd somehow overlooked the office-skills part of his résumé, and even more desirable than GI Joes were GI No-Typos. The problem was you didn't have to stay in the army as long if you were being shot at, as opposed to wielding correction fluid. More important, at least to Dad, was that he'd trained and fought with a bunch of guys for almost a year. What are you supposed to say to your buddies: "Uh, yeah, they found out I can alphabetize faster than I can shoot"?

When Dad was discharged from the army in 1953, he returned to his parents' two-bedroom apartment on Long Island, dumped his uniform, dog tags, three bronze stars, and assorted medals in the garbage, and went back to school under the GI Bill to become a court reporter.

❃ ❃ ❃

Though times were tough in the Depression, as well as during and after World War II, my father's family always had enough to eat. It helped that Grandpa was employed at a restaurant and was best friends with the owner and chef. But they survived largely because he worked hard as a waiter seven days a week. (Grandma was just embarking upon her stock trading.)

Grandpa began work in the early afternoon, leaving an hour before Dad returned from school and arriving home long after his son was in bed. He waited tables all day on Saturday, Sunday, and holidays. When Dad sang a solo a cappella version of "Old Man River" at his high school graduation in a stunning bass voice, Grandpa had no idea that his son was able to sing at all.

My parents are both from the waste-not-want-not era where

everything was used, conserved, and reused. As a result, while I was growing up in the sixties, seventies, and eighties, there was never any talk about "the good old days" of the thirties, forties, and fifties.

Despite straight As in all her academic subjects, my mother took the secretarial track in high school, which was common for girls at that time. After graduating in 1955, she found a job at the unemployment office in downtown Buffalo. Personally, I've always liked the ironic sound of "I work at the unemployment office." Mom earned eighty dollars a week while the claimants received about seventy, but they only had to come in one day a week instead of five. It was mostly clerical work and typing forms in triplicate. If there's one genetic marker that runs on both sides of the family, it's for typing.

The unemployment office happened to be where my father was reporting some hearings, and that's where my parents first met. It being Buffalo, he asked her out for a Friday night beer-batter fish fry.

A court reporter uses shorthand to record everything that's said in the courtroom (quite different from a journalist assigned to report on court proceedings). After court was dismissed for the day, reporters were expected to translate their notes into typed transcripts and make them available to the parties involved. At least that's how it worked up through the eighties, when high technology arrived.

My mother and father were married by a justice of the peace in Buffalo on February 14, 1958. Despite the romance of Valentine's Day, none of their parents made it to the wedding, and my mom wore a blue suit. Though one could argue that in a typically white Buffalo winter this was simply a safety precaution.

Overnight, Mom went from being Ellen Watson to Mrs. John A. Pedersen. Going forward, that name would be on her charge cards, her mail and invitations, and in the phone book. There wasn't any designation of Ms. If you were a woman, people could determine by your title of Miss or Mrs. whether you were single or not (unless you were a widow); but men had no such indicator, except maybe the tan line from where their wedding ring was supposed to be, or a slight lisp if it was temporarily hidden under the tongue.

In 1963, two years before I was born, my parents moved from Buffalo to the leafy suburb of Amherst, New York, twelve miles northeast of downtown. It was a plain, modest, yellow-brick ranch-style house with three bedrooms, a living room, dining room, kitchen, and attached single-car garage on a pie-shaped lot at 419 Frankhauser Road. Although the two thousand dollars for the down payment came out of my mother's savings, her name wasn't put on the title.

In those days, Amherst was truly a small town—a gentle blend of farmland and subdivision where most everyone knew their neighbors, all of their neighbors, and the police blotter was replete with barking dogs, burning leaves, and the nefarious doings of a large squirrel population. The new home was set on a recently paved winding road that had served as a cow path in the not-so-distant past and prior to that was swampland. By the sixties, Amherst had grown into a bedroom community inhabited by sixty thousand residents, a mix of working-class and professional families who fell firmly in the middle of the middle class. People didn't ask where you "summered," and if they did, you'd have told them "outside."

The area wouldn't be completely overrun with housing and strip malls until a decade later, when the University of Buffalo designated the edge of our neighborhood as the site of their new North Campus. The population quickly exploded and has more than doubled since those early days. They paved paradise and put up a parking lot, as Joni Mitchell sang in "Big Yellow Taxi."

Living in close proximity to one of the Great Lakes meant year-round dampness, and we didn't know a family without silverfish in their basement. When you're a kid, they look big enough to saddle up and ride over to the sump pump. Silverfish are more wingless insects than fish, though they really are silver and practically glow in the dark. Their hobby is to slither rapidly in droves out from underneath objects and scare the bejesus out of you. Silverfish thrive in cool, dark, wet places, and their favorite foods are bookbindings, wallpaper, clothing, and small children. If you want to see The Running of the Silverfish, go into any Buffalo-area basement and lift an old can of paint off the concrete floor. To make it extra scary, wait until dark and use a flashlight.

Mr. and Mrs. John A. Pedersen went marching to suburbia with a basset hound named Herbert. Shortly after they arrived, a man campaigning for the local town council rang the bell, introduced himself as Herbert, and asked the name of their dog. My mother quickly said the dog was called Snoopy, and he remained Snoopy from that day on. At least until he bit my mother, and then his name was again changed, this time to Sleep Tight.

Unlike the suburb in which we lived, I was not a fast developer. I didn't turn over, walk, or talk anywhere near the pediatrician's timetable. The first few years, I was more or less a turnip in a sleeper with a room temperature IQ, despite being breast-fed and having a humidifier. Eventually I was taken for tests, and a doctor informed my mother that I was retarded. (There was no *differently abled* or *mentally challenged* back then—just *slightly retarded*, *retarded*, and *very retarded*.) Mom was sent for counseling and given pamphlets with such titles as "How to Deal with Your Retarded Child." But she told them no, I was just on my own schedule.

And what a schedule it was. By age four I was finally up and running, and a glimmer of comprehension kicked in around six. My teeth were mostly in place by the time I was a teenager, and my top molars dropped down at age twenty-five.

Seven

Onward Catholic Soldiers...Everything's Good in the Hood...The Sinusitis Capital

My youth was whiled away primarily during the 1970s. And though the world was a complicated place, it was a simple time to grow up in small-town Middle America, a time that is no more. Or perhaps it never was.

I realize that geographically Buffalo is located in the Northeast of the United States; I do own a place mat with a map on it. However, having spent my first seventeen years in upstate New York and the rest of the time in Manhattan, I've taken the liberty of reclassifying Buffalo as the Midwest, at least during the time I was living there. Back then it had much more in common with Cincinnati, Des Moines, and Moline than with Boston, Manhattan, and Philadelphia. Even now, despite explosive population growth, the town of Amherst consistently ranks as one of the safest places to live in the United States.

Also, Buffalonians sound much more like midwesterners than New Yorkers. Living with all that dampness, we're somewhat nasal voiced. And most of us suffer from a disease of the vowels, flattening them out to the point where they can be walked across, in particular the letter *a*. What would be pronounced as *ferry* in most places, to rhyme with Ireland's County Kerry, comes out as *fairy*, to rhyme with *dairy*, in upstate New York.

Perhaps the age and place can best be summed up with a maxim that was popular at the time: "Never return an empty tray." When there was a function or a funeral, and people brought casseroles and baked goods in glassware or finger foods arranged on china serving platters, they placed a piece of masking tape on the bottom of the dish with their name printed on it in black Magic Marker. Not only was the dish returned clean, but usually filled with a different homemade goody such as sticky buns, oatmeal cookies, or apple brown betty. Another common courtesy dictated that if you were in the supermarket and discovered a coupon you'd brought along wasn't needed, you placed it on a shelf near the product so that some other housewife could take advantage of the savings.

Mothers instructed daughters to always count the silverware after the good utensils had been used. This wasn't for fear of theft, since neighbors didn't steal pieces of your silverware and no one we knew employed servants, but in case a spoon had accidentally gone into the garbage and a massive dig needed to be organized, usually performed by children in the backyard or garage. The trash could be spread out and sifted through, with an adult operating in a strictly supervisory capacity.

Back then, if a child restlessly hopped about, the grown-ups asked if you were suffering from Saint Vitus's dance. Or they'd inquire if you had *shpilkes*—the Yiddish equivalent of "ants in your pants." Bad kids were told they were going to "get it in the keister." For people who talked a lot it was said, "His mouth goes like a duck's ass in huckleberry season" or else "His lips move like a whip-poor-will's ass." Of folks more than "slightly touched" they said, "He's crazier than a shit-house rat." The grandparents among us still remembered how chemicals used to treat outhouses made the rats crazy, much like the mad hatters in England. If you were just slightly off in any number of ways, someone politely whispered "not quite right" or "home-knitted" as you skipped past on one leg with binoculars pointed skyward. Or else, "a half-bubble off plumb." Eccentricity was much more of a vocation in those days, before everyone started taking medication.

When leaving a place inhabited by people raised on the gospel they said, "See you soon if the good Lord's willin' and the creeks don't rise." If you arrived appearing disheveled, exhausted, or as if you'd been caught in a storm, it was bound to be noted that you looked as if you'd been "ridden hard and put away wet." When someone was ravenous and not against working slightly blue he might announce, "I'm so hungry I could eat a rag doll's crotch." If you became lost in a bad section of the city late at night, you were sure to say, "We're going to get screwed, blued, and tattooed."

If mothers disapproved of an outfit, haircut, or overuse of makeup, but were too exhausted to fight it or didn't have solid grounds to make you change, they said, "suit yourself," though their mouths twitched with censure. This translated to "Do not expect me to admit that I am your mother when the police call, or to bail you out of the county jail."

Commercial airline flights had only been available for nine years when I was born, and to get on a plane people dressed up as if they were going to a wedding. Stereos were "hi-fis," for "high fidelity." A new labor-saving device or invention, such as automatic transmissions in cars, was usually viewed with mistrust by the older generation and derisively referred to as "newfangled." Any of these gadgets that stopped working were said to be "on the fritz."

Amherst was a predominantly Catholic town and home to a high percentage of Irish, Poles, Germans, Italians, and Greeks, as was the city of Buffalo. If you need proof that Buffalo is ethnically diverse, just look at the list of mayors since my birth: Frank A. Sedita, Stanley Makowski, Jimmy Griffin, Tony Masiello. Byron W. Brown, the first African American mayor, was installed in January of 2006. He's a wake-going, turkey-giving Democrat, but a Baptist, of all things. Rather than state the neighborhood in which a home is for sale, real-estate ads often list the church parish in which a house is located, such as Assumption, Our Lady of Loretto, or Infant of Prague. And workers regularly take off Dyngus Day, Saint Joseph's Day, Saint Patrick's Day, Saint Stanislaus Day, and Ash Wednesday.

The Irish ran most of the political machinery in Buffalo while I was growing up. Many an Irish wake was described as open bar, closed casket. And people liked to say that at a Jewish wedding they break a glass, while at an Irish wedding they break everything.

The huge population of Poles kept us in kielbasa (spicy smoked sausage), pierogi (dumplings filled with meat, cheese, cabbage, or prune), and accordion music, especially polkas such as the "Hinky Dinky, Parley Voo." A *Polish porch* is a garage used as a substitute living room during the summer months by installing a large screen where the garage door normally goes. And when a Buffalonian sees a car wash with a Free Polish sign, we read *Polish* with a long *o*, and at first glance think they're giving away people born in Warsaw rather than a wax job. In addition to a handful of O'Neals, O'Malleys, and Mahoneys, it wasn't unusual to have several neighbors and teachers with Polish last names that were almost unpronounceable (forget about spelling them), so kids were told to simply call them Mr. K. or Mrs. W.

The Germans ate bratwurst, knockwurst, blutwurst, bauernwurst, weisswurst, Wiener schnitzel, and sauerbraten with red cabbage, and played schottisches and mazurkas on their glockenspiels, tubas, trombones, euphoniums, and flügelhorns in the battle of the oompah-pah bands. Almost everyone went out for a Friday-night fish fry, a result of the Catholic prohibition of eating meat on that day (considered a sin because Jesus died on a Friday, and so one should abstain from pleasure).

Buffalo butcher shops carried at least a dozen varieties of sausage: hot or mild, Italian, Polish, turkey, wienerwurst, pork roll, beer, blood, beef, barley, summer, veal, and liver. This was the same for bacon: Canadian, slab, double-smoked hunter, pancetta, pepper coated, and so on. Salami ran a close third with hard, soft, chicken, hot, dry, pork, Genoa, and other types. Most women had a borscht recipe. Most men had a heart attack.

The many different ethnic groups held annual street festivals, with the Greek and Italian ones especially well known for having delicious food and lively music. The raise-your-glass-and-sing Irish put on a lively Saint Patrick's Day celebration, and the Poles organized the Pułaski Day parade, honoring the Polish American general who served under George Washington in the Revolutionary War. I don't have the satellite photographs to prove it, but Buffalo boasts the largest Saint Patrick's Day parade west of Manhattan (despite a population of three hundred thousand to Manhattan's 8 million) and the largest Pułaski Day parade east of Chicago, which has a total population of 3 million, ten times that of Buffalo. African Americans hold a well-attended Juneteenth festival.

Even the saffron-robed Hare Krishna had a Buffalo office for a number of years. They could be counted on to incessantly chant throughout the many street fairs, "Hare Hare, Krishna Krishna," to the point where it was something we kids would do for fun. I once asked Dad about the Danish parade, and he said that as far as he knew it was just the two of us, so every time we went outside together it was a parade.

Despite a high concentration of Irish, Poles, Germans, and Italians, it's safe to say that Buffalo can produce at least a few of just about every nationality. In the eighties, a popular Gypsy leader was receiving treatment at a local hospital when a contingent of followers attempted a ceremony that involved roasting a goat on the hospital steps; officials eventually put a stop to the outdoor shish kebab, though whether it was based on a health ordinance or for blocking the fire lanes, I don't know.

The area is currently three-quarters Catholic, according to the American Religion Data Archive, and was even more so back in the sixties and seventies. It could be considered just plain efficient to have such a prayer-centric religion in the majority, as Buffalonians spend a good deal of their time hoping the car starts and the pipes don't freeze.

Even though there were plenty of Jews and Protestants, you felt the Catholicism wherever you went. For instance, at a birthday party there was a 90 percent chance that following "Happy Birthday" there would be a rousing round of "May the Good Lord Bless You." Roadways and parking lots were full of the vans and station wagons necessary to cart around large families. The matriarch of one Polish household containing fifteen children required all the boys to eat at least one hot dog *before* sitting down at the dinner table.

The Second Vatican Council ended on December 8, 1965, and alleviated a considerable amount of heavy lifting for Catholics. However, these decisions were regarded much the same way Buffalonians view volcanoes—as disasters that happen to other people in faraway places. Nuns didn't suddenly start to dress down, rump roast didn't appear on the table on Friday night, and the Virgin Mary was as blessed and ever present as before. Few of the faithful truly looked or listened hard enough to determine whether or not the priests had turned around and shifted from Latin to English. And just try to get an old Polish Catholic woman to stop wearing a doily on her head.

Regarding Roman Catholics, James Joyce once said, "Here comes everybody," because Catholics tend to live out loud. Whether it's because there aren't enough bedrooms in their houses or because ritual and music are so embedded in their traditions is up for debate. But it makes for an energetic community, with street parades and enormous picnics and going all-out for the many Catholic holidays.

Even if you went to public school, as I did, you couldn't escape the overarching influence of the Catholic Church. Friends were constantly off to first communion, Catholic Youth Organization (CYO), confirmation classes, and confession. On Fridays, all the public schools served a breaded fish patty as a nod to the large number of Catholic students. And whenever the kids uncovered a student with a secret life as an altar boy, he was mercilessly teased about it right up until graduation.

Why didn't all the Catholic kids go to parochial schools? Because the public school system was free, had better sports facilities and more advanced-placement classes, and included transportation. Also, many parents were Cafeteria Catholics—they took the pieces of the religion that suited them, and left other parts aside, most often the ban on premarital sex and birth control, and sending their children to parochial schools.

Even with these public school defections, thousands of local children did indeed attend Catholic schools, and the area overflowed with churches, priests, nuns, Catholic hospitals, nursing homes, and cemeteries. Basically, there was a cloaked figure around every corner, ready to remind you that sex is for procreation, not recreation. And you couldn't go three blocks without hearing a chorus of "Kumbaya" drifting out of a school bus or classroom window. The career elementary teachers could simultaneously perform the song in sign language as they sang. If you yelled questions from the Baltimore Catechism across a crowded playground, you'd surely get an 80 percent response rate.

(Q: Who made us? A: God made us. Q: Who is God? A: God is our Father in heaven.) A housewife busy preparing three meals a day for a dozen or so people could often be heard calling upon Saint Thérèse of Lisieux, who declared, "God is in the pots and pans."

Because of its high concentration of God-fearing Catholics, this godforsaken landscape is a natural flash point for battles between the pro-choicers and right-to-lifers. Representatives of both factions regularly descend upon the city from all over the country to protest. The 1998 murder of Amherst resident Dr. Barnett Slepian made national headlines. One of a few local doctors who provided abortion services, he was shot in his home by God Squad activist James Kopp.

Another sign of the strong Catholic heritage is the goodly number of older adults in my hometown who are ambidextrous. The pro-right nuns were still converting lefties to righties in the late sixties, more often than not by tying the offending hand behind the back of the chair to relieve them of temptation. The Latin word for "left" is *sinister*, and so it's painfully obvious why this was necessary. Judas, betrayer of Jesus, sat to his left.

The main difference between children who attended Catholic school and those who went to neighborhood public schools is bladder control. The nuns believed a bladder could be trained and constrained just like every other part of the mind and body. Thus from the first day of kindergarten, Catholic kids were conditioned to pee only once during the school day, right after lunch. Despite some embarrassing accidents early on, it's worth noting that the nuns were correct on this point. In any group of adult women, the one skipping the bathroom break is a Catholic-school graduate.

At Christmastime, my Catholic friends made Advent calendars, arranged mangers underneath their trees, and attended midnight Mass. The mangers were an endless source of fun. We'd rearrange them so the donkeys and sheep were biting the wise men in the ass, poor, tired Joseph was doing headstands, and we'd hide the baby Jesus or send him on endless train rides around the base of the tree, hanging off the back of the caboose by his tiny plastic feet.

In small suburban neighborhoods like mine, families lived in ranch, split-level, and two-story houses with three or four bedrooms and one or two bathrooms, purchased for between $15,000 and $40,000 in the fifties or sixties. Adjacent to the driveway was a front lawn with a few trees and shrubs, and in the back, a yard large enough for a garden, shed, and swing set, or an aboveground swimming pool. There was also a grill and a redwood picnic table for that suburban specialty, the Summer Barbecue Olympics. Gentlemen, start your briquettes.

The backyard was where kids were sent to shuck corn, shell peas, peel spuds, and hull strawberries. And, of course, eat watermelon on warm summer evenings, during which monumental seed-spitting wars erupted. These were the days before the big black seeds had been hybridized out of the melon (along with the flavor) for eating efficiency, and prior to the advent of the mini-watermelon; if you dropped one of these industrial-sized footballs, the result was a broken foot, a hole in the floor, or a dead dog. Meanwhile, the grown-ups had a separate watermelon, one inside of which a bottle of vodka or champagne had been poured the day before.

Lawn statuary was popular and consisted mostly of faux deer and a generous sprinkling of Madonnas. In the heavily Polish neighborhoods of Cheektowaga (sometimes called Cheektowarsaw), Depew, and Sloan, one could often find a Mary on the half shell—the Virgin Mary in a shell grotto or, more commonly, a partially buried upright claw-foot bathtub, or a hot pink flamingo.

If Dad's job was steady, you might eventually add on a Florida room, a glass-enclosed greenhouse for sun-starved humans. Otherwise, most homes had a rumpus room where the kids could lounge on bean-bag chairs, engage in active play that mothers referred to as *roughhousing* and constantly warned against, and watch TV (most sat atop a large wooden console containing an older TV that was too costly to repair). This area was either a family room on the main floor or a basement redone with knotty pinewood paneling, indoor/outdoor carpeting, a spring-shot sofa, and a dartboard. Though in large Catholic families, the luxury of an extra room was not something to be enjoyed until the oldest children began moving out.

The mantel over the fireplace held a few Hummel figurines, and the coffee table was home to a snow globe and souvenir ashtray from someplace warm, with S & H Green Stamps stored in the drawer below. A particleboard bookcase was laminated with faux walnut veneer and filled with a set of encyclopedias that stopped at World War II and was devoid of pages containing information that had to do with sex. Catholic homes had a picture of Jesus somewhere, along with a few statues of Mary, small wooden or plastic crucifixes over the beds, and usually a plaque inscribed with grace above the kitchen table. Being modern meant track lighting on the ceiling and a bottle of Blue Nun on the Formica countertop.

There was one telephone per house (no cordless phones, cell phones, or car phones), and this resulted in much synchronizing of watches, designated meeting places, and waiting in the freezing cold for people who never showed up. It was a decade before answering machines, so if no one was home, the phone just rang and rang and rang. Large families fought over whose turn it was to answer the phone, especially if everyone was lounging in front of the television, and the phone could easily ring a dozen times while this was being resolved. Or you could pretend not to be home and let it ring until the caller eventually gave up.

Call waiting, Star 69, voice mail, and e-mail were just a glint in some electrical engineer's eye. When we phoned someone and the line was engaged, we heard a busy signal, which sounded like a dryer buzzer going off over the phone. People regularly capitalized on the busy signal and the fact that there were no answering machines. It was easy to fib and say that you'd been trying to call someone *for weeks*, and there was no way for them to prove you hadn't.

A call from outside the area code was expensive, oftentimes bad news, and almost always for parents. Everyone knew that these exchanges should be kept brief to avoid a big phone bill, and so we ran scattershot through the house shouting, "Hurry! It's long distance!"

If someone phoned and we didn't write down the message or else forgot to tell the person, especially a parent, then we were in *big trouble*. A constant refrain was "How would *you* like it if we didn't remember to give you *your messages?*" Sometimes a younger child scrawled down the message and it would forever remain a mystery due to his undeveloped listening skills, poor spelling, or disastrous penmanship (for example, "M. Flub canxl turs").

In homes containing one or more teenagers, it was possible for the phone line to be engaged for hours every night, and callers would give up trying to get through, deciding instead to drive over or write a letter. In large families with older children expecting calls from girlfriends and boyfriends, the fights to use the phone were monumental. Eventually a moratorium would be declared after a grown-up had been unsuccessful in trying to make contact with Dad about a work matter and he found out about it the next day at the factory or office. Fortunately he hadn't seen the episode of *The Brady Bunch* where Mike installed a pay phone inside the house.

Teenage girls were constantly scolded to get off the phone. They also received a good tongue-lashing for absentmindedly twisting and pulling the stretchy cord while talking (and applying Bonne Bell Lip Smacker). In an effort to dodge eavesdroppers, it was necessary to sequester yourself behind a door, in the pantry, or under a table, and this left an extended spiral cord about ten inches off the ground, perfect to trip Mom as she carried the laundry basket up from the basement, or to clothesline little brothers and sisters.

Kids developed phone signals with their friends because it was so difficult to talk with any degree of privacy. If your phone rang only once and stopped before anyone was able to answer it, a parent could be pretty sure that something was up. And if right after the single ring one of the kids disappeared from the table, Mom and Dad *definitely* knew that there was a bad moon on the rise.

By the time I entered junior high, sledding was no longer considered a cool pastime, but my longtime friend and classmate Debbie

Kohnstamm, who lived up the street, and I loved it so we'd head out at midnight, when the hill was empty. Because parents didn't like the phone ringing after nine, if you wanted to rouse a pal late at night it was necessary to go to her house and toss gravel at the window. This looks easy enough in old movies, but in real life there's a good chance of hitting the wrong window; plus, a small stone tossed with the necessary force to ensure accuracy had enough velocity to crack the glass.

Back then, a computer was a building-sized contraption in a science-fiction movie. Calculators had just become affordable to the general public and were selling at Kmart for $7.99. Parents and kids alike were thrilled to toss out complicated slide rules and adding machines that were heavier than today's portable computers. A few well-heeled families were just starting to buy these newfangled appliances called microwave ovens and install second phone lines to keep chatty teen-agers from tying up the main one.

Many people tended flower and vegetable gardens in their backyards. In the rich upstate soil, just about anything you plant and water will grow. And also a lot of stuff you didn't. Acres of buttercups, Queen Anne's lace, and daisies could be found gracefully swaying in empty fields and along roadsides; goldenrod, bachelor's buttons, cattails, and pussy willows grew wild down by the creek. The tomatoes and zucchini in our gardens all seemed to ripen on the same day in early August, and after fantasizing about them for eleven long months, we were suddenly inundated and couldn't give them away. By the beginning of October, our backyards held pumpkins the size of medicine balls (a large piece of athletic equipment that served no apparent purpose, but was much favored by gym teachers back then). In fact, this mineral-rich soil in which cabbages grow to the size of meteors was one of the main reasons the Indians had originally made their homes in that region. It certainly wasn't the sunbathing.

The only drawback is that the growing season is a short ninety days, give or take—mostly take. However, beer and bingo eventually alleviated the tedium of staying indoors throughout the long winters.

There still weren't any video games—handheld, arcade, or other-wise. Just pinball machines, skeeball, foosball, and, when the carnival came to town, shooting galleries, the ring toss, and the baseball throw. *Pong* arrived in 1972, when I was in second grade. It was followed by *Space Invaders* in 1978, and in 1979 there were *Asteroids* and *Galaxian*. However, these games couldn't be played in the comfort of your own home. You had to go to an arcade or 7-Eleven or the bowling alley, and usually wait behind some guy who played video games all day like it was his job and could make a quarter last an hour. His initials filled every space of the on-screen high-score chart. *Pac-Man* came on the scene in 1980 and *Donkey Kong* in 1981. That's as far as most of us got, aside from some minor flirtations with *Tetris* in college.

I was in elementary school when designer sneakers became a cultural phenomenon, with Nike, Adidas, and Puma using new technologies and introducing fresh styles that incorporated leather, suede, stripes, and nonprimary colors. Nike struck a particular chord with its introduction of the waffle outsole in 1974. We'd all been playing hide-and-seek in boring old canvas Keds and Converse up until then.

Even vending machines were still somewhat primitive, constantly stealing your change or spewing out a windfall. The most sadistic were the beverage machines that let you watch your soda, coffee, or hot chocolate squirt into the drain and then plopped the empty paper cup down as an afterthought.

The Good Humor man parked his ice-cream truck at the end of our street every summer afternoon and played psychotic merry-go-round music to announce his presence. The Kirby vacuum-cleaner man appeared by appointment and showed housewives his wares. Moms on a budget knew that if you were having a party and your household allowance was gone, you could get at least one carpet cleaned for free by requesting a demonstration. My mother remembered the Fuller Brush man, and my father told stories about the iceman, but they had both cleared the landscape by the time I arrived. You could often tell the old-timers who had been around for the iceman because when it hailed in the summertime they'd run out with a bucket to catch the hailstones in order to make their own ice cream. And they always referred to the freezer as the icebox. Encyclopedia peddlers still traipsed from door to door, along with a few Bible salesmen, but not so much of the latter in our part of the country. The Catholics didn't have the same appetite for scripture as the Protestants and Baptists farther south.

A trip to the Erie County Fair signaled that summer was coming to a close. Begun in Buffalo in 1819, and moved to nearby Hamburg in 1868, it has since become the second largest county fair in North America. The only other local event that could compare on an entertainment scale for a child was going to Crystal Beach Amusement Park across the border in Canada, where you rode the famous Comet roller coaster and stuffed yourself with sugar waffles.

The Erie County Fair featured pie-eating contests, midway rides, fireworks at night, clown school, horse pulls, barrel racing, roasted onions, corn dogs on a stick, loganberry, goat dressing, dairy cattle, pig races, beef cattle, sheep contests, rabbits, chickens, llamas, wood carvings, vegetable displays, afghans, knitting, needlepoint, crocheting, and quilts. And of course the moo-ternity barn, which housed expecting cows.

My mom wouldn't ride the Ferris wheel because once someone had vomited on her from above. Dad told me not to play the arcade games—tossing hoops over stuffed animals, racing ducks, throwing Ping-Pong balls into fishbowls, rolling balls at wooden pins, and shooting baskets—because they were rigged so that you didn't have much chance of succeeding. And even if you did win, the prize wasn't worth the cost of playing. But if I really wanted a stuffed dog, he would carefully place his cigarette on the counter so the ashes would fall onto the ground and win one for me by clearing out the red star with an air rifle in the shooting gallery. The Korean War had been good for something after all.

Campbell's soup played a starring role in many dishes, making them into "an occasion all on their own," as housewives liked to say. Tomato soup enhanced chili and stew, cream of celery soup went into tuna casserole, and cream of mushroom soup was used for pretty much everything else, such as Tater Tot hotdish (spread crumbled potato chips on top for desired level of sodium) and any entrée that contained the word *surprise* in it. The more adventurous chefs experimented with aerosol cheese and Parkay Squeeze margarine. Frozen fish sticks were basically the only fish you could get a kid to eat, and even that could be a struggle without strawberry-flavored Nestlé Quik to wash them down.

When Mom left the kids with Dad, they usually heated up Swanson TV dinners or picked up a pizza from Bocce or Santora's. Children left to their own devices made sandwiches, anything that came in a Chef Boyardee can, or homemade "pizza"—slices of Wonder Bread slathered with ketchup and topped with a slice of bright orange American cheese.

Most moms baked regularly, and dessert was usually apple pie, apple crisp, apple upside-down cake, apple turnovers, apple cobbler, or apple strudel. We were comforted with apples not because of the Bible, but because New York State has about seven hundred varieties, they're inexpensive, and readily available. There was plenty of apple cider to drink in the fall, and apple-mint jelly could be found in most refrigerators. Boys liked to put firecrackers into mushy crab apples and throw them into open windows.

If you didn't like apples, God forbid, there was chocolate pudding or Jell-O. Jell-O was often tarted up with canned fruit or tiny marshmallows. It wasn't until you headed west to Michigan and Minnesota that they started adding vegetables, like carrots. School lunch desserts were homemade cookies or one of the recently introduced Hostess snack cakes, such as Suzy Qs, Ho Hos, Twinkies, and Ding Dongs.

In the summertime, kids lived for frozen Kool-Aid pops, more Jell-O, and lots of Buffalo's own Perry's or Charlap's ice cream with extra jimmies (sprinkles). At the candy counter one could find everything from licorice whips and Dubble Bubble to wax lips and candy cigarettes.

Saturday mornings were synonymous with cartoon characters, such as the Road Runner, Fat Albert, Scooby-Doo, and Prince Planet. Tots liked Mr. Rogers, Captain Kangaroo, and, of course, *Sesame Street,* which went on the air in 1969. Rocky wasn't Sylvester Stallone, but a flying squirrel that was pals with a dim-witted moose named Bullwinkle. After school, kids watched reruns of *The Three Stooges, The Partridge Family, Gilligan's Island, The Brady Bunch,* and *The Little Rascals.*

We looked forward to the televised jumps of motorcycle daredevil

Evel Knievel, who performed such stunts as riding through walls of fire and vaulting over live rattlesnakes, tanks of sharks, mountain lions, and even canyons. The high ratings were due not so much to the exploits themselves as to the fact that they often ended badly. Moms disliked such televised spectacles since they provoked copycat stunts among us kids, many more of which ended badly.

Then there were the commercials. The crying Indian taught us not to be litterbugs, while Smokey the Bear warned that "Only you can prevent forest fires." A person born in America in the sixties may not know who was president then, but he or she can score 100 percent on the following matching quiz:

1) Lucky Charms	a) They're Greeeeeeeat!
2) Frosted Flakes	b) Toucan Sam
3) Rice Krispies	c) Are for kids.
4) Fruit Loops	d) Magically delicious.
5) Trix	e) Cuckoo for them.
6) Cocoa Puffs	f) Snap. Crackle. Pop.

A kid had one commencement, and that was from high school, not kindergarten or any other grade. You didn't graduate from junior high—you finished it, the same way you finished dinner. The only way to get a graduation other than from high school was if you completed a vocational program like cosmetology school, or else college. Nothing in between mattered.

The only rite of passage upon completing junior high school was to avoid the librarian on the way out the door. The book gestapo, who'd gone to school with Mary Todd Lincoln, believed that a full body-cavity search was not unwarranted if she had reason to believe you were still in possession of one of her tomes.

The most fun to be had starting a new grade was examining the inside front cover of your textbooks to see if any older siblings, baby-sitters, or neighbors had once possessed them. Some kids had all new school clothes, but many received hand-me-downs from older brothers and sisters. However, it didn't matter much because there weren't any cup holders in cars or movie theaters back then, so we all went around with dark stains on our crotches.

Many of us also walked around with bowling ball bags. Not as a fashion statement, but to hold our Yellow Dot—a polyester ball made by Columbia, known for its good roll and hit. That my parents were not league bowlers placed them squarely in the minority for the Buffalo area. In the seventies there were almost as many bowling alleys as bingo parlors. And there were a *lot* of places to play bingo, since games were usually run in church basements and a Roman Catholic church could be found in every neighborhood.

To Buffalo teenagers back then, safe sex meant having your boyfriend over on league bowling night, when it was a sure thing your parents would be out late. We were such a bowling-centric culture that parents explained thunderstorms to frightened children as God bowling in his big alley up in the sky.

Uncle Jim started working as a pinspotter at Bowlaway on Niagara Street in 1952, when he was fifteen. Before machines, the pins had to be reset by hand after every throw. The pay was twelve cents per game, but Uncle Jim soon received an offer of eighteen cents per game over at the Knights of Columbus on Delaware Avenue. And at the Knights, the guys would often tip the pinspotters by tossing quarters down the lanes.

What's the connection between bowling and blue-collar, immigrant-filled industrial cities like Chicago, Detroit, Cleveland, Saint Louis, and Buffalo? "The modern game of bowling originated in the factory, was popularized by the factory, and projected the ethos and acoustic ambience of the factory," according to Gideon Bosker in *Bowled Over: A Roll Down Memory Lane*. "From the dull roar, thunderous claps, and mechanical clang-jangle of automated pinsetters to the arrangement of the alleys, with their clean geometry and mechanics reminiscent of a conveyor-belt line, bowling was a workingman's game that put a premium on precision, piecework, and team play. Here was a recreational setting where the sound of machines prevailed over the sound of human voices, and where the body's movements were governed by a single imperative—to hook a rolling sphere made of hard rubber into the 1–3 pin pocket and knock ten pins to the floor."

The televised bowling competition *Strikes, Spares, and Misses* seemed to play in a continuous loop. Every time you passed a TV set ("the idiot box," according to striving parents and local intellectuals), the hushed and tension-filled voice of an announcer best suited to narrating documentaries on glaciers was sizing up the complexity of the next throw. Every kid knew *bedposts* (seven and ten pins remain standing on the ends, also called *goal posts*), *grandma's teeth* (a random gap-filled group of pins left standing), a *dead apple* (a ball with no power when it reaches the pins), and the *Moses ball* (parts the pins like the Red Sea and turns a spare into a strike). Though most of us couldn't read by the time we started school, we'd learned how to score bowling by hand, using a black-and-white chart and a pencil stub with no eraser, and were adept at the complicated math involving two strikes followed by a spare. Electronic scoring wouldn't arrive until after we'd finished high school.

The bowling alley also served as a primary source for the industrial-sized rolls of toilet paper that we used to decorate houses. These could be easily removed from the premises in bowling bags without arousing suspicion. Raising hell on a Saturday night meant being tossed out of the bowling alley for extreme bowling (purposefully hurling a ball into the next lane to mess up hypersensitive league bowlers and watch them go berserk), toilet-papering your teacher's home on a double-dog dare, and then locating a pig to grease and let run through the school on prank day.

The lanes also served as a good place to find guinea pigs. It was widely rumored that if you ate Pop Rocks with soda, the combination would blow up your stomach and you'd die, so older kids regularly offered the young and gullible free supplies if they were willing to experiment.

My looks were pretty well set by age three—skin that started to crisp the second the sun came up (even if only in conversation), green eyes in a permanent squint, matching green freckles (add red sunburn to brown freckles and somehow you get lime green), a nose way too big for my face, and an unruly tangle of strawberry blond hair that was the envy of nesting animals during the winter months. My nose was clown red year-round, and there were undoubtedly neighbors who speculated that I was a child alcoholic.

The only event I can recall from my early years was a hospital visit at age three to have my tonsils and adenoids removed. In the few decades between Dad and Mom's childhood in the thirties and forties and mine in the late sixties and seventies, many deadly diseases had been reined in through vaccines, sanitation improvements, and antibiotics. These included tuberculosis, typhoid, smallpox, diphtheria, German measles, mumps, pneumonia, infantile paralysis, scarlet fever (to a large degree), and the dreaded polio. Mine was the first generation without the all-too-common limp or shoe lift found on so many of our parents and teachers who'd contracted polio in the forties. Only a decade before our arrival, the American microbiologist Jonas Edward Salk had developed the first effective vaccine, and we are eternally grateful to him for getting us back into the public swimming pools.

Like many children who don't thrive in dampness, I was constantly sick with colds, bronchitis, sinusitis, tonsillitis, strep throat, walking pneumonia, and chronic earaches. Alas, no vaccinations had as yet been invented to ward off these annoying scourges. By age five I'd had enough chest X-rays to qualify for a photo finish with Madame Curie in the radiation-poisoning marathon. Penicillin was such a large part of my diet that I eventually became immune to it, along with several other antibiotics. One theory bandied about regarding my apparent feeblemindedness was the possibility that partial deafness had occurred as a result of numerous ear infections, and so my hearing was constantly being tested. I carried codeine cough syrup around like a Bowery bum with a flask of Thunderbird stuffed in a hip pocket and was self-medicating by age six. (Though it turns out this is rather common among Irish and Scandinavians, who are for the most part too cheap, stubborn, cynical, or just plain dim-witted to visit doctors.)

In every picture taken with Santa Claus at the local Hengerer's department store, I am a pasty white waif with half-closed eyes, leaning into Santa more for support than to secretly share my Christmas list, which had an iron lung near the top, right below the oxygen tent.

This is not to say that I was considered a sickly child, like those who missed weeks of school due to asthma, heart problems, or other more serious ailments. As people say they are "living with cancer" or "living with AIDS," we Buffalo kids simply "lived with upper respiratory distress." Science tells us that heat kills germs and bacteria, and between the long, harsh winters and the energy crisis, we were in short supply of heat—natural or manufactured. The germs easily located these gaps. At any given time, over half the class was hacking, sniffing, sneezing, and wheezing. If the government ever needs a group of individuals highly resistant to infectious disease for a mission into some plague-infested area, my suggestion would be the Buffalo public school teachers. And based on the amount of time they spent on strike and without a contract when I was growing up, it's safe to say they'd jump at the extra money.

Upon arriving at a sleepover, I simply handed all my medications to the mother in charge and she lined them up on the counter with the other twenty or so bottles. For those who forgot their Robitussin, St. Joseph's children's aspirin, and Mentholatum (our locally manufactured version of Vick's VapoRub), there were vats on hand.

Mothers had to be philosophical about contagion or we'd all have been confined to bed for the duration of our childhoods. If you were able to walk the length of the house you were allowed to go out. They just figured that while playing or sleeping with all the other diseased kids, you'd either build up your immune system or give whatever it was you had to someone else.

By the time we were in school, most of us no longer needed the measuring spoons and cups that came with our medications. Moms would just toss the bottle into the backseat of the car, and the kids would take a swig or two, hitting somewhere within range of the recommended dosage. We were champion pill swallowers by age eight.

Not only could most of us knock back big chunks of vitamin C and what looked to be doses of antibiotics for horses, but we did so without having anything to wash them down.

Mothers of large families acted as pharmacists to save on visits to the doctor and costly prescriptions. If a child recovered before the medication ran out or there was an unused refill, then it was stowed in a cabinet along with fifty or sixty bottles of accumulated liquids and pills. The next time someone took sick, Mom searched through her stash and tried to match up the symptoms with whatever the doctor had previously prescribed for a similar ailment, whether it had belonged to that child or another member of the family. Pets were often included in this system.

Sometimes there would be a week in May, right at the tail end of cold and flu season and just before allergies hit, that I'd emerge for a breath of fresh air while enjoying a brief moment of perfect health. I'd sit underneath the weeping willow tree out front, its long skirt hanging down to the ground. This canopy of leaves formed an enchanting secret playhouse through which I could see out while the inside was shady and protected. I passed lilac and rosebushes on the side of the house and the yellow forsythia blooming directly below my window, all of which would attempt to collapse my lungs and choke me starting in another few days when thick clouds of pollen darkened the summer skies. And if they didn't fully succeed, winter and bronchitis would be back with a vengeance soon enough.

Eight

Buffalo Runs Riot

Though I don't remember it, support for the Vietnam War began wearing extremely thin during my toddler years. The war was complicated, to say the least. However two things were certain: (1) in Vietnam there were two huge armies, the North equipped by the Soviet Union and the South by the Americans; and (2) the United States had lost the Korean War in 1953, thereby demonstrating that we couldn't win a land war in Asia.

In 1966, four California housewives attempted to block a shipment of napalm bombs. Napalm was a highly combustible and controversial fuel produced primarily by Dow Chemical Company and had a tendency to stick to anything it hit (including civilians) and burn uncontrollably.

In 1967, a few days before my second birthday, folksinger Woody Guthrie died. Among the many popular tunes he'd penned was "This Land Is Your Land," a song that could go a long way as our national anthem, being that it's in a sensible key and contains fewer polysyllabic words.

Two weeks after my second birthday, 50,000 antiwar demonstrators gathered to march on the Pentagon. There were now almost 500,000 United States troops in South Vietnam. The nation had become its most divided since the Civil War. From inside the White House, President Lyndon B. Johnson could hear the chant: "Hey! Hey! L-B-J! How many kids did you kill today?"

While Johnson was making his momentous decision not to run for reelection in 1968, I was enrolled in a local preschool. Back then, preschool was not the norm for children the way it is now. Such souped-up socialization was primarily for those with means, or it was intended to keep an only child from becoming an inappropriately behaving life-long loner (read: homicidal maniac). For me, it was a halcyon period of playing with trucks, singing songs, and painting, during which time it was a commonly held belief that I was mildly autistic. I recall enjoying the school rabbit and playing off by myself with a load in my pants.

The Summer of Love was followed by The Year of Hate. Dr. Martin Luther King Jr. was shot to death by a sniper on April 4, 1968, while standing on the second-story balcony of the Lorraine Motel in Memphis, Tennessee. Dr. King was there to support a strike by the city's sanitation workers. The night before he died, Dr. King gave a speech at the Memphis Temple Church in which he said, "I've seen the promised land. I may not get there with you. But I want you to know tonight that we, as a people, will get to the promised land." Okay, what did *he* know and when did he know it?

Robert F. Kennedy was assassinated just eight weeks later, on June 5, 1968. But I have no real-time recollection of either of these tragedies. I was vaguely aware of talk about busing children from the inner city to the suburbs and vice versa in order to desegregate the schools. And that popular songs included "Blowin' in the Wind" and "The Times They Are A-Changin'" by a young folksinger from Minnesota named Bob Dylan.

The evening news showed demonstrations and occasionally riots in downtown Buffalo. With its racial, ethnic, and income diversity, the city was a flash point during a time heavily focused on civil rights, desegregation, women's liberation, war protests, and growing mistrust of the government. Most black leaders were against the Vietnam War because of the high incidence of casualties among blacks—they made up only 11 percent of the United States population but comprised 16 percent of the army's casualties in 1967, and 15 percent for the entire war. Others were against the draft because the system favored the wealthy and well connected through student deferments and coveted positions in the National Guard (which was not deployed overseas back then) that weren't easily accessible to the lower classes.

Bomb threats were constantly being phoned in to universities and government buildings. The courts where my dad worked happened to be a favorite target, and sometimes he'd spend hours standing outside in the cold or arrive home early if the call came late in the afternoon.

Further complicating matters was growing unemployment. As with other Rust Belt cities, there had been a great migration of blacks to Buffalo in the forties and fifties. They had come to take industrial jobs and escape the rural poverty of the South. Only, many of these jobs were now heading overseas. Residents became increasingly unhappy with poor housing, insufficient employment opportunities, and the fact that most of the work available to them offered no future. Between June 26 and July 1, 1967, rioting on the east side of Buffalo virtually shut down the city. On the night of June 28, forty people were injured, fourteen with gunshot wounds.

During these turbulent times, my aunt Sue was a teacher at one of the most troubled and overcrowded public high schools in Buffalo. A faculty meeting was called to assign teachers a riot-duty position—the place they'd head in an uprising, so as to maintain control of the agitated student body. My tall, willowy, and anemic aunt was assigned the front doors of a high school housing over two thousand inner-city students. She was to lock the doors, use her body as a barricade to prevent the stampeding mob from exiting, and insist that they calmly and quietly return to their classrooms.

Fortunately, Aunt Sue was a bit more creative when chaos did indeed erupt in the weeks following the assassination of Dr. Martin Luther King Jr. She went directly to her riot station, flung the doors wide open, told the students to have a lovely day as they tore out of the building, and offered change from her own pocketbook in case anyone needed to make a phone call or was short on bus fare.

At Berkeley in California and Columbia in New York City, college students were staging uprisings and administrators were scrambling to meet their demands by organizing black studies programs and allowing teach-ins (a day set aside for discussion of the Vietnam War). Tensions escalated on May 4, 1970, after four students at Kent State University in Ohio were killed when National Guardsmen opened fire into a crowd protesting the United States' bombing of Cambodia. This set off demonstrations at many other schools across the country that up until then had been relatively peaceful.

The historical event I recall most clearly from those years is the moon landing in July of 1969, when I was almost four. This is because I rose at dawn and switched on the TV, anticipating a fun-filled morning of cartoons. However, in place of my beloved *Flintstones*, this damned slow-bouncing man in a white space suit was on *every channel*—the same footage played over and over and over. It wasn't exactly rife with the special effects we'd later see in movies like *Star Wars*, just a big, white tin can, some guys in asbestos-removal outfits, and an American flag being stuck into the ground. A scratchy soundtrack played Neil Armstrong nattering away about a small step for man and a giant leap for mankind, and a big hello to his neighbors back down on Earth.

Meantime, I just wanted him to float off the screen for good so we could get going with Fred and Barney. They didn't stop the coverage, and my day was essentially ruined. Thank you, NASA. Had they told me I was watching half a billion dollars being squandered while millions of Americans were still living in poverty, I might have been slightly more interested. At the time, proponents of the space program insisted that the scientific value of a moon landing would add ten years to a man's life. The best I can tell, all that's happened so far is that a lot of dentists raked it in after people ended up with cavities from drinking Tang. And Ralph Cramden blustering that he was going to send Alice to the moon was no longer just an idle threat.

It was the same summer as the famous Woodstock concert in upstate New York. But that event didn't interrupt my TV viewing and no one we knew attended, so I don't remember it. Plus, I was still operating under the "not quite right" designation, and adults were ready to call it a day if they could just get me to learn my name, address, and phone number, in case I should wander off.

In the fall of 1969, Yale University admitted its first female under-graduates. Back in my hometown, O. J. Simpson started playing his first of ten seasons for the Buffalo Bills. During that decade, he would set numerous records, including most career rushing yards (10,183) and highest career rushing average (4.8 yards per carry). In 1973, O. J. became the first pro runner to gain 2,000 yards in one season, finishing the year with 2,003 in just fourteen games. The excitement was enough to cause my church to move the Sunday morning service from 11:00 AM to 10:30 AM so that no devout fan should risk being late for a game, heaven forbid.

The Vietnam War went on and on, a constant buzz in the back-ground that could at any moment erupt into World War III. My memo-ries of it are isolated jigsaw pieces from a much larger puzzle that I didn't understand at the time. Convoys of army jeeps rumbled along the New York State Thruway as we made our way to Long Island to visit my father's parents for a week every summer. Children might suddenly be silenced with a ferocious hush when the radio was turned to certain newscasts; the names of the dead were read on the radio in the morn-ing, during which time grown-ups were silent and had a faraway look or tears in their eyes. Afterward, they might glance at their young sons and take a deep breath. At the end of the lists were usually the names of journalists who'd recently been killed while covering the war.

Additionally, I recall an awful lot of talk about birds. Supporters of American intervention were "hawks." Critics were labeled "doves." Senator George D. Aiken of Vermont insisted that the country needed more owls. Senator Warren Magnuson of Washington declared himself an American eagle. And political humorist Art Buchwald admitted to being a bird as well, specifically a chicken.

Antiwar protests peaked on November 15, 1969, with 250,000 people marching through Washington, DC. The chant "Hell no, we won't go!" entered the lexicon. On the evening news, things were con-stantly on fire—tires, draft cards, flags, and even people. Although bra burning was often discussed, I don't recall seeing any cups going up in flames. However, I do remember plenty of fiery arguments breaking out over politics, people exiting parties and family gatherings in a huff, doors slamming and tires screeching as they roared out of the driveway. Before leaving the house, women cautioned their men, "Remember, don't talk about the war."

I regularly heard discussions about a lottery, only it wasn't the kind where someone won money or a new car. And the draft wasn't the usual type that blew through the windows, causing us to catch bronchitis. David Lance Goines, a student active in the free speech movement at the University of California at Berkeley, wrote to his draft board in 1966, "Gentlemen: Please remove my name from your mailing list, as I am no longer interested in your organization."

The older boys known to my family were classified as 1A or 4F, and they all had numbers, but I didn't understand what that meant. Same with "Going to Canada," where 50,000 to 100,000 Vietnam protesters headed since that government refused to extradite draft resisters; I thought they were planning a vacation. On the other hand, one could say I had access to as much factual information about the war as the government was willing to provide the American public at the time, which is to say, not very much.

Nine

A Full House

When not in school, I played with my neighbor Mary Pyne. We sometimes phoned or hollered over the fence, but usually we just walked into each other's houses as if they were our own. Mary was half German, half Irish, and twice as wild as her wild red hair. She was ten months older and scheduled to start kindergarten the same fall; thus we would serve out our school sentence in tandem.

Mary was the older sister I didn't have and taught me everything worth knowing about growing up. She happened to be so well-informed as a result of having four older brothers and four older sisters. These eight siblings had read every page in "A Child's Garden of Tricks." Through the trickle-down effect we learned how to escape school by placing a thermometer near the radiator or under a light bulb, the right way to put tape over locks so that after sneaking out we could get back in again, and which classes to avoid because the teachers were tough. When it came time to learn how to drive, Mary explained that if you *have* to hit a car while backing out, make sure to pick the one without anyone in it.

If we took all the large families in the neighborhood into account, there was an endless pipeline of information fueling future generations. They instructed us how to prepare for prank day—where to get the thousand marbles that would be dropped down the stairwell of the science wing and to tell everyone to put alarm clocks in their lockers, all set for noon, right in the middle of a class. They knew how to get into the school through the air shaft in order to rearrange the furniture. Teenage boys could jimmy most locks and hot-wire cars, trucks, and even earth-moving equipment at local construction sites. Parents and teachers didn't stand a chance.

Mary's home contained eleven people (two parents and nine children), two dogs, and a cat. Upstairs were five bedrooms: one for her parents, two rooms with two boys apiece, one with the two oldest girls, and a room added on over the garage for the three youngest girls. Mary's room reminded me of something out of a storybook because there were three twin beds, three dressers, three closets, and three desks, all exactly the same, evenly spaced, in a neat row. Mrs. Pyne sewed the bedspreads and curtains, and they all matched. She also made clothes, tablecloths, pillows, and even wedding dresses for a few of the girls, despite Mary and me ruining at least one cutting board by employing it as a sled to fly down the stairs, and several pairs of pinking shears by fashioning snowflakes out of cardboard.

The myriad Pyne children often had friends over. Mary's dad would occasionally glance at a child and not be able to recall who was in front of him. In these situations he'd start at the top of the list, saying, "Diana, Melinda, Barbara, Kathy..." and either he'd eventually arrive at the bottom, or to hurry things along my friend would chime in, "I'm Mary."

In Mr. Pyne's defense, Mary and Kathy both had red hair, Kathy and David were twins, Barbara and Melinda both had long dark hair, and people regularly said that Mary and I were easily confused for one another. Mr. Pyne was also somewhat hard of hearing from gunfire in World War II, and this worked enormously in our favor when planning any sort of escapade.

I particularly enjoyed when Mr. Pyne attempted to instill order on those late June evenings when it stays light until nine at night and we kids were recovering from being winter-worn and snow-shocked. The charge out the front door would begin as soon as the dinner plates were cleared, and Mary's father, who was a burly six foot seven and worked as a detective for United States customs, would stand on the porch and make a vain attempt at crowd control.

"Kevin, stay in and do homework!" Kevin had graduated the year before.

"Melinda, stay in and do homework!" Her parochial school had already let out for the summer.

"Mary, stay in and do homework!" We were starting kindergarten in the fall. There wasn't any homework.

Eventually he'd give up these attempts at discipline, rub at the red rivers of capillaries etched into his nose, and shout, "Dammitol!" This was Mr. Pyne's favorite exclamation, and when he bought a boat and asked all the kids to vote on a name, they were unanimously in favor of *The Dammitol*.

However, Mr. Pyne did have one significant weapon in his arsenal, and that was access to government files, which he'd regularly employ to perform deep background checks on any boys who might come a-courting. This substantial database turned up everything from traffic violations to an arrest record to unpaid child support. Next, the suitors experienced a full interrogation, during which he might casually leave his badge lying on the coffee table. Though my favorite use of the badge was the time he was cut off in the church parking lot after Mass at Saint Leo's and flashed it at the driver who'd committed this sin.

In my opinion, large families had several advantages. If a vase is broken in a house with many children, it's very hard to pin the blame on anyone. Furthermore, teachers tended to give the same tests year after year, and these could be passed down like a favorite sweatshirt. Best of all was the school science project. The Pynes had a plaster volcano painted to look real and wired to produce smoke. While other students toiled away for weeks on their projects, the Pyne children dug this old standby out of the basement on the morning of their presentation and lugged it to class, along with the two note cards taped to the base explaining how volcanoes work. It was pretty beat up by the time Mary brought it to school, the smoke nothing but a wisp, though still good for an easy B.

In charge of feeding and clothing such a large brood, Mary's mom was an energetic saver. She sewed most of the family's clothes and made as much food from scratch as possible. Several bushels of McIntosh apples would remain in the Pyne garage throughout the year, and any child who complained of hunger was instructed to eat an apple. The remainder would become pie filling, preserves, and canned fruit to sustain the family through the long winter months. Fresh fruit of every variety wasn't flown to supermarkets around the country on a daily basis back then, and what wasn't in season, if available at all, came with a hefty price tag.

When a grocery store advertised an especially good sale, Mrs. Pyne would load as many of us as she could find into the station wagon. Sitting behind the wheel of the car was perhaps the only time I saw her sit down—ever. The seat in the back pointed toward the cars behind us, and was convenient for making faces at other drivers while not being seen by our own chauffeur.

These sales were almost always one per customer. Mary's mom would marshal the troops outside the supermarket entrance and hand us each a dollar along with the coupon. We'd go in one by one and purchase the item, more often than not a half gallon of milk. Sometimes she'd send six of us through the checkout three times, and by the end of the maneuver we'd have eighteen half gallons of milk. This supply lasted nine kids between the ages of five and nineteen about four days, then everyone had to drink powdered milk until shopping day the following week. In my neighborhood, *shopping day* was synonymous with *payday*.

When Mary and I were small, we'd sometimes play in the mountains of laundry in her basement. Our families weren't clothes conscious, and kids under ten didn't care what they put on, so long as it was warm in the winter and cool in the summer. For a period of time when all the Pyne offspring were young, there weren't many individually owned garments so much as a boys' pile and a girls' pile, and you grabbed something that looked to be about the right size.

When a child angled for a new coat, shirt, swimsuit, or Scout uniform, she was usually sent to the hand-me-down bag. The objective became to prove, beyond a reasonable doubt, that nothing in that bag could possibly work, that the coveted article was nothing that Mrs. Pyne could possibly sew, and that a trip to the store was absolutely necessary.

Mary, being the youngest, had the odds stacked against her, and I doubt she wants to hear about the hand-me-down bag ever again.

One day a week Mrs. Pyne baked bread, and when we arrived home from school, a dozen loaves were spread across cooling racks on the kitchen table. The entire house smelled delicious, like an enormous bakery. At the time, kids looked down on homemade bread and instead wanted store-bought bread. Wonder Bread, to be specific. It wasn't until adulthood that I realized we'd enjoyed the best bread in the world, fresh from the oven.

Mary's mom was a terrific baker. And it was a good thing because there was a birthday almost every month. She regularly made delicious cakes, cupcakes, and cookies, even if they didn't last more than a few minutes. We learned fractions by dividing up the beaters after she finished with the icing. We'd get to lick one-quarter of one beater under strict surveillance from the others, to make sure our tongues didn't "accidentally" slip onto their section.

Everyone in our neighborhood knew the saying "Eat what you can and can what you can't." It was especially popular during the seventies, when inflation had sent the cost of groceries soaring. Most people planted a garden and went fruit picking in local orchards and then canned a portion of it to be used throughout the year. That way, in the middle of winter, we could enjoy tasty creamed corn and glazed carrots, freshly baked apple crumble, and for breakfast, smear some strawberry jam across a thick slab of homemade bread. The pantries of the most adventurous canners also contained tomato sauce, corn relish, and watermelon pickles.

Folks with any sort of a yard grew lettuce, tomato, radishes, peppers, and cucumber for salads, and then peas, beans, corn, onions, and carrots for the table, followed by zucchini and broccoli for quiches, watermelons for dessert, and of course, pumpkins for the kids to carve into jack-o'-lanterns at Halloween. The surplus cucumbers were loaded into jars of brine along with some white vinegar and various ingredients that hinted of voodoo practices—celery seed, turmeric, ground cloves, and dry mustard—and miraculously transformed into pickles.

However, the excess zucchini would meet a less-glamorous fate. When the prolific squash started overtaking the yard and creeping in through the windows, as it always did around the middle of August, the wayward zucchini would be gathered up in large shopping bags and surreptitiously abandoned in the middle of the night on the front porches of neighbors without vegetable gardens. This practice was known as "zucchini dumping."

Also collected and sent to the kitchen for canning were buckets of raspberries grown on trellises next to the shed or against the fence in the backyard, and the apples and peaches from nearby pick-your-own orchards.

Mary's mom regularly took us apple and berry picking. By patrolling the fields and issuing regular reprimands, Mrs. Pyne attempted to keep her platoon focused on the task at hand. But the day would grow long, the sun fiercely hot, and inevitably a fruit war would break out. The strawberry patch was particularly susceptible to uprisings, with tangled vines that made ideal ramparts and tiny green unripened berries not all that different from BB-gun pellets. Meanwhile, their overripe counterparts had fallen to the ground and become mushy and bug infested—perfect for splatball.

Peak canning time at Mary's house was early September, and amazingly there was always a zero absentee rate from school during those two weeks. Because unless you were dead and had a certificate to prove it, you'd get stuck cleaning fruit, leaning over steaming pots, and stirring vats of gucky jam until it was ready to be put in jars and sealed with wax. The kitchen was over a hundred degrees, every surface covered with sugar, pectin, funnels, strainers, Ball jars, Mason jars, brass lids, and red rubber rings. Canning even had its own lingo—we "put up" or "put by" vegetables and preserves. If you were planning to feast on peach melba in March, you packed the fruit in halves in wide-mouthed jars with a light corn syrup. People liked to joke, "You can't put peaches up yourself."

If a child did get conscripted into the canning brigade, there was at least one exciting scenario to contemplate—it was common knowledge that a tiny error could lead to the dreaded botulism and the entire family would die slow, horrible deaths. Only mothers were two steps ahead of bacteria, and in addition to keeping the process sanitary, twenty-four hours after canning they checked all the seals by pushing down on the flat metal lids; the top was supposed to be slightly concave and not move when pressed in the center. To be extra safe, they'd test the seal by tapping the lid with the bottom of a teaspoon to make sure it made a high-pitched ringing sound. If there was a dull thud, then the jar wasn't sealed properly, or the food was in contact with the underside of the lid. In this case, the jar went into the garbage and a shout went up the back stairs: "Who sealed the peach halves?"... Silence.

Mr. Pyne was a large, gruff-voiced Irishman, so we all toed the line whenever he was around. But that was only during the evenings and some weekends, since, in addition to working downtown from nine to five, he was also in the Army Reserves. Mary's mom was petite, about five foot nothing, and yet the offspring all inherited their father's genes, absolutely towering over her by age twelve, girls and boys alike. So she was constantly swatting at us with spatulas, hairbrushes, and frying pans, especially for sneaking into the pantry and eating applesauce that was supposed to last until spring. Mrs. Pyne used to hide the keys to the pantry and the spare freezer, but we were constantly finding them or sneaking them from out of her purse. One of the older boys could pick the pantry lock, while another had an actual copy of the freezer key.

Mrs. Pyne didn't have the time or necessary hidden video equipment to determine who was responsible for such infractions, and, like the Irish Republican Army, no kid was about to tell on another. Thus, if something went missing, such as three gallons of ice cream meant to go with that night's birthday cake, then everyone was going to get it. A shout would go up and we'd all race down the stairs toward the front door, neighborhood kids included, and Mrs. Pyne would be standing on the landing with a wooden spoon in hand. We'd fly out the door like a flock of excited birds, shrieking and laughing, knowing there was safety in numbers. Mary and I had the least to worry about since we were the smallest and not only viewed as low on the responsibility chain, but hardest to catch in a crowd. To discipline the boys, who often raided the freezer for hamburgers and steaks, Mrs. Pyne would stand on a chair and twist their ears. But even this only made them wince slightly or laugh.

Had the Pyne household not been Roman Catholic and strictly antievolution, it could best be described as survival of the fittest. Playing the card game bloody knuckles with Mary's brothers meant that's exactly what I was going to end up with. The loose tooth of a younger sibling was extracted by attaching it to the garage door with fishing line and then slamming the door shut. Belching contests were a serious matter, and some Olympic burpers were brought up through the ranks at that long wooden kitchen table. I remember being challenged to a soup-eating contest, and after the word *go* was hollered, I was the only idiot to reach for a spoon. By that time they'd all gulped their soup in one swallow and slammed the bowls back onto the table. I learned. The best food went to the swift and the tricky. Fights broke out, bones were broken, and favorite objects could fly out open windows, sometimes with small children still attached to them.

Mary's father installed an aboveground pool in the backyard, and during the summer gleeful shouts from all of us kids splashing around echoed throughout the neighborhood. The pool wasn't heated, and to dive in during the month of June could cause one to momentarily lose consciousness and then hallucinate about being aboard an icebreaker in the North Atlantic. But we passed many joyful hours playing Marco Polo and other games, jumping out every once in a while to go and pee in the grass.

When the pool became grimy with leaves and dirt, we'd move clockwise around the edge and create a giant whirlpool that would bring the debris to the center so it could be easily scooped out. However, the whirlpool always became so strong that we little kids couldn't even cling to the stairs long enough to climb out before getting sucked around again. Much like a roller coaster, it was terrifying but fun. Similarly, we were supposed to wait a half hour after eating lunch to go back in, but never did. This served to add another element of exciting danger: that a child would suddenly get a cramp and drown, or vomit all over everyone.

When winter arrived, Mr. Pyne made an outdoor skating rink by flooding the backyard. We'd play tag, broomball, and, if Mrs. Pyne wasn't on the lookout, we'd bowl with the frozen chickens she'd picked up on sale and stored in the freezer, or play hamburger hockey using frozen beef patties as pucks. True, when she did catch us it was harder to escape the yard wearing skates, but out on the safety of the ice, it was also more difficult for her to clock us with that frying pan.

Ten

Egg Salad Days...Beads of Paradise

Sweet Home is a school district about eight miles northeast of Buffalo in the town of Amherst, where the suburbs melt into farmland. At least they did when I was a kid; now it's all strip malls, office buildings, multiplexes, and Hooters. Even my old jawbreaker and Slurpee dealer, 7-Eleven, home of the brain freeze, has become a medical center.

As for the name Sweet Home, it's obvious that someone inhaled too much eraser dust. The surrounding school districts were mostly named after their respective towns: Kenmore, Williamsville, Cheektowaga, Maryvale, and Tonawanda. An Amherst school district already existed, and the Armory, which would have been a suitable name, based on the bunker-style construction scheme, was also taken. Fortunately, a person couldn't beat up an entire student body for its name, or else I'm certain we would have all graduated to the morgue. Though at basketball games, "Sweet Home Sweeties" was not used in a complimentary fashion by the opposing teams.

Sweet Home High School and Junior High were, at the time, fed by six elementary schools. I attended the one in our neighborhood, Maplemere, walking the quarter mile from home every day to warnings of "step on a crack and break your mother's back."

Although the name Sweet Home conjures up a picture of a cozy Frog and Toad–type dwelling, most buildings in this peculiarly named district were Cold War–inspired tributes to the functional brick architecture of the sixties. This included a brave use of turquoise and mud brown as accent colors, and grayish white asbestos icicles that hung down from the ceilings. Most of the roofs leaked, and we became adept at jumping over puddles and zigzagging around buckets in the hallways, while the windows seeped air to the point where snowdrifts were inside the classrooms. In 2005, long after I'd graduated, a student would plot to blow up the high school, though it turned out not to be an architecturally motivated crime, as I immediately assumed, but rather inspired by the Columbine school shootings in Colorado several years earlier.

The Northeast was hit hard by the utilitarian movement, and industrial cinder-block structures became the cornerstone of the "What Were They Thinking?" school of architecture, where old-world charm meets reinforced concrete. The nearby north campus of the University at Buffalo, just a Molotov cocktail's throw away from my home and school, was fast becoming another funereal example. There's apparently a fine line between the Prairie School and the penal system, one that was quickly crossed after the riots of the midsixties.

The area was still home to prominently displayed yellow-and-black fallout-shelter signs, which had started appearing in 1963, as the Cuban missile crisis heated the Cold War up to a full boil. These were originally placed outside any building that possessed what the Army Corps of Engineers determined to be the proper amount of radiation shielding. Every day, the TV and radio stations interrupted programming and played a recorded announcement: "This is a test of the Emergency Broadcasting System." In the event of an emergency (translation: nuclear war), they were supposedly going to tell us what to do and where to go.

This was shortly after the rage to build home bomb shelters had swept the nation. These concrete dugouts covered with two feet of pit-run gravel still existed on the properties of the middle and upper classes. In addition to stockpiling provisions and converting a covered garbage pail to serve as a toilet, many bunker owners also opted to have a gun on hand. What to do about a pesky nonshelter-owning neighbor wanting to escape the radiation and play pinochle with your family while snarfing all your pretzel rods? The editor of the Jesuit magazine *America* advised shooting him, just like you would any trespasser. Hence the birth of the eleventh commandment: thou shalt not covet thy neighbor's bomb shelter.

Consequently, the Cold War was still being felt, and, in keeping with the Communist decor, schoolchildren were regularly marched through duck-and-cover drills as a way of preparing for nuclear Armageddon. Ticktock went the doomsday clock. We were informed that nearby Niagara Falls, power source for the Northeast Corridor, was the number one target for a Ruskie bomb. Later I found out that kids in Pittsburgh were being told the same thing because of their steel plants, and Detroit children for their truck and automobile manufacturers.

Best I could figure it, if we did survive a bomb by hiding beneath our partly wooden desks (translation: kindling) or under the hall coat-rack, we'd be spending the next hundred years in school, waiting for the radiation to subside—much like the prospect of an endless Thanksgiving. Or as Soviet leader Nikita Kruschev put it, "The living would envy the dead." But if we didn't survive, the bright side, at least for our organization-minded teachers, must have been that we'd perish in alphabetical order.

Although the risk of bombings and nuclear accidents only increased over the years, for whatever reason, the drills stopped in the late seventies. At some point, an official must have figured out that the hall coatrack might not in fact operate as the defense mechanism they originally thought it to be.

We also had frequent fire drills, which I never understood since all the buildings in that school district were going to be the last things left on Earth after the Apocalypse, along with the cockroaches, pet rocks, and my mother's homemade rolls. During a fire drill on a sunny day, it was safe to say we'd lose about 10 percent of the school population, especially if the exercise came after lunch. There was a low fence at the edge of the playground, making it a simple matter of up-and-over followed by cutting through a few backyards. Winter fire drills posed a challenge because we weren't allowed to stop and pick up our coats; thus 10 percent of the students would still be lost, only in this case to hypothermia.

However, if you showed up at home without a coat in winter you were going to hear about it, usually in a loud sentence containing your full name. While my mom was angry didn't seem the right moment to point out that shouting *"Laura Elizabeth Pedersen!"* when I was the only other person there was obviously a bit silly.

When it came to naming children, none of our parents ventured far from what was standard issue for the day. There were about three of each of the following in every class: Linda, Susan, Lisa, Wendy, and Amy for girls; Jim, Mike, Mark, Paul, and Bill for boys. Being a Catholic town we also had our fair share of Marys, Virginias, Matthews, and Johns. It was the previous generation who had changed their names to Sunbeam and Starshine, and it would be those hippie parents who'd give birth to the plethora of Rainbows, Jasmines, and Moonglows that would follow us.

There were plenty of twins in my school—fraternal, identical, and Irish. None were the result of fertility treatments, which didn't exist back then. A woman wasn't even aware that she was having twins until the first one was born, she was about to hop off the table, and the doctor called out, "Whoa, not so fast!" Nor did people know ahead of time what sex their baby was going to be. Though a multitude of old wives' tales existed about how a woman was carrying the baby (high for a boy, low for a girl), it was a big guessing game. Paint stores sold plenty of primary colors, and parents could never go wrong with the circus wallpaper.

My school was a vibrant mix of Northern European blonds, Irish redheads, and Eastern European and Mediterranean brunettes. Reginald Sutton was the only black child in my kindergarten class. He was friendly and smart, and in the middle of the year he gave all of us chicken pox. When I was born, people with dark skin were going from being called "coloreds" to "Negroes." During my school years, they became "black," and sometime after high school graduation it was changed to "African American."

Students weren't allowed to wear shorts or sweatpants to school, and sneakers were only supposed to be for gym day. Kindergarten was largely about tying shoes bunny ears–style, forming lines, and learning letters, none of which I was capable of accomplishing (where were the shoes with Velcro?). I was the last to comprehend whatever was happening, if I caught on at all, and thus remained silent most of the time. Another battery of tests followed—a jumble of shapes and pictures that I was supposed to connect or arrange, only I ended up randomly coloring them in (and not very well). The results were clear: big dummy with coordination problems, despite normal vision and hearing.

It was suggested that my difficulties could be the result of my left-handedness, or that perhaps my unruly hair was impairing my vision. Polar bears are left-handed, survive in cold climates, and have thick, woolly hair. They might have considered testing to see if I was a polar bear.

My mother had to meet with another counselor who, once again, attempted to help her cope with raising a mentally challenged child. And once again, she completely rejected such conclusions and informed the doctors that I was simply operating on my own timetable. (Perhaps one dating as far back as the Julius Caesar calendar.) But that was the good thing about being of Irish descent—Mom had a sizable capacity for denial. Sigmund Freud once said about the Irish, "This is one race of people for whom psychoanalysis is of no use whatsoever."

In first grade, we were told to raise our hands when the teacher called out the month of our birthday. Finally, an instruction that I could understand. My birthday is October 8. It transpired that most birthdays were in September and October. Obviously there's nothing like only three TV channels combined with a long, cold winter and the high cost of heat to feel the love.

When leaving elementary school at the end of each day during the winter, kids were checked to make sure they wouldn't die from exposure on the way home. And when Buffalonians talk about exposure, we don't mean streaking or attracting publicity. If we didn't have a hat, scarf, mittens, and boots, we were sent down to the lost-and-found trunk near the main entrance to borrow the necessary articles. After a half hour of fumbling with zippers and snaps, wrapping scarves so as to be protected but not completely blinded, and fastening rusty metal boot buckles, we were lined up for a final inspection and then shoved out into the blowing snow looking like an army of Michelin midgets.

We weren't proprietary about our winter garments. Any ski mask would do the job. Even in a house like mine, with just three people, the hallway was a jumble of outerwear. In large families, kids didn't have their own stuff for long and eventually just grabbed from the heaping pile underneath the stairs. Boots didn't always match, and neither did mittens. It wasn't unusual for a child to have a mitten on one hand and a glove on the other, or a coat a few sizes too large.

It was always possible to borrow something if the weather turned nasty, or if we arrived at a friend's house unprepared to go outside and play. At the bottom of every winterwear heap were the colorful accessories knitted and crocheted by elderly aunts and well-meaning grandmas who were lying around with broken hips and had become unstoppable handicraft mills. These collections always included hats made of multihued wool yarn that looked ridiculous on anyone. And not only did they give us hat head, but also static head. The thing to do was yank the brim down low and wrap a scarf over your face so as not to be recognizable, other than as a one-person Village People.

The dreaded dickey also managed to weave its way into the tapestry of daily life. A dickey is the top part of a shirt, usually a turtleneck, with no fabric for arms, nothing below the chest, and was less expensive than a real turtleneck. The biblike garment is tucked into a sweater, and *supposedly* no one can tell it's not a full turtleneck, especially if they can't see the very obvious half-moon outline across the chest. Children wearing dickeys were routinely tortured by having them yanked over their heads while walking down the hallways at school, resulting in demented shouts of "Give me back my dickey!" The dickey was flung atop the lockers, where it was impossible to retrieve without a ladder. I never went after one but can only imagine that it was a regular dickey graveyard up there.

While kids in Kansas were being trained to make a run for the root cellar in case of a cyclone, we were taught what to do if caught in a blizzard. According to our teachers, this entailed digging into the lee side of a snowbank and then removing our clothes and using them to insulate the "igloo" in order to survive on combined body warmth. In second grade, a question immediately arose: "How can we remove our clothes if we're trapped in a storm with boys?" It was a time when spraying for cooties was commonplace, and often required, and that was when the boys in the vicinity were fully clothed. However, by junior high, most girls were trying to arrange to get caught in a snowstorm with the boys of their choice.

Elementary school was an enjoyable time of making things out of colored construction paper in sync with the seasons. Most classes had several paste-eaters and magnifying-glass bug-burners. The teacher gave me lefty scissors with green plastic handles, but there was still no telling my snowflakes from my leaves.

As a left-handed writer, I was classified as a "pusher"—one who clutches the pen between thumb and forefinger and smears as she goes. The slant travels anywhere from left to straight up and down to a hard right, and changes every inch or so. For some reason this style of writing looks physically painful, though it isn't, and strangers often ask pushers if it hurts them to write. Lefties can alternatively be "hookers"—they hunch over and curl their hands around a pen so they're practically imitating the right-handed slant. For the most part, hookers and pushers alike smudge their work, can't see what they've written, and have an uneven scrawl. This being the case, calligraphy with a steel-tipped pen and a bottle of India ink is not a good pursuit for the lefty. Perhaps the nuns were right.

Somewhere around the third grade, my academic classification was upgraded from *probably retarded* to *below average*. And though slow of wit, I was not faint of heart. I became convinced that I could fly like the superheroes in my Saturday morning cartoons and loved the sensation of being airborne. By age five, I was regularly donning a blanket as a cape and taking flying leaps off the stone bench in front of the fireplace. At seven, I was jumping off rooftops at nearby construction sites or from the branches of our oak tree, sometimes holding an umbrella above my head. I'd like to blame it on peer pressure, but that wasn't a factor, since I often leapt alone. Eventually I managed to crack my head open five times. With such an accumulation of scars, my scalp now resembles a map of the moon. Or, as Dad likes to say, my head has eight corners.

It was obvious I wasn't going to win any beauty contests, talent shows, or athletic competitions. Family members were willing to consider themselves fortunate if I became semiliterate. By the end of third grade, my teachers were exasperated that I still couldn't tell time. It was the year before digital watches arrived on the scene, and if Debbie hadn't become tired of me constantly asking her the time, I still wouldn't understand the little hand to this day. One afternoon she took me up to her room and explained the process by using an alarm clock. It was no easy task, but she eventually prevailed. If you really want to teach something to an eight-year-old, find another eight-year-old.

Thus, I didn't distinguish myself in elementary school, other than to garner a membership in Monkey Club, which meant I'd climbed a rope to the top of the gymnasium. Basically anyone with two arms and legs could do it.

When it came to socializing, I was incredibly shy and had two friends: Mary, who lived in the house behind mine, and Debbie, from the next block. In fourth grade, our teacher, Mrs. Franz, asked Heather Osgood to be my friend. The woman should have been a matchmaker, since more than three decades later, we're still great friends.

My favorite memory from elementary school would have to be of my third-grade teacher, who was fond of stopping at the Scotch 'n Sirloin on the way home, tossing back a few gin rickeys to dull the pain of explaining long division, and then making late-night Nixon-like phone calls to parents. It was a small school in a small town, and people tended to overlook such idiosyncrasies, especially as it went without saying that only working at a nuclear power plant could be more stressful than teaching third grade. However, one night my spirits-addled instructor made the mistake of dialing Debbie's mom. No-Nonsense Nina took education seriously, particularly when it was mixed three parts to one with inebriation and given a twist. That was the end of the phone calls.

When I began elementary school it was the early seventies, and I have vague memories of flowers as fashion accessories, Afros like cater-pillar tents, peace signs, tie-dyed clothes, headbands, striped bell-bottoms so flared a person could hide a cat curled up around each ankle, and pasted everywhere, yellow happy faces with black eyes. Then there were beads, beads, beads—as jewelry, purses, furniture, chairs, vests, and even doors. The ultimate sign of friendship was to give a necklace or bracelet of colorful love beads. No teenager's room was complete without a lava lamp, incense burner, dream catcher, bricks-and-boards bookcases, patchouli oil, disco ball, empty Chianti bottle as a candleholder, and black-light posters that glowed with fluorescent abandon when the regular lightbulb was replaced with a special dark purple one, much to every mother's dismay.

We couldn't walk through someone's living room without tripping over driftwood sculptures, sand art, and homemade candles. My dad elevated candle making to new heights by polishing rocks in a tumbler, mixing them with hot colored wax, and using a blowtorch to shape the concoction around a wick. When friends saw the safety mask and blowtorch in the basement, I think they were inclined to give him a wide berth. Since Dad was already the absentminded professor type, wandering around in a plaid, double-brimmed Sherlock Holmes hat with a smoke dangling from his lower lip, this merely added to a sort of serial-killer detachment.

My mother covered the entire dining room wall with a forest mural, a bold decor statement that could only have been considered a good idea during the psychotropic seventies. As a result, holidays and birthdays were spent in perpetual autumn. Even the cat was freaked out, sometimes heading outside thinking he was going in, or peeing against the birch tree near the electrical outlet. Anyway, the mural covered the doorbell chime, so when that broke we no longer had a doorbell, as my mother wasn't willing to hollow out a tree trunk to fix it.

During the seventies, it was virtually impossible to approach a patio, porch, or bathroom without clunking your head on a fern or spider plant in a handmade macramé hanger. A 1973 book, *The Secret Life of Plants,* informed us that house- and garden plants possess extraordinary powers to feel emotions, diagnose diseases, act as lie detectors, and read minds. Meantime, macramé was thought capable of solving all life's problems and was employed to weave owls, cloche hats, ponchos, caftans, guitar straps, place mats, belts, bracelets, headbands, and tote bags. The sartorial possibilities were endless, hence the phrase *wearable art*. World peace through macramé was undoubtedly just around the next nubby wall hanging.

At parties, our mothers took pictures using Instamatic cameras with Sylvania Blue Dot flashbulbs that left us temporarily blind. We are white faced and red eyed in all these photos, not unlike albino guinea pigs.

Brightly hued Volkswagen Beetles and microbuses were parked on every street, complete with Saint Christopher statues on the dashboard and bumper stickers proclaiming Make Love, Not War, and Join the army: Travel to exotic distant lands, meet exciting, unusual people and kill them. Station wagons the length of hearses were avocado green, turd brown, or harvest gold, with simulated-wood paneling along the sides. Sort of a den on wheels.

It was about this time that the electric bug zapper arrived in the suburban Midwest. I didn't notice any reduction in the bug population, but it certainly provided people eating outdoors with a whole new topic of conversation. The chirping of crickets and tinkling of wind chimes would suddenly be interrupted by a tremendous charge of electric current, and someone would exclaim, "Wow, that must have been a real hugger-mugger!"

My friends' older brothers and sisters scraped together money from paper routes, babysitting, and mowing lawns to buy cars—used Pintos, Novas, and Gremlins were favored by the girls, and for the boys, muscle cars like Camaros, AMC Pacers, Monte Carlos, and Firebirds that were souped up with larger tires and louder engines. The cat's meow was to have a big pair of fuzzy dice dangling from the rearview mirror above the dashboard, while faux leopard or zebra velvet covered the bucket seats. All interior space was taken up by speakers, stereo equipment, and eight-track Queen cassettes in order to effectively blast "We Are the Champions," "We Will Rock You," and "Bohemian Rhapsody." Girl-friends finished off back windows by attaching a stuffed Garfield with suction-cup feet. The end result was known as The Love Machine. A van tricked out with mattresses in the back was called a Shaggin' Wagon.

The Main Street novelty shop did a good trade in whoopee cushions, Mad Libs, rubber dog doo, plastic vomit, black soap, red-hot chewing gum, joy buzzers, and fake cans of peanut brittle that surprised the opener with flying fabric snakes. These were the main attractions at parties, along with piercing each other's ears using a needle, ice cube, and potato. Over the next decade, such forms of entertainment would slowly be replaced by handheld video games, ear-piercing guns, and prescription drugs.

The Attica Prison riots, the bloodiest battle between Americans since the Civil War, made national news in 1971. More than a thousand of the state's worst criminals staged a revolt at the overcrowded Attica Correctional Facility, thirty miles southeast of Buffalo, during which they took thirty-three guards and four civilian employees hostage. Inmates stormed the prison yard and seized the central guard station. Windows were broken, buildings torched, and fire hoses cut. Eventually the prisoners issued a list of demands, including minimum wage for their work, elimination of overcrowded cells, freedom to practice their religion, an end to censorship of reading materials, better rehabilitation services, less pork in the dining hall, and amnesty from punishment for the uprising.

Negotiators agreed to almost all the prisoners' demands, except for amnesty, which became especially difficult after one of the injured guards died in a Rochester hospital. After the state issued an ultimatum demanding the release of the hostages, the prisoners dangled some of them over gasoline-filled trenches in public view and displayed others with knives held to their throats.

On September 13, four days after the riot began, one thousand New York State police officers and National Guardsmen moved in with tear gas and guns blazing, while helicopters hovered overhead. The prison was reclaimed after four hours, but the cost was heavy: four guards, ten hostages, and twenty-nine prisoners were dead or mortally wounded. Subsequent autopsies revealed that all the hostages had died of police fire—not at the hands of prisoners, as many claimed at the time. After examining the bodies and finding the bullets of law enforcement weapons, the coroner described it as a "turkey shoot."

Being a New York State Supreme Court reporter, my father was oftentimes required to accompany judges to Attica Prison for trials. Dad would spend half the morning going back and forth through the metal detector, emptying his pockets and removing his shoes and socks and layer after layer of clothing, until he was down to the metal fillings in his mouth and his boxers with metal snaps. The judge was permitted to go around the metal detector. Perhaps they'd heard about Dad's blowtorch.

Influenced by what we'd seen on TV, and aware of the prisoners' complaints about the food service, for many years after the prison riot, kids at school would bang their trays in the lunchroom and shout, "Attica! Attica!"

In school we were often asked to give money to plant trees in Israel and to save pagan babies in Africa by funding their conversion to Christianity. On the evening news, I watched the trees in Israel burning amidst war and terrorism and the pagan babies in Africa dying of malaria and starving to death in famine after famine.

In the wider world, Governor George C. Wallace was shot on May 16, 1972, while giving a speech for his third presidential bid. The news described it as the bullet of a would-be assassin. This begged the question: Exactly how important must one be in order to be assassinated as opposed to just shot? Wallace was the man who famously stood in front of the schoolhouse door at the University of Alabama to block desegregation in 1962 during his first term as governor, and who proclaimed, "Segregation now, segregation tomorrow, and segregation forever." He lived another twenty-six years, but was permanently paralyzed from the waist down and eventually turned the corner on the segregation issue.

The radio played Joan Baez's version of "The Night They Drove Old Dixie Down," Janis Joplin's cover of "Me and Bobby McGee," The Doors' "Riders on the Storm," and Cat Stevens's "Wild World." In the fall of 1970, rock-and-roll icons Jimi Hendrix and Janis Joplin overdosed on drugs. He was twenty-seven and she was twenty-eight.

At any given moment, at least one radio station was playing Judy Collins singing "Amazing Grace," though, based on the news updates that followed, people felt much more lost than found.

Eleven

The Tundra Years

The energy crisis of the seventies loomed large and still comes to mind every time I see a light left on in an empty room or enter a house where I don't begin to shiver uncontrollably without a sweater. My childhood was a never-ending cold blast of parents yelling: "Turn it off!" "Do you think I'm made of money?" "Are we heating the entire neighborhood?" "Who left the lights on?" and "Who was the last person in this room?" When my mom dies, she'll see the light at the end of the tunnel and then promptly switch it to *off.*

There are almost as many theories surrounding the energy crisis and whether it was real or manufactured as there are about the assassination of President John F. Kennedy. No matter. The fact remains that just as Kennedy was undeniably gone, we were undeniably cold. And it wasn't a dry cold, either, but a really, really damp one.

It's common knowledge that in the sixties and seventies, energy consumption in this country increased by 50 percent. United States' oil production could no longer keep pace with demand and, thus, we became reliant on the Organization of Petroleum Exporting Countries (OPEC), which translates to buying oil from the Middle East. In 1972, OPEC began raising their prices. In 1973, when Israel won a decisive victory in the Yom Kippur War with assistance from the United States, angry Arabs retaliated by raising oil prices again. On October 17, 1973, OPEC increased the price of oil from $3 a barrel to more than $5 a barrel. A day later, production was cut by 5 percent a month. Then Iran, with the consent of other oil-producing nations, called for an additional price hike to $11.65 per barrel. The result was a new phrase in the lexicon of the American motorist: gas lines.

For the Middle East, it meant the start of petrodollars pouring into countries like Kuwait, which had until then been devastatingly poor, and an overnight transition from riding camels to flying Learjets. For the United States' economy, which was heavily dependent on industry, it translated into a huge drop in growth, the start of hyperinflation, double-digit interest rates, unemployment, and an increase in the poverty rate. Or what President Jimmy Carter so poetically summed up as a "terrible malaise." (Fortunately we had the comic relief of his boozy, chain-smoking brother, Billy, acting as a paid lobbyist for the anti-American Libyan government and introducing his own line of beer, Billy Beer.)

In the midseventies, the energy crisis temporarily subsided, and although prices didn't drop back down to previous lows, fuel became more available. In 1979, however, OPEC again jacked up prices and curtailed production. A major cause was the revolution in Iran, one of our largest oil suppliers, where fifty-two United States embassy employees were taken hostage. We quickly halted imports from Iran as they enthusiastically canceled our contracts. All this touched off another round of inflation combined with a stagnant economy. Eventually, in the early eighties, OPEC was no longer able to keep some members from overproducing and once again prices dropped.

For most of the seventies, 30-watt bulbs were put in light fixtures meant for 60s. Kitchen ovens were left on with the door open for extra heat, and, as a result, this was usually the warmest room in the house. Grown-ups huddled in chairs around the oven to talk, while children played cards on the floor, as if the stove was a campfire. When it came time for bed, families would fight over who was sleeping with the dog, nature's very own electric blanket. I'd be surprised if it wasn't a Buffalonian who came up with the expressions "two-dog night" and "three-dog night," which describe how many hounds are necessary to keep a body warm in a punishing climate.

People talked about America generating more of its own power.

This would supposedly be done through nuclear reactors. On March 28, 1979, a plan to shift toward nuclear power turned nightmarish when a major accident occurred at "fail-safe" Three Mile Island near Middleton, Pennsylvania, only 230 miles southeast of us. For a few tense days, we fretted about being annihilated by radiation poisoning in what Walter Cronkite described on the evening news as the "worst nuclear power accident of the atomic age," followed by the dire warning that "the potential is there for the ultimate risk of a meltdown." Some Catholic churches in the Middleton area were giving entire congregations general absolution, a sacrament offered only when death is imminent and usually reserved for armies going into battle.

There were no casualties, but citizens would think twice about welcoming a nuclear reactor into their town, city, or even state. A growing number of Americans questioned the safety of nuclear power and marched on Washington carrying placards that said Babies Die First! and Hell No, We Won't Glow! Witness the birth of NIMBY—it's a great idea, but Not In My Back Yard—which would also extend to the construction of low-income housing, prisons, mental institutions, and other necessary but undesirable or unsightly facilities.

Inflation approached 14 percent in 1979 and climbed to over 20 percent in 1980, the worst level in decades. In October of 1981, the interest on a fixed-rate thirty-year mortgage reached 18.5 percent. Unemployment hovered around 6 percent in 1979 and by December 1982 was 10.8 percent nationwide, the worst since the Great Depression. With Buffalo losing its manufacturing base, the local jobless rate was about twice that of the national average.

Residents continued to leave in search of work. Over the short space of three decades, Buffalo had gone from a thriving industrial center to a resort town—people would resort to anything to escape. It became the first city to allocate money for a self-esteem campaign (Talkin' Proud), designed not to attract visitors so much as to aid the psyche of locals. While we hoped for the best, we expected the worst.

Having come of age during this stagflation, I'm told that my first conversation opener was "Can you believe the price of sugar?" and that

I finally learned addition by counting cars lined up at the gas pump, and subtraction by counting the number of locals who lost their jobs at the Bethlehem Steel plant, one of the largest steel mills in the world, which kept laying off workers.

People recycled like pioneers, not for the sake of the environment, but because of budget constraints. We saved and reused everything, from paper plates, cardboard boxes, egg cartons, and jam jars to rubber bands, butcher string, and pencil stubs. These last three items were usually stuffed into a messy kitchen drawer that eventually could no longer be opened, which was mostly a relief. Mothers had crumpled tissues in their purses dating back to the Eisenhower era. ("It's perfectly fine—just blow your nose.") Kids were constantly told, "Eat your dinner because there are starving children who would love to have that food!" "Can we send the peas to them?" was a dicey response if Dad arrived home grouchy after working all day.

Fuel prices climbed higher and higher. At one point, license plates that ended with even numbers could get gas only on certain days and odd numbers on the others. Oftentimes, large signs proclaimed No Gas Today! While driving in our Oldsmobile station wagon, which was approximately the size of a living room set, we could actually watch the needle drop while braking and wondered if we were looking at the gas gauge or speedometer. It wasn't uncommon to rummage through the seats, ashtrays, and one's pants pockets for change, and then buy gas in the amount of $1.22, which basically got us as far as the next filling-station line. Hence, large, inefficient Detroit gas-guzzlers came to be known as "fossil burners."

President Carter reduced the speed limit so that we not only lived like hibernating bears, in dark, cold houses and schools, but now had to travel slowly in order to reach them. My parents saw new signs on the thruway that said 55 Saves Lives and apparently thought they referred to the thermostat, because every month the heat continued to be turned down, down, down. Dad's bedroom/office became positively Dickensian as he warmed his fingers over candles while typing court transcripts.

The day those heating bills arrived in the mail from National Fuel, the local gas company to which all local families tithed a large portion of their income, was the worst. That night we could hear fathers throughout the neighborhood going ballistic as they dragged their La-Z-Boy chairs next to the thermostat to stand (or rather recline) guard over it. And while dads were at work, red-lettered cardboard signs posted above the thermostat warned DO NOT TOUCH! A line made with a black Magic Marker was usually drawn somewhere around fifty-eight degrees to indicate that the red arrow should not be seen even slightly above woolly mammoth territory. The dads who were handy with tools found ways to lock the dial right where they wanted it, on *subarctic*. Clustered around the television in afghans, we thought the kids in *Little House on the Prairie* and *The Waltons* didn't know how good they had it.

The heat was turned way down or off at bedtime, so when we woke up for school, the house resembled the inside of a meat locker. After a blustery night there'd be a little snowdrift on my window ledge—inside! The most frigid zones were the bedrooms, since they were generally farthest from the furnace. Kids realized that the smart thing to do was take a shower or bath at night and sleep in our school clothes, like minutemen during the Revolutionary War. This way we could leap onto the freezing floor in the morning, pray that someone else's butt had preheated the icy toilet seat, throw on our shoes and coats, and run to catch the bus. Sleeping in a "Little Match Girl"–cold room also had the effect of curtailing any bed-wetting. One would probably freeze to death.

If there happened to be an unoccupied room in the house (not much chance in my heavily Catholic neighborhood), then the radiator in that room was switched off and the door was closed. Voilà! The family had a walk-in freezer at no extra cost. Or, for maximum economizing, we used duct tape to seal the door until spring.

With an ice-pick wind screaming off Lake Erie and rattling the windows, indoors we wrapped ourselves in blankets or else jumped around to keep warm. There was a small minority of citizens with heat—those who lived in apartments where utilities were included and they happened to reside closest to the furnace, old people with thin blood, and rich people, who set their thermostats to an extravagant seventy degrees.

When I walked into one of these homes after being refrigerated for so long, I stumbled over to the couch and passed out as if I'd just eaten three Thanksgiving dinners.

However, the people hoarding the heat got their just desserts in the form of dry, flaky skin and chronic dandruff. With wool hats, coats, and socks constantly being put on and taken off, the inside of our homes were laboratories for experiments with static electricity. Shuffle across the floor in a pair of fuzzy slippers and then go electrocute the cat or, in the case of my friends, zap a younger brother or sister. When Dad came to kiss me good night with those leather soles scraping along the gold shag carpet, he could basically set my hair on fire with a single peck to the forehead.

Sure, we could use a humidifier to try and avoid middle-of-the-night nosebleeds. But the old-fashioned machines increased the mold and microbes in the air, and eventually we'd end up with pleurisy in addition to well-entrenched bronchitis.

There was no doubt that the cold was a beauty treatment all its own. Any Manhattan modeling agency will tell you that the best finds in fashion photography of the seventies were Polish girls from Buffalo, with their flawless skin, chilled to perfection. Or as my childhood friend Heather puts it, "Buffalonians are the *other* white meat."

As kids, when one of us complained of being cold, we were told to move around. We were told to wear layers. We were told to stop complaining because did we think we were the only ones who were cold? Jimmy Carter wore a cardigan sweater, thus earning him the nickname Jimmy Cardigan. Apparently he was cold too. But did we see him complaining? No, we did not. Catholic children were of course instructed to "offer it up," meaning to suffer in peace so that God could use their sacrifice for the good of the church or a specific intention close to their heart.

Yet we loved to play in the snow, and our parents didn't seem to worry about us dying out there. They knew how to do it right, like sun-tanning—start 'em young with a few hours out in the cold every day until they build a base and can stay out until bedtime.

We kids regularly heard rumors that the school district maintained in its files a study concluding that children learn better when the heat in the building is kept extremely low. And that cold builds moral fiber. However, I think they made a mistake between the thermostat being low and completely off—we were being kept fresh like minnows. For us, the problem wasn't so much the shivering as the telltale sign of whispering to a friend; even though the teacher couldn't *hear* us talking, she could *see* the steam created by the warm breath rising from our mouths.

The Energy Police were everywhere. Classroom light-switch plates had bright blue stickers warning KEEP THE MIDDLE SWITCH OFF! This was before people connected the high rate of depression and suicide in Buffalo with seasonal affective disorder (translation: foul-weather fatigue). It's one of the few places where a person can open her window shades in the morning and the rooms actually become darker. I grew up two decades before the University of Buffalo school newspaper started running ads in March asking if students needed to talk to a counselor or sit under a sunlamp. The dark side to the nearby and popular Niagara Falls is that one person takes the plunge at least every two weeks—and it's not for lack of guardrails and warning signs.

Statistically, Buffalo is right up there with Seattle when it comes to the number of overcast days, and Lands' End wouldn't be off base in creating a sweater color resembling dried mud and calling it Buffalo beige. A local newspaper ran a cartoon of a mother taking the hand of her frightened little girl and saying, "Don't be afraid, dear, it's only the sun." At any given time, the city is half under skies the color of duct tape and half under indictment. That being the case, Buffalo is not used as the backdrop for many romantic comedies. Or in the rare case that it is supposedly the setting, such as in the Jim Carrey movie *Bruce Almighty*, most of the filming is done elsewhere.

If someone encounters native Buffalonians now residing in other parts of the world, he should never ask them about the weather when deciding what to wear. "Fine" to them means it isn't a blinding blizzard. "Nice" implies that the mercury is above thirty degrees Fahrenheit, with a low windchill factor. And "hot as blazes" is anything above fifty.

Likewise, most Buffalonians who move away (deserters) tend not to be big consumers of air-conditioning. Hot air will eternally be looked upon as a luxury, something for which we once paid almost an entire month's salary. Also, we're not raised to view a continuous blasting of cold air as climate control so much as a draft; it was the thing that came seeping through our windows and underneath doors, caused flu, pneumonia, and sent Grandpa to an early grave.

Buffalo should be called the City of Space Heaters. For denizens of the Magnolia Belt, these are operated with gas or kerosene (though nowadays they tend to be portable electric devices that plug into a wall), and they can more or less heat a room. However, space heaters were and still are responsible for a lot of fires. We may as well have had a pile of newspaper (which people often left next to the heater, go figure) doused with lighter fluid lying around the house. For this reason, older Buffalonians are terrified of fire, especially mothers; before leaving the house they shout, "Is everything turned off? Is everything out?" while frantically dashing from room to room searching for lit candles, plugged-in curling irons, and electric blankets with short circuits.

Twelve

Mary Tyler Moore for President...Hit Parade... The Americans with No Abilities Act

The only political drama other than the Vietnam War and the Attica Prison riots to enter my early consciousness was Watergate—a word that has since become shorthand for an amalgam of scandals and disclosures that culminated in President Richard Nixon's decision to resign in 1974 rather than face impeachment. And, it also led to the guilty pleas and convictions of more than thirty White House and Nixon campaign officials.

This one made absolutely no sense to me. I'm certain there were more-aware-and-intelligent eight-year-olds around who not only understood it, but could have gone so far as to explain why Gerald Ford issued a pardon so that Nixon couldn't be indicted for any crimes he may have committed while president. I, on the other hand, was still coming to grips with the fact that the letter *y* could sometimes be used as a vowel. This information alone was so overwhelming that I was barely able to absorb anything else that was happening at the time.

In fact, the only reason I even recall President Nixon resigning is because my mother made me watch it on TV during dinner that night. I couldn't have been less interested, but she insisted this "historic moment" required our full attention. Thus were the drawbacks of living with someone who came from a newspaper family.

Eventually we'd start watching *The Mary Tyler Moore Show* while eating dinner. That's how we all knew when to arrive at the table—at

6:01, when the daily *MTM* reruns played on channel twenty-nine. (The actual show ran from 1970 to 1977.) Watching TV during dinner every night helped disguise a Chekhovian household where my mother and father only spoke to each other when necessary, which pretty much meant when snow tires and storm windows needed to be put on and taken off. We lived more like roommates, with the subtext that everyone was on the way to something else more permanent that didn't involve the others, and this was merely a way station, albeit one with a resplendent lemon-and-tangerine-colored kitchen. My parents took separate cars wherever they went and slept in separate bedrooms as far back as I could remember. The hallway outside my room had always been Kashmir, with Mom (India) living off to the east and Dad (Pakistan) to the west.

As one character put it in Michael Bennett's hit Broadway show *A Chorus Line*, "It wasn't paradise, but it was home." Though he also said that suicide in Buffalo is redundant. It was meant to be an inside joke, since Bennett was a native Buffalonian. Or perhaps an outside joke, if he was taking the harsh winters into account. (I've since heard that this wonderful line was contributed by the playwright Neil Simon.)

As a kid, I simply enjoyed the characters and jokes on *The Mary Tyler Moore Show*. In retrospect, I think the groundbreaking sitcom had a deeper impact. I'd occasionally hear how a woman could pursue almost any career, live on her own, and put off having children, but I didn't see much of it in my neighborhood. Most women were homemakers. If an older woman passed away and her husband died a few months later, people said it was a result of a broken heart. But deep down, they suspected he killed himself with his own cooking and housekeeping, or lack thereof.

If the women in my neighborhood went to work, it was usually as teachers, nurses, or secretaries. In local businesses, women made coffee, not policy. Otherwise, they volunteered at the blood bank, book-mobile, or their church. Buffalo was always slightly behind when it came to social progress. In fact, the cowboy comedian Will Rogers once said he wanted to be in Buffalo when the world ended because it would happen there five years later. Outside of my Unitarian church, few people I knew declared themselves to be women's libbers.

To me, Mary Tyler Moore's career-girl life felt like a realistic possibility, whereas women my mom's age saw her as a feminist, or part of a new generation, for better or worse. It was logical to assume that I'd work in a place like Mary's newsroom, with male colleagues, and that in the managerial hierarchy some men would be above me and some below me. I imagined someday moving into an apartment like Mary's, except with a big *L* on the wall instead of an *M*. I'd have entertaining and neurotic friends, and we'd have sitcom-worthy times together. Mary's theme song constantly reassured me: "You're gonna make it after all."

Designer jeans, along with disco, didn't reach the Midwest until I was in junior high. In elementary school, kids wore Levi's from the Gap if they were with it, and Toughskins from Sears if they weren't. My Toughskins were a particularly vibrant purple. Cool or clueless, everyone carried a comb in his or her back pocket.

For the hip crowd, the music of the moment was Swedish pop sensation ABBA, courageously sacrificing lyrics that plumbed the depths of sophistication for ones that rhymed in English. The nature lovers had "Rocky Mountain High" and "Take Me Home, Country Roads" by John Denver and "Seasons in the Sun" by Terry Jacks, while teens sang and smooched to the Partridge Family's greatest hits, including "I Think I Love You" and "Come On Get Happy," and the entire Captain & Tennille oeuvre, which featured "Love Will Keep Us Together" and "Muskrat Love." Lyrics from the latter still sparkle like tiny jewels in the snowbanks of my mind: "They whirl and they twirl and they tango, singin' and jinglin' the jango."

If we wanted to make a mix tape of favorite songs, there was no Internet from which to download music. We had to call our request in to the radio station, wait an hour or three for it to be played, and then start the tape recorder at exactly the right second. The disc jockey usually talked over the first and last parts of the song, and because it wasn't a direct feed, if the dog barked, our mothers yelled, or the phone rang, that was on the tape too.

A favorite album of elementary school children was *Free to Be...You and Me*, which, through a variety of catchy songs and stories with generous banjo accompaniment, insisted that it was okay to be different. This meant everyone from the beleaguered William, who desperately wanted a doll (Grandma arrived and finally had the good sense to buy it for him), to the athletic Princess Atalanta, who recoiled in horror at the idea of Daddy selecting her husband; a race was organized to determine her mate, which she handily won, and she went on to marry her true love. The king eventually realized that the times were indeed a-changing.

However, this album paled in popularity compared to Sonny and Cher's hit song "I Got You Babe." In the early seventies, *The Sonny and Cher Comedy Hour* was the must-see TV of its day. Other popular variety shows were *The Captain & Tennille* and *Donny and Marie* (that would be Osmond).

On school field trips we'd sing "Ninety-Nine Bottles of Beer," "John Jacob Jingleheimer Schmidt," and "Bingo" until one of the drivers probably quit and went on to invent Prozac. Everyone's favorite bus song (of which there are different versions) was:

> Miss Suzy had a tugboat,
> Her tugboat had a bell,
> Miss Suzy went to heaven,
> Her tugboat went to
> Hello, operator, please get me number nine,
> And if you disconnect me, I'll kick you from
> Behind the 'frigerator, there was a piece of glass,
> Miss Suzy sat upon it
> And cut her little
> Ask me no more questions,
> I'll tell you no more lies,
> The boys are in the bathroom
> Zipping up their
> Flies are in the park,
> Bees are in their hives
> The boys and girls are kissing
> In the D-A-R-K, D-A-R-K, dark, dark, dark!

When the teachers finished all the aspirin, we moved on to "I Met a Bear" and "On Top of Spaghetti."

A portion of almost every school day was dedicated to learning the metric system—converting back and forth between inches and centimeters, gallons and liters, miles and kilometers. Teachers warned us that a rude awakening was coming soon and we'd find that Fahrenheit, pounds, and acres would all be suddenly gone! Science teachers explained that our system of measurement was decidedly stupid to begin with—based on the length of someone's body parts—and all truly modern countries used the metric system, which made sense since everything was divisible by ten. We sat there, day after day, bent over our desks dividing by five-ninths and multiplying by nine-fifths and subtracting thirty, or whatever it was. The Metric Conversion Act to change over the United States was passed in 1975, but it had about as much effect as Prohibition and Vatican II. President Reagan canceled funding for the Metric Board in 1982, and it was as if the whole thing had been a bad dream, like the idea of Americans learning how to speak foreign languages. It wouldn't be until twenty years later, when NASA scientists (my age) started forgetting to convert English units into metric, and millions of dollars in equipment was lost or ruined, that people began saying, "Hey, what ever happened to that whole metric thing?" Otherwise, the United States stands proudly alongside Liberia and Myanmar, the only other nonmetric countries in the world.

After school we rode banana-seat bikes, played by the creek (a paradise for budding botanists and pyromaniacs), and started impromptu games of kickball, dodgeball, street hockey, and freeze tag in neighborhood cul-de-sacs. Compared to nowadays, life moved at a tea-party tempo.

Few kids had lessons or organized sporting events to attend. And no one had heard of a playdate or quality time with parents. The word *parent* was still regarded as a noun, and it was at least a decade before it would become firmly entrenched as a verb. We were responsible for making our own friends, and parents were viewed as an impediment to enjoying life's finer things, such as homemade milk shakes, prank phone calls, and playing with matches. They were adversaries to be ditched as soon as possible. A day spent with Mom was a day spent in suburban purgatory—standing around the shoe-repair shop and the dry cleaner's, returning something at the mall, and then being dragged through the supermarket. Not only that, we weren't of much value to our parents, aside from doing typical chores like cleaning, taking out the trash, and bringing in the groceries; their lives weren't loaded with complicated gadgetry that only young people knew how to operate.

The girls played in many of the ball games with the boys, but also gyrated inside hula hoops, skated down sidewalks, played hopscotch, school, and house. Boys went to war using toy soldiers or cap pistols and amused themselves with yo-yos, marbles, and slingshots. Many fine hours were devoted to shadow puppetry. However, we were the last generation to give these activities any serious consideration. The first primitive video game had arrived while I was in elementary school. And I mean primitive—a flashing dot that moved across a screen, pretending to be a Ping-Pong ball.

In winter, we built snowmen and forts and had snowball wars. When I went to elementary school it was still the Woolen Age, and so we had to go inside when our mittens eventually became sopping wet and froze, along with our fingers.

Some of the more expensive boots *claimed* to be waterproof—a bit like ads for mail-order sea monkeys promising hours of entertainment—but the technology hadn't arrived yet, and they really weren't. So we pulled plastic bags over our feet before placing them inside our boots. We mostly used Wonder Bread bags, and you could see the red, yellow, and blue polka dots sticking out above our shins. For this reason, no one ever threw out a bread bag. They were kept in a pile near the back door or in the mudroom. And if we planned to be out for a long time, we double-bagged to reduce the chance of leakage.

When it was too rainy or snowy to go outside, we'd stay in and play board games such as Life, Stratego, Chutes and Ladders, Parcheesi, Candy Land, Monopoly, and Clue, work jigsaw puzzles, build strip malls out of Legos and cabins out of Lincoln Logs, or watch the hamsters scamper around in the Habitrail, a rodent terrarium. Card games were popular, and many a rainy afternoon was whiled away playing war, old maid, go fish, concentration, slapjack, crazy eights, and bloody knuckles. For the more imaginative (or friend challenged) there was the Spirograph (creating hallucinogenic curves on paper), the Slinky (a tension spring that went down the stairs, sort of), and Silly Putty (the result of a failed experiment in making artificial rubber). After it grew dark, we'd play blindman's buff in Mary's basement with her multitude of brothers and sisters and their friends. The blindfold was usually an itchy woolen scarf, and so there was an added incentive to find and identify someone else to be It.

At the beginning of June, the school nurse examined us for head lice. Most of the year it was too cold for ringworm and insect-related problems, and so she dealt with extremely chapped lips, windburn, and the dry, itchy patches of frostbite that would appear on our wrists and ankles where chunks of snow had managed to sneak inside mittens and boots and remained unnoticed for an hour or so.

When the glorious summer vacation finally arrived, kids burst out of their houses by eight every morning and didn't come in contact with parents again until bedtime, except for a quick lunch provided by somebody's mom. That said, the neighborhood was a honeycomb of stay-at-home moms rarely too far out of reach, most able to recognize the sound of an M-80 being dropped into the sewer or an eyeball splattering against a tree trunk. Nannies were unheard of and babysitters a rare extravagance. If younger children weren't being watched by older ones, then they went into the playpen. (Suburban secret: On a pleasant day, the playpen could be moved to the backyard and flipped over, making a nice outdoor cage.)

Staying indoors was *not* an option in the seventies. First off, if we weren't sick, and if we attempted to stay around the house, our parents would likely find some horrible chores for us, like edging the lawn or cleaning the basement. Second, remaining inside was thought to be injurious to a child's health. Third, large broods in close quarters resulted in brawls that began with the innocent-enough sounding she won't stop looking at me." When siblings started knock-down, drag-out fights in the house, moms would say, "Go and murder each other outside so I don't have to clean up the mess" or "Don't get blood on my carpets!"

Parents attempted to annihilate their children on a daily basis, and it was perfectly legal. In the morning we'd hear: "Eat your bacon and fried eggs! Go out and play in the sunshine!" There were no hel-mets or knee pads or wrist guards for cycling and skating. After the first nighttime bike wreck, we usually took safety into our own hands by inserting yellow tennis balls between the spokes of our wheels. Seat belts in cars were either nonexistent or buried under the seat with old gum, loose change, and melted chocolate. We didn't have car air bags, just windbags—older people who wouldn't stop blabbing about grow-ing up in the economic ashes of the Depression.

No one wore hats or sunscreen. We inhaled gasoline fumes from corroded pumps, model-airplane glue, and helium (to make our voices sound high and funny). Our cribs were covered with brightly colored lead paint. When a thermometer broke, parents gave kids the mercury to play with. There was no bottled water as an alternative to the stuff that had killed all the fish in Lake Erie. The only health directive we were given was that if we sat too close to the television set we could go blind. And when the first childproof medicine caps, with two barely visible arrows that needed lining up, arrived on the scene, kids were the only ones able to open them, especially if the grown-up had the tiniest bit of arthritis or vision trouble. It was not uncommon to hear an adult instructing a seven-year-old to "open Mommy's quaaludes."

Good friends became blood brothers or blood sisters by making a cut in a finger with a needle or knife (preexisting wounds were not okay) and rubbing them together. Today this is certainly viewed as being not only disturbingly vampirish but completely unsanitary.

Otherwise, childproofing our homes meant letting the kids get burned by a hot stove and shocked from sticking a knife into the toaster; they did it once, learned not to do it again, and the house was officially childproof. Maximum childproofing meant making sure the kids were raised right so they didn't return home after graduation and the parents wouldn't suffer from full-nest syndrome.

We'd climb trees in the nearby woods, build forts down by the creek, and walk or ride bikes to the school playground to use the swings, the slide, and the merry-go-round. In addition to ball games, we played Mother, may I, cops and robbers, cowboys and Indians, red light/green light, king of the castle, and statue. There were cutthroat games of red rover, the patron saint of dislocated shoulders. During hide-and-seek, when we reached home base we shouted, "Olly, olly oxen free!"

Caucasian children turned a riot of pink, red, and peach—a combination of too much sun, calamine lotion slopped across bug bites, Band-Aids pasted over cuts, and scrapes painted with Mercurochrome (a vivid red antiseptic mixture). These were set off by chalky-white casts applied at the local emergency room to heal broken bones. And I was doomed to wear a skunklike stripe of stark white zinc oxide down my nose to try and prevent an already brightly hued snot locker from veering off in a Ringling Brothers direction.

On hot days we'd dash back and forth through the sprinkler, have water balloon wars, and if we knew someone with a pool, there was swimming, or else we could go to the public pool a few blocks away. There were hours of shouting and splashing, and everyone knew that the time to pee in the public pool was right before the thirty-minute adult swim. Then we wriggled on the hot pavement to dry off.

For girls, entire afternoons could be whiled away sitting on the curb or up in a tree with only a piece of string for entertainment, fashioning it into cat's cradle, witch's broom, and Jacob's ladder. Then they'd move on to clapping games that went with songs such as:

Miss Mary Mack, Mack, Mack
All dressed in black, black, black
With silver buttons, buttons, buttons
Down her back, back, back
She asked her mother, mother, mother
For fifty cents, cents, cents

To see an elephant, elephant, elephant
Jump the fence, fence, fence.
He jumped so high, high, high
That he touched the sky, sky, sky
And he didn't come back, back, back
'Til the Fourth of July!

Girls also jumped rope into the twilight, and their singsong rhymes echoed throughout the neighborhood as the mosquitoes emerged in hard-driving, bloodsucking platoons.

Baby, baby in the tub
Mama forgot to pull the plug
Oh what sorrow! Oh what pain!
There goes baby down the drain!

And...

The King of France
Wet his pants
Right in the middle
Of his wedding dance
How many puddles did he make?
1, 2, 3...

The fun only stopped when the come-home whistles started to blow and the cowbells rang. Kids didn't have watches because they were still expensive, so large families like the Gundermans, Rudewiczes, and Pynes answered to a police whistle recognizable by a particular signal—two longs and a short, three shorts and a long. Mrs. Greenan was a coloratura soprano who'd let a couple of notes fly out across the neighborhood. The sounds of summer.

Standing atop the hill at Cindy Park, I watched as kids cupped hands to ears in order to determine who was being called in. If the bell

114

or whistle went three times and they weren't inside, a paddle-wielding parent was often waiting by the door. After the first round, the rest would follow within ten minutes, as if the parents had phoned one another and conspired to end the fun. I had no bell or whistle, or time to be in. However, once my friends had all been requisitioned home, there wasn't anyone left to play with.

❀ ❀ ❀

Meantime, back at the ranch house, the late sixties and early seventies constituted my mother's frantic-housewife period. She cooked and sewed and gardened. Mom attended adult education classes that enabled her to fashion scarecrow centerpieces out of Styrofoam balls, arrange dried flowers, and make stew in a Crock-Pot. This was closely followed by the homemade-pickle phase, where one couldn't move through the house without tripping over a vat of brine.

She became a Girl Scout leader and for a while I was a Brownie, though not a very successful one. My indoor pallor and allergies did not serve to generate any enthusiasm for huddling around campfires or marking a trail. Group activities in general rarely succeeded in holding my interest.

The rest of the time, Hurricane Ellen papered walls, stained kitchen cabinets, laid floor tile, and lined shelves with contact paper. She sewed all of my clothes until I went to elementary school, and many of her own. For the house she made bedspreads, dust ruffles, drapes, and pillow shams. In the bathroom, she not only sewed the shower curtain, window treatments, and toilet-seat cover, but, using matching fabric and adhesive, she covered the scale, tissue box, and toilet-paper holder. Basically everything was given some sort of treatment, except for the disposable Dixie riddle cups, which she declared to be more sanitary than drinking glasses.

However, Mom appeared increasingly frustrated with every Halloween costume, trip to the craft store, and new McCall's pattern. It all came to an end when I was eight years old, probably the result of three incidents that happened in quick succession.

The first was when Mom accidentally made two left sleeves for a dress she was planning on wearing to a party. When she went to buy more of the expensive fabric to correct the error, they'd run out. The dress and the pattern went into a bag. She folded up the cutting board, unplugged the sewing machine, let the garden go to hell, abandoned the kitchen, closed the laundry, and applied to college.

The second episode was when she invited her family over to dinner to celebrate my uncle's birthday. We were sitting around the dining room table in the faux forest munching salad when we heard a thumping down in the basement. It was winter, so we assumed the furnace was making its usual haunted-house noises. But when it was time for the main course, Mom went to get the roast from the kitchen table and it was gone! Our cat, Spaz, had dragged the roast down the basement steps (thus explaining the thumpety-thump) and begun feasting at the bottom. Without a word to our guests, Mom quickly scooped up the roast, sliced off the section he'd been devouring, turned the oven on high, and put it back in for another twenty minutes. She quietly explained to me that this would kill any germs.

The final, and most pyrotechnically satisfying, event occurred when Mom decided to make fruitcakes for Christmas. After excessive basting with Bacardi rum, they literally exploded, blew off the oven door, singed Mom's eyebrows, and took out the kitchen light. However, like the unflappable Julia Child, Mom pronounced the survivors edible. I actually heard several guests announce it was the best fruitcake they'd ever tasted. So at least she went out with a bang.

It was around this time that my first romance occurred. His name was Bill Alleyne. At the drinking fountain in elementary school, he "asked me out." Bill wrote me a poem, and that was about the end of it. In fact, technically, since nothing has ever been done to dissolve this contract, even though I haven't seen him in over thirty years, we're still going out. Likewise, I'm pretty sure that some of Mary's brothers and sisters are still grounded, even though they're now in their fifties.

It's safe to say that I went right through junior high school without attracting the attention of any scouts for television quiz shows. On the contrary, my academic output served to demonstrate that I had fewer talents than most. I'd finally learned to read, but my comprehension wasn't good. When first introduced to the alphabet as a toddler, I could see that one day it might be useful when it came to reading street signs and the like. But later, when teachers suggested adding the letters together along with numbers, that's where I parted ways with Donald Duck in Mathmagic Land. To this day I can't figure out how many square feet of carpet are needed to cover a room.

Science—what *were* they talking about? I'm still not sure if the moon rises in the south and sets in the north, or if the Earth revolves around space junk or space junk revolves around it. And why don't we fall off the bottom during half the year? If gravity is holding us to the ground, then why don't we at least *feel* as if we're upside-down, with blood rushing to our faces and bad sinus headaches? I can't make out one single constellation or find the North Star. The only thing I'm convinced of as an adult is that the rings around Saturn are made up of my lost luggage.

The extracurricular activities in school turned out to be an even greater disaster. I was a total failure in art. In addition to having absolutely no aptitude, my hands shake like a junkie on the first day of rehab. My mother claims that I inherited this "benign tremor" from her dad. I'm wondering if I inherited the D.T.s from my grandfather. Mr. Schmidt, the art teacher, decided it was dangerous to put X-Acto knives and skinny garrote-style paintbrushes into my trembling hands and substituted a harmless lump of clay for me to work with during these sessions.

It was the same story with music. I was tone-deaf, pitch-deaf, note-blind, and unable to warble anything. There would be the select chorus, the training chorus, and those of us who stood in the training chorus and mouthed the words so as not to throw off the actual singers. I attempted playing the clarinet and quickly gave that up. I sawed away on the guitar for several years because it came so easily to my dad, and now use it as a doorstop. During tap dancing lessons, while everyone was doing step I was doing ball change. Similarly, a series of ballet and tumbling classes did nothing but perhaps accentuate my sheer gracelessness.

My mother and I soon made a pact to abandon the arts altogether. Whatever we would slave away to learn, whether it was painting, calligraphy, or woodworking, my father would waltz in and do it like a professional, without ever having tried the thing before in his life. My mother was the first to bring home a guitar, planning to take lessons. Dad picked it up and played by ear. Forgot your chess set? Give Dad some cedar, polyurethane, and stain, and inside a few hours he'll whip one up that can later be exhibited at a folk-art museum. Mom came home with some oil paints, and Dad knocked out a terrific portrait of a friend's daughter.

This phenomenal hand-eye coordination carried over to his driving. Dad could balance his twin addictions of nicotine and caffeine while steering with his knees for miles, occasionally employing his elbows for tight turns, all while simultaneously operating a butterfly window (the small triangular window that could be found in cars with long front doors) so the freezing air and sleet wouldn't come in (much) and the cigarette ashes wouldn't blow into the backseat and set me ablaze (much). Raymond Carver described himself as a cigarette with a body attached to it; Dad was a cigarette and a coffee mug with a body attached to it.

However, the magnitude of Dad's natural talents was not only unnatural, but downright discouraging. It wasn't the kind of innate ability that excited me with the thought of how he could help on school projects; in fact, it made people want him to go live in the woods by himself, since it was obvious they'd always be rank amateurs in comparison. Even Dad has learned not to pursue artistic activities anymore because it only loses him friends.

Along with everything else, I got off to a slow start in physical education and was unable to comprehend the rules of games or execute a simple play. Through sheer fearlessness and a love of being airborne, I managed to survive tumbling between ages eight and eleven. However, I soon became too healthy (as we politely say about big-boned girls in the Midwest) to be a dainty gymnast. Also a certain lack of natural poise made the balance beam into a nerve-wracking tightrope walk over Niagara Falls. Roller derby would have required a cool nickname like Luna Chick, and so I turned to soccer. How much trouble could I get in running and kicking?

As it turned out, not much. In four years as a fullback, I never scored a goal, but I possessed enough speed to clear a ball out of our end zone and enough bulk to briefly stun forwards on the opposing team. Being a sweeper or a fullback is not so much about being an athlete as it is about being a security guard. And it's not entirely true that I *never* scored a goal. I did score one. Only, it was for the opposing team. The ball got behind me, and, with my heel, I accidentally tapped it between our goalposts.

I was equally klutzy at home, and after I upset a table, broke a glass, or knocked over a lamp, Dad liked to say, "You're the banana peel on the doorstep of progress."

The school natatorium was an overchlorinated Dante's cave that I managed to avoid all the years of my academic incarceration. This was accomplished by cultivating athlete's foot—not because it was unsightly or itched uncontrollably, but so there'd never be the suggestion of a group swim or entrance into the equally skanky showers. The real trick wasn't keeping the highly contagious athlete's foot from causing toe decomposition so much as hiding it from my mother, Nurse Ellen. Aside from avoiding her fungus-sensitive gaze, it wasn't a difficult condition to keep under wraps. Having had my feet frozen several times as a kid, I've always been a sock person, even on the hottest days of the year. When swimming ended in senior year of high school, my graduation gift to myself was a team-sized container of Tough Actin' Tinactin antifungal spray.

Several friends employed another good dodge to avoid having to swim laps. At the first session, a teacher asked if there were any non-swimmers. A few authentic landlubbers raised their hands, but a number of very competent swimmers also claimed to be strokeless. For the next two months, they stood talking and laughing in the shallow end, pausing only to use a kickboard if the instructor looked over. During the last class, these impostors were tested, and by the grace of God they had learned to swim! Fortunately, the gym teachers were Catholic and believed in miracles. Some still insist that those contested waters were a regular Lourdes.

Likewise, I dodged home economics after the first year. This was accomplished by taking refuge in the industrial arts room. However, I turned out to be one of the few students whose mechanical drawings had wavy lines, even when employing a ruler and T square. Unfortunately, this was just before Frank Gehry brought his curvy architectural style into fashion. Furthermore, you don't ever want a lefty using a power saw, trust me.

Thirteen

Born in the UUA...Keeping Kosher

When I was nine years old, the ever-present war that we'd been fighting on the other side of the world at last came to an end, and body bags containing American soldiers stopped being a regular feature on the evening news. Everyone was relieved, especially since Vietnam had become, in writer Michael Arlen's enduring phrase, the living-room war.

Saigon fell at the end of April 1975, and the television showed mobs of South Vietnamese trying to scale a fourteen-foot wall in an effort to reach evacuation helicopters as the last Americans departed the city.

On April 30, Communist North Vietnamese forces captured Saigon (now Ho Chi Minh City), forcing the surrender of South Vietnam. The war had necessitated eleven years of United States military involvement, longer than I'd been alive, and resulted in the deaths of 58,000 American troops and around 2 million Vietnamese, about half of them civilians.

Gerald Ford was president, and the country lingered in its deepest recession since the Great Depression of the thirties. In the seventies, the value of common shares on the New York Stock Exchange fell by 42 percent. It was as large as the collapse under President Herbert Hoover, only spread out over a longer period of time. And thus it was no coincidence that an economic indicator called "the misery index" was created, a gauge combining unemployment and inflation rates.

Vietnam proved that a war of occupation can seldom be won,

unless the intruder is willing to proceed in the way that Rome finally defeated the Carthaginians: kill all the fighters, enslave the remaining populace, raze the cities, and sow the fields with salt. Sadly enough, this fact would soon be forgotten—or conveniently overlooked. It seems our politicians and military strategists suffer from collective amnesia every two or three decades, since the futility of occupying foreign soil had already made itself evident when we lost the Korean War in 1953.

Thinking back, I wonder how parents, particularly mothers, felt when giving birth during those eleven long years. Did they hope the war would end by the time their newborn son turned eighteen? Did they pray for a girl? I imagine it was much like it is today, even though there isn't a draft, with regard to those who ask why anyone would bring a child into this world; we just have to believe that they will grow up to help make the world a better and safer place.

I've often heard, "Your folks must have been hippies." Only my parents were anything but hippies. They both came of age in northeastern working-class families during the forties and fifties. And they never used any recreational drugs.

The hippies were from the generation between my parents and my classmates. The only flower children we knew were offspring of slightly older neighbors and had moved to communes, geodesic domes, and wherever hippies went to practice Kundalini yoga and smoke cigarettes with no writing on them and appear on the evening news, which was where we got most of our information about them. We occasionally had wardrobe crossover—sandals; patchwork vests; violently hued, polyester, zigzag-print shirts; medallions that brought to mind Olympic champions; and long hair. But that was about it.

The hippie confusion about my family probably resulted because we were out-of-the-closet Unitarian Universalists. In short, UUs believe that there is truth to be found in all religions, but no one religion holds all the truth. On any Sunday morning you're most likely to encounter a coterie of dialectic agnostics and social activists waving petitions and signup sheets to tighten DUI sentencing laws, operate food drives, and fight global warming. (That last group is recognizable by their I Brake for Butterflies bumper stickers). You won't, however, find any Bibles in the chapel. But that doesn't mean you can't bring one. Or the Torah. Or a cookbook.

Another way of attempting to sum up UUism is to say that it's Emersonian (Ralph Waldo Emerson was a Unitarian minister), with a strong inclination toward self-determination and personal responsibility. If we wear a T-shirt that says WWJD, it probably means "What Would Jefferson Do?" The emphasis is on deeds, not creeds. "Noisy Quakers" is another popular definition. The basic difference between UUs and the pacifist Quakers is we believe that on occasion arms must be taken up to discourage the more megalomaniacal and murderous of our species.

Some early Americans, based on their beliefs and activities, were tagged borderline UUs. These included Benjamin Franklin, Walt Whitman, and Emily Dickinson. As a child I assumed this was like being borderline schizophrenic.

It's natural to want to take pride in a religion that, while representing less than 1 percent of the population, claims several signers of the Declaration of Independence and five presidents. However, it's also necessary to point out the flip side. The architect of the *Titanic* was a Unitarian. The captain of the *Titanic* was a Unitarian. And, "Nearer, My God, to Thee," the hymn played while the *Titanic* went down, was written by a Unitarian. Our very own trinity of disaster.

People don't really become UUs, convert to UUism, or accept UUism as their personal savior (unless perhaps they're drowning during a failed Greenpeace mission) so much as one day just discover that they *are* UU, have been all along, and find there is a name and place for it, possibly like discovering that one is gay or has a natural aptitude for clog dancing.

Mom was raised Roman Catholic on her mother's side and Spiritualist on her father's. Though my uncle Jim claims that his father was actually Church of England, and a meeting with a Spiritualist who declared himself able to communicate with the dead (undead?) raised the prospect that the man might be able to select winners at the racetrack for Grandpa Watson.

This schism made for some heavy fireworks around the house, especially the day Grandma took my mother to be confirmed. My mom doesn't appreciate being told what to think, plain and simple. For her, the UU church was the last stop in organized religion. It's a place where she can believe as she likes, and yet do so in the company of others. Mom doesn't believe in heaven, hell, or reincarnation, but she insists that if anyone smokes at her funeral she will find a way to come back and put a stop to it.

If anyone was going to commune with spirits, it would be my father, given the clouds of cigarette smoke trailing behind him like phantoms and gray eyes beneath thick wavy hair that turned gray in his thirties. Decades of puffing unfiltered Luckys left his skin such a deathly pallor that I was often tempted to put a mirror under his nose when he napped, in order to make sure the nicotine was still coursing through his veins. Fortunately, Dad's glasses have dark brown frames, or on a particularly overcast Buffalo day we might have lost him for good. I'm constantly amazed that Ingmar Bergman never tapped him to play the part of Death in one of his productions.

Dad was raised a no-nonsense Lutheran. They have a reputation for being a staid, industrious, and sensible people, and my father's folks were no exception. Or, as the joke goes, did you hear the one about the Lutheran who loved his wife so much that he told her? Danish Lutherans are known for being slightly on the dour side, though not to the same extent as the Swedes and Norwegians. Still, I tend to think there's a reason that *Hamlet* was set in Denmark.

When my dad was a teenager, there were plans for him to become a Lutheran minister. However, he began to notice that his pastor spent more time excoriating Catholics than extolling the virtues of a model Lutheran. So Dad decided that in his adult life he wanted a religion defined by what it favored rather than what it forbade.

Being drafted at twenty-one and sent to the front line in the Korean War further shaped his religious views. As a forward observer locating the people his government had decided needed killing, it occurred to Dad that many wars are fought over God. And that whether it was the Crusades, the Balkans, or Sinai, killing was more often than not in some way related to believing in the "wrong" god. If Dad returned home in one piece, he was determined to find a religion where another person's god was not incorrect, just different, and it was okay to have a dozen gods, or no gods at all, or to just sit on the god sidelines while considering which team to back.

Thus it happened that shortly before I was born, my parents cast off their old religions once and for all and joined the Unitarian Universalist Church in Amherst, which billed itself as a place of religious tolerance with an emphasis on social reform through protests, petitions, pickets, and other types of civic action. In the early seventies, buttons like Committee to Reject the President and Suppose They Had a War and Nobody Came? could be found in my church, but rarely in my school or neighborhood.

Many UUs attend church to ferret out individuals they concur with as much as to find some feisty arguments. During the Vietnam War, the Buffalo Unitarian Church provided sanctuary for conscientious objectors. The Amherst church debated the issue and voted against following suit. If local churches in the same denomination can't reach an accord on the issues of the day, certainly no one expects the individual members to agree on everything. Even my parents regularly voted for different political candidates.

One joke has it that UUs go around burning question marks on people's front lawns. Another is that if you cross a Unitarian with a Jehovah's Witness, you get a person who goes door to door for no apparent reason. A favorite yarn says that when a house of worship catches fire, the priest grabs the crucifix, the rabbi saves the Torah scrolls, and the UU minister rescues the coffee urn. Coffee is one of the three UU sacraments, and the church is like a political convention in that all the wheeling and dealing takes place during coffee hour, which usually runs twice as long as the sermon. The other two sacraments are the clipboard and the Birkenstock. We realize that an uncomfortable protestor is a less-effective protestor. Comfort is also synonymous with safety, although UUs still account for over 80 percent of all clipboard injuries.

When two UUs produce a child, there is, of course, great cause for celebration, since a future committee member has been born unto us.

However, instead of a traditional christening, the congregation has a naming ceremony. This consists of a few minutes worked into the regular Sunday service when everyone welcomes the newborn into the community and makes a note of when the child will be old enough to take petitions out to be signed, sell UNICEF greeting cards, and paint placards.

UUs are absolutely wild about committees and discussion groups, even more so than the federal government. We can have a congregation of three hundred members, but over four hundred committees. They say that when UUs die they are faced with three choices: heaven, hell, and a discussion on heaven and hell. It's a well-known fact that a metal clipboard can better withstand any fiery furnace than a wooden cross.

Though many UUs profess to believe in a single god, there are not many who believe that a single god created the universe in one week. This doesn't relate to dogma so much as to the fact that when we work entirely by committee, the idea of anything being accomplished in such a short time is unfathomable. Rather than a comment on the prowess of its members, having sent five of our faithful to the Oval Office more accurately reflects the view of committee-addicted UUs that the presidency means being in charge of the biggest committee of them all, the American People.

To be sure, some UUs pray. However, many address these prayers "to whom it may concern" or, alternatively, "the party of the first part." UUs take summers off to go election-watching in Africa, backpack through Bhutan, and frolic in the sea while avoiding person-eating sharks. For the most part, these small churches on shoestring budgets can't afford to operate during the summer, but members prefer to say that God trusts them. In the end they're looking more for a feeling of closure than salvation.

With regard to finances, UUs don't tend to be well-heeled investment bankers, but instead teachers, social workers, master potters, and minor poets. Therefore our edifices incline toward the modest. Usually the only stained glass to be found is in the sink. And during winter, it's strictly BYOH—bring your own heat. Which also saves money because then we don't need a lot of coatracks.

Though UUs may not be able to afford high-class entertaining, they still love a party. A lively social occasion with drinking and dancing isn't considered to be in any way sinful; if anything, we believe a party is good for the economy and keeps profits flowing for wineries in northern California and cheddar manufacturers in Wisconsin. UUs believe that we have a friend in cheeses. Crackers too.

A good thing about being an only child is that I could join in adult gatherings. Not that UUs are very vigilant about keeping children segregated in the first place, but at my house I was always allowed to remain at a party until I was too tired to stay awake. For many years there were handprints on our living room ceiling from one particular soiree where people danced and apparently walked across the furniture to the asymmetric rhythms of Ravi Shankar's Hindu ragas. Political arguments often took place in Hungarian or German, followed by the appearance of bongos, maracas, and a hurdy-gurdy. My *mother* actually belly danced at a party, wearing a silk turquoise scarf fashioned into a low-slung sarong and playing zills with her fingertips. And Dad, who'd lost his sense of smell, dropped an atomic bug bomb in the backyard right before one barbecue that succeeded in welding partygoers' contact lenses to their corneas.

There were always visitors from foreign countries at these get-togethers. Invited guests called an hour beforehand and asked if they could bring the people staying with them—exchange students, a Bengali family, visiting professors from Kenya or Sofia, someone seeking political asylum from wherever for whatever. There was certain to be at least *one* other person who spoke Bengali or Bulgarian. Neighbors peered over the fence to see if the United Nations was in town.

As a small child, I was sent to an interracial day camp organized by our church and operated on its premises. My mother was on the board of directors. I was one of a half-dozen white children spending the summer making clay creations and jumping rope with a busload of inner-city youth. At the time, I didn't notice anything different about my camp versus the ones attended by my friends—mostly vacation Bible school and Girl Scout camp. Colors were what we used to paint and draw with, not to describe people.

One might charge some particularly zealous UUs with using their offspring to further their social agendas. I recall one Sunday morning spent digging a mock fallout shelter along Main Street and surrounding it with charred dolls to protest nuclear proliferation. Meantime, the church newsletter was a veritable menu of rallies to attend and bills heading for Congress that required phone calls and letters from local constituents.

On weekends, many a UU child could be found accompanying Mom on the ERA bus trip to Washington, or pressed into service painting signs with Dad to protest the treatment of fruit pickers at an afternoon march in front of a local supermarket. Adult UUs regularly volunteered as bodyguards at women's clinics. And if that wasn't enough to prove that we had a dangerous side, Nixon's White House investigated the Unitarian Universalist Association after its publishing arm, Beacon Press, brought out the first full edition of the *Pentagon Papers*.

Even though I was only seven at the time, I recall that extra wine and cheese was needed at the UU church during the first month of 1973. The first cause for celebration was the Supreme Court decision *Roe v. Wade*, which overturned antiabortion laws in forty-six states on January 22; the second was the end of the draft five days later, on January 27.

In the eighties, my minister handed out Trojan condoms to his flock as part of a sermon on AIDS awareness and prevention. The national media dubbed him The Condom Cleric and wanted to know what in God's name he was doing. I can't say the resulting paparazzi carnival affected membership at our church, but it certainly increased attendance at the Baptist church across the street, as they apparently wanted to get a good look at who they were praying for.

There are a few drawbacks, in addition to sore feet, to being born into this low-density religion. The UU child is not exposed to the Bible to the extent that most Christians and Jews are, so we tend to fail the test on *The Grapes of Wrath* in high school. Religious symbolism usually went right over our heads. There's the story of the little UU girl who describes Easter to her teacher: Jesus is resurrected, they roll back the stone of his cave, and if he sees his shadow there will be six more weeks of winter.

The church offers no specific guidelines for raising a UU child. Parents are left to use their own judgment. And so as horrifying as this may sound to the many of today's self-actualized parents, I *was* spanked as a child. Though my father halted corporal punishment when I reached the age of reason, i.e., when I understood that I wasn't supposed to dash out into the road because I could get run over by a car. My mother stopped spanking me when I was able to run faster than she could. I attribute this ability to evolutionary biology: we develop the traits we need in order to survive.

All religions have their taglines. The Irish say "God willing" after everything, e.g., I'm going to take out the trash, God willing. UUs like to say "as you are able," e.g., stand as you are able, give as you are able. It's too bad that most aren't able to sing, though people claim this is really because they're too busy looking ahead to see if they agree with the words.

Also, UUs are rampant revisionists. Some of them are working to change the word *women* (look what it ends with!) to *Estrogen Americans*. The old standard "Onward, Christian Soldiers" has actually been rewritten in our hymnbook as "Forward through the Ages." The holiday pageant can easily become *Coincidence on Thirty-fourth Street*, complete with wise persons bringing gifts and gingerbread persons served afterward. Around President's Day they get busy considering a petition to change *Founding Fathers* to *Founding Parents*. And many will say that Moses came down Mount Sinai with the Ten Suggestions.

Every Sunday, we sang our modified hymns along with life-affirming poetry put to music and songs from other religious traditions, all to the piano stylings of a longtime church member named Charlotte. By the time I began attending the service, she was quite elderly and losing her eyesight. However, Charlotte knew the hymns by heart, so being unable to see the music wasn't a problem. As the years passed, she often unknowingly repeated verses, added a few new ones, or segued into other hymns entirely. For the congregation, it was like being participants in a fast-moving volleyball game—we didn't know what was going to happen from moment to moment, so everyone remained alert, anxiously glancing from their text to Charlotte for a clue as to where she was headed. More often than not we managed to catch up by the time we saw her lean over for that last big chord.

The UUs made a lot of statements while I was growing up, however fashion was never one of them. Back in the seventies, a typical Sunday put the following on display: a beaded necklace from an African or Far Eastern country where one had gone on sabbatical or to serve as a human-rights observer, a protest T-shirt, a long, flowing peasant skirt, a brightly colored madras shirt sold by village-women's collectives, jeans painted with peace signs, Dr. Scholl's, Birkenstocks, and clogs. Put UUs in suits or dresses for their funerals and they'd most likely consider it a waste—all dressed up with no place to go.

Despite talk of separation of church and state, prayer and religion were everywhere in the Buffalo area, the village atheist be damned. My public school teachers were mostly Catholic and Evangelical Christian, so there was a fine line between homework and the Lord's work. One administrator was fond of reminding me that Saint Laura was a ninth-century Spanish martyr who became a nun after being widowed and was later scalded to death in a vat of molten lead by her Moorish captors. Was this a threat or a promise? Prayers were said before most athletic events at my *public* high school, and I would think, *If we win, then that must mean God doesn't like the opposing team.* Even the chorus sang mostly religious music. Once a year, a student who was Jewish or agnostic would ask our Bible-backed music teacher why all the songs featured God, Jesus, Mary, the Twenty-Third Psalm, and other religious references. She always replied that some of the best chorale music is religious. I don't doubt this. However, we might want to consider that this was coming from a woman who believed that during the Rapture she was going to be sucked out of her Buick Skylark up to heaven while the rest of us went over the guardrail to die a fiery death in a roadside ditch.

Because of my friends' diverse beliefs, they had several religious holidays when they were able to stay home from school. And that's the only change I'd recommend for UUs—how about a day off for the kids? Susan B. Anthony's birthday, February 15, would be good.

She was put on trial and fined for voting in Rochester, New York, in 1872, because only men were allowed to vote until 1920. My idea is that we all go sledding and drink hot cocoa to honor Susan the way people have barbecues and three-legged races to celebrate Memorial Day.

I was actually raised Jewnitarian, or as a U-Jew. My little church was constantly on the brink of financial disaster and, in order to survive, depended on the Jewish Congregation Havaruh to rent space from us. As a result, my Sunday school featured a papier-mâché mountain with Moses and God having a tête-à-tête, along with timelines of Jewish history papered over the walls.

More significantly, my godparents were Jewish, somewhere between Orthodox and Reformed, depending on whether or not they had to drive their five children anywhere. We regularly went to their home for dinner, including Shabbat on Friday, when Betty would bless the bread and Irving would sing the prayers. I knew the answers to the four questions asked at a Passover seder before I knew the three parts of the Holy Trinity. Every fall, we celebrated the harvest festival of Succoth around a lean-to shelter built in their backyard to remember the forty years that the Israelites wandered in the wilderness.

The sound of Harry Belafonte singing "Hava Nagila" and "Matilda" could usually be heard throughout their house. Don't ask me why all the midwestern Jews in the seventies adopted a brown-skinned Caribbean entertainer, but they did.

My godmother was a kind woman with a warm smile, porcelain-doll skin, and a lap that always held a child. My mother once told me that her shoulders were on backward, but as many times as I stole a glance, I couldn't see anything wrong. Betty was a terrific cook who made wonderful matzo-ball soup, latkes, and kugel. If something boiled over she'd say, "Oh, Christmas," instead of a curse word. And when she hugged us good-bye she almost always said, "Next year in Jerusalem." I used to wonder if when I became old I'd start saying, "Next year in Copenhagen."

My godfather, Irving, had a rapid-fire temper, and all of us kids were terrified of him. My mother told me he was a genius, so I didn't associate the word with anything complimentary. He refused to read directions, and whenever he put a bike or toy together, there'd always be a pile of "extra" parts. Once he couldn't get a can of Raid insect repellent to work and, rather than read the plastic cap that was clearly marked Twist to open, he banged the can against the counter so hard that it exploded.

Betty and Irving's oldest child suffered brain damage at birth. Technically, I suppose he is what's called an idiot savant—a mentally disabled person who exhibits superior intellect in highly specialized areas, such as math or music. When I later saw the movie *Rain Man,* I immediately thought, *It's Clifford!* Clifford could give anyone's telephone number or date of birth off the top of his head. But what he really excelled at were directions. My godmother would be driving, become lost, and ask Clifford the route. This was thirty years before GPS. Without so much as a map, he'd reel off a list of highways, exits, detours, mile markers, turns, and alternatives like a modern-day MapQuest. Clifford was also very definite about his likes and dislikes, especially when it came to people. Someone would arrive at the house and he'd immediately and loudly announce whether he liked that person or not—and then repeat the verdict several times until no one could be unaware of his preferences.

Since I rarely saw my Long Island grandparents, I easily adopted my godparents' parents as grandparents—Bubbe Zelda, Zada Joe, and Bubbe Dora. When I was in eighth grade, my godfather died from complications of diabetes, at age fifty-three. As soon as the casket was lowered, Bubbe Dora flung herself into the grave. However, the nephews and grandsons were standing by and ready to seize her because apparently this a longstanding and revered tradition among Jewish mothers, especially when the son was a doctor.

My godparents' five children were like brothers and sisters to me. Together we played dreidel, danced the hora, and attended Purim parties, and when they began having bar mitzvahs and bat mitzvahs, I was surprised to find out that I wouldn't be having one too. (At age sixteen, I was invited by the UUs to sign the membership book, and they gave me a necklace with a flaming-chalice charm. *No* money arrived. In fact, a few years later they began asking *me* for money.)

I regularly helped friends rehearse for their bar and bat mitzvahs (drink lots of orange juice to get the throat-clearing sound just right). My first kiss was at a record hop following a bar mitzvah. The Jewish boys were definitely faster than the Catholics. Maybe it had to do with getting all that money on their thirteenth birthday. Or perhaps it was the whole ceremony about becoming a man. No matter. Most of the Catholic boys were still pulling our hair and dropping rubber snakes in our bags.

Buffalo has a large population of Jews. Although there was a private Jewish school called Kadimah that went through the eighth grade, most Jewish children attended the local public schools. However, I happen to know that Kadimah was an excellent school. When Andy Freedman transferred from there to my junior high school, he knew all the presidents. I mean, he had them memorized, in order. We public-school kids were truly stunned. Yet Andy didn't view this tremendous knowledge as a big deal and didn't even attempt to show off. Once, our eighth-grade teacher, Mr. Heffley, was struggling to remember who came after John Tyler, and Andy just casually ticked off the presidents on his fingers starting with George Washington. (It would later come to light that he also knew vice presidents and state capitals!)

From my godparents and their extended family, I learned that every large Jewish family has, somewhere within it, two brothers or cousins or brothers-in-law who aren't speaking to each other. And it is the job of every party organizer to make sure these two are seated at opposite ends of the room. Sort of like every Irish wedding has one designated drinker who must be pointed out to the photographer in advance so as to get that picture taken first.

Fourteen

Water Hazard...Is That Your Child?

The Great Lakes, found in the upper eastern part of the Midwest, contain one-fifth of the world's surface freshwater. I'll save you the trouble of learning their names by providing the mnemonic device straight off—HOMES: Huron, Ontario, Michigan, Erie, and Superior.

Lake Erie makes up the western border of the city of Buffalo, continues above Ohio, and has its northern shore on the Canadian province of Ontario. To the Indians who lived there in the 1600s, Lake Erie was known as one of the Sweetwater Seas. Before colonization, it teemed with northern pike, lake sturgeon, smallmouth bass, walleye, cisco, and whitefish. From the first explorer to see the lake in 1669 to the settlers of the 1820s, conditions in the region remained about the same. It wouldn't be until the mid-1900s that the white man would flock to the Seneca Nation Indian Reservation for tax-free gas, cigarettes, and bingo.

However, starting in the 1820s, milldams were constructed on nearly every stream that entered Lake Erie. This spelled doom for many of the abundant species of fish that needed to be able to migrate up tributaries to reproduce. Meanwhile, the human population soared in lakefront cities such as Buffalo and Cleveland, and so did the discharge of oil, sawdust, animal carcasses, agricultural residue, flour, and human waste.

By the early 1970s, the lake bore little resemblance to the one enjoyed by Native Americans, who happen to have this proverb: "We did not inherit the land from our fathers. We are borrowing it from our children." Years of indiscriminate industry dumping of chemicals

(PCBs, mercury, DDT, dioxins) and wastewater, along with the release of millions of gallons of untreated sewage, had fouled the once-great lake to the extent that Erie was officially declared a dead lake. Advisories were issued warning locals against any contact with the water.

Actually, the lake was filled with life, just not the right kind. Excessive algae became the dominant plant species, covering beaches in slimy moss and killing off native aquatic species by soaking up all the oxygen. This overabundance was primarily caused by the overload of nutrients, such as phosphorous, in the lake. Oily sludge allowed spontaneous fires to erupt. Fishing now meant scooping the dead and discolored sturgeon off the top of the lake, though I doubt anyone would have wanted to eat them.

Buffalo was once again a national joke. Lake Erie was too thick to drink and too thin to plow. Johnny Carson claimed it was the place that fish went to die. The situation was referenced in an environmentally themed Dr. Seuss book called *The Lorax*. ("I hear things are just as bad up in Lake Erie.")

Suffice it to say that the perennial Seuss best seller didn't attract the tourists the way that Lucy Maud Montgomery's *Anne of Green Gables* brought them to Prince Edward Island. The poor conditions in Lake Erie during the early seventies were a major factor in the decline of the fishing industry and also limited the lake's recreational use. It smelled bad. With an abundance of dead fish and decaying algae, only three beaches were declared clean along the entire shoreline.

Finally, Canadian prime minister Pierre Trudeau and President Richard Nixon signed the Great Lakes Water Quality Agreement on April 15, 1972, and both Canada and the United States committed themselves to restoring the Great Lakes environment. The agreement established guidelines for reducing pollutants and improving treatment of human sewage.

And that's why I swim with my eyes closed.

Is that your child? No, mine is the bright green one.

Love Canal is about ten miles northwest from where I was raised. This ironically named neighborhood near Niagara Falls is the country's best-known hazardous-waste site. It provided much of the local news while I was growing up, especially after evacuations started in 1978, when I was twelve.

In 1942, Hooker Chemicals and Plastics Corporation (now Occidental Petroleum Corporation) began dumping tons of chemical waste, including carcinogenic dioxin, into Love Canal (a three-thousand-foot trench). Shortly after they stopped, in 1953, the land was sold to the Niagara Falls School Board for the price of one dollar, and two years later the Ninety-ninth Street Elementary School was built. Families moved in and soon the area became a thriving working-class suburb.

In 1976, following a wet winter and spring, portions of the land-fill sank and large drums began to bob up. Chemicals seeped into the groundwater, leached into basements, contaminated ponds, and made for strangely colored puddles, while foul odors filled the air. Add to that Bethlehem Steel's blast furnaces and smokestacks belching fumes from the southwest and the stench of rotting fish coming off now-dead Lake Erie, and it was hard to tell which way the wind was blowing.

A study by the Agency for Toxic Substance and Disease Registry would list 418 instances of chemical pollution in air, water, and soil samples. High incidences of birth defects, miscarriages, cancers, and other illnesses started to occur in the area. Led by housewife Lois Gibbs, whose children suffered from recurring health problems, residents pressured state and federal officials with protests and lawsuits. In April 1978, New York health commissioner Robert Whalen declared Love Canal a threat to human health, ordered that the area near the old landfill site be fenced off, and a few months later closed the school. President Jimmy Carter assigned federal funds and ordered the Federal Disaster Assistance Agency to help the city of Niagara Falls. The case sparked the creation of the Superfund law, which would force polluters to pay for cleanups and make them more cautious about the disposal of waste.

The state decided to pay for the relocation of 239 Love Canal families, leaving 700 behind in worthless homes, their inhabitants suffering from illnesses and caring for children with birth defects. After two years, the patience of the remaining residents ran out, and they took two EPA workers hostage until President Carter approved moving the rest of the families.

As environmental cleanup became a national issue, more than thirty thousand toxic sites were found across the country. Americans had something new to fear—the very ground they walked on.

In 1990, the government declared Love Canal hazard-free, and houses are for sale again. They're a national bargain, starting at thirty thousand dollars apiece.

Fifteen

Will Joke for Food...It's a Mad, Mad House... How I Learned to Cook

Where I believe things took a turn away from how "normal" kids were raised, at least among my middle-class friends in the Buffalo suburbs, is that I don't recall my parents telling me to do this or do that. Sure, they gave a few general directions, but I clearly remember being the architect of my day. Rather than *The Pedersens*, the label on our mailbox should have read *The Existentialsens*.

When Mary and I played hooky together, we'd have lunch at the local mall, enjoying free samples at Hickory Farms and York Steak House, and then stop to hear the mynah bird at Sattler's department store say the curse words that kids had taught him over the years. Afterward, we'd ride our bikes downtown to check out boys. Mary was excellent at finding guys anywhere, anytime, and she would always generously give me her extras or castoffs. By the time we were teenagers she could stop traffic with her Marilyn Monroe figure, long red hair, and sparkling green eyes. I can recall more than one instance when drivers took their eyes off the road for that extra second to stare or wave at Mary, and then hit the car in front of them or swerved up onto the curb and crashed into a signpost or mailbox. Meantime, it's safe to say that I've never caused a driver to so much as accidentally cross a dotted white line.

We'd often pass my dad walking through Main Place Mall, which was only a block away from the courthouse where he worked. Dad never noticed us because he operates in a parallel universe. People claim the Internet wasn't rolled out until the eighties, but I'm quite certain he was surfing some kind of intergalactic wireless network back in the sixties and seventies. If we stopped Dad to say hello, we always had a story ready about there being teacher conferences, in case he wondered why we had so much leisure time on a school day. But he never did. And we skillfully avoided Mary's father because he worked in law enforcement, and the school situation would definitely have crossed his mind, first thing.

Visiting Mom at work was always an education. She supervised a nursing home and then a psych center. At both places, the patients would stop me and make unusual requests. For instance: Would I please call Bob Hope and fly them all to the Caribbean?

On the low end of the parent-child chain of command, I wasn't ordered to straighten my room, make my bed, finish dinner, or eat vegetables. (I became a vegetarian, so maybe there's some reverse psychology in that.) Fifi, our poodle, was always more than happy to finish leftovers. My room was an area of cyclonic chaos, not unlike a Manhattan garbage strike in its fourth week, and Mom simply closed the door, refusing to clean it or even scout the perimeter for any reason. If I was given one instruction as a child, it was from my mother, and that was to put on a coat and hat in the winter "or else you'll perish from hypothermia." Though once I recall her reading a brochure a local politician dropped off and advising me, "I can't tell you whether to vote Democrat or Republican, but make sure the candidate was a B-student or better." My mother is clearly not interested in a world run by C-students or dropouts. Or people who spit in public. One afternoon she witnessed a campaigning councilman hack up a giant phlegm wad on our front lawn and quickly scratched his name off her list of candidates.

On the advanced end of parental surveillance, I was never bothered about homework, ordered to study, or asked about my grades. When a dinner guest used a word that began with a *k*, my parents never turned to me and asked, "What other words do we know that start with a *k*?"

My parents were not ones for insisting that I attend school or church, even if my reason for not going was simply that I didn't feel like it or preferred to sleep late. I don't know what would've happened if I'd started skipping four days a week, but I often said that I'd headed to the racetrack, gone to the home of an elderly neighbor for a day of gin rummy, or just stayed inside to read, and they didn't seem concerned. During high school, I became quite taken with the novels of German-born Swiss writer Hermann Hesse. What teenager isn't entranced by the duality of human existence and alienation? Had I possessed any musical ability, I'm convinced that some truly horrid punk rock songs could have emerged from this period.

Sometimes I rode my bike downtown and watched Dad work in a courtroom. It was fascinating to observe real-life trials starring prostitutes in short skirts, lawyers in shiny three-piece suits, policemen wearing uniforms and badges, and the gavel-banging judge in his black robe on the bench high above me—just like in a movie.

Seeing the judicial system up close, particularly in this hotbed of ethnic politics, also squelched any desire I might have had to pursue legal work. However, the smooth marble floors and long staircases of the courthouse did much to improve my skateboarding. Through the protracted snowy winters, I could bring my board to Erie County Hall, and, after everyone cleared out at five o'clock, the place was ideally suited to whizzing around pillars and hanging ten while Dad typed transcripts of the day's proceedings. The bull pen where all the court reporters had their desks and lockers was a perfect place for jumping metal garbage cans.

Although the other twenty or so reporters must have wondered why my particular public school had so many days off, I was given special dispensation to monkey around for two reasons. The first was that I had a rubber stamp–making kit, and for the reasonable price of twenty dollars I'd print postcards for the reporters to use when billing for transcript copies, thus saving them a substantial amount of time handwriting invoices and envelopes. (It was Dad's idea.) The second was that the reporters liked my dad; not only was he friendly, funny, and kind, but his desk was a veritable Woolworth's, containing everything from stationery to plumbing supplies. Dad had pens, markers, scissors, hole punchers (single, double, and triple), chalk, caulk, hole reinforcements, a stapler, paper towels, silverware, and several varieties of tape including masking, strapping, double-sided, gaffer, and duct. Most of these were chained to his desk like bank pens so that people could enjoy the items without accidentally borrowing them. He also had a large toaster oven that he allowed everyone to use. Never underestimate the value of a hot lunch in a cold clime.

Furthermore, Dad carried at least two hundred pounds of cat litter in the trunk of his car. Between November and April, downtown Buffalo was the Boulevard of Broken Hips, and all we did on weekends was visit older relatives who'd slipped on the ice. Judges received special up-close-parking passes, but court reporters were on their own. Most had to park a half mile away and walk under an expressway viaduct to get to work. In the dead of winter, the slope became a sheet of ice. Dad would arrive with his cat litter, and people used it to keep from skidding down and then to get some traction for the climb back up. He arrived early, but occasionally people who came before him would slide down and get stuck at the bottom and have to wait for him. Even with the added traction, they sometimes had to crawl up the other side on their hands and knees. I'd hate to think what would've happened had Dad missed a day of work in the wintertime. There might not have been any court reporters or county clerks. But he never did. Those dutiful Scandinavians with their Viking heritage only miss work for a funeral—their own. And even then they usually call in the night before to say they'll be dead.

It's possible that, because I'm an only child, my parents simply forgot that I was not an adult, couldn't drive or cook, and was legally supposed to be in school. However, they were busy with work. Around the time I turned eight, my mother went back to school, and becoming a nurse involved classes during the day and evening shifts at local hospitals. Meanwhile, my father was trying to keep up with inflation by working late into the night. He not only had to finish transcribing everything that was said that day in the courtroom, but he also had to proofread and bind the final copies. Those who could afford it hired typists.

Until that time, the three of us occasionally did things together, mostly with my godparents and their five children. My dad and I enjoyed playing chess, Ping-Pong, shooting pool, and going to Mel Brooks movies. If an entertainer came to Buffalo, such as the magician Harry Blackstone Jr. or the famous Spanish guitarist Andrés Segovia, he'd take me to see him.

Segovia was amazing. The enormous stage of the grand old Shea's Buffalo Theater, which was usually home to large productions of *The King and I* and *Camelot*, had only a tiny stool in the center. A small man with a guitar walked out and kept the full house captivated for three hours. Once we went to see Segovia when I was ten and experiencing a particularly bad bout of bronchitis. Thus I arrived equipped with a large supply of tissues and cough lozenges. A few minutes before the famed guitarist came out from the wings, I released a pants-wetting cough and blew phlegm chunks like a patient in the final moments of a tuberculosis death. The dowager next to me peered over her spectacles and inquired, "Will you be hacking like that throughout the performance?" I said, "No, ma'am. I'm getting it all out now."

During the summer, my dad and I continued traveling to Long Island to visit my grandfather. My mother stopped joining us when I was eleven, which was a relief in a way because this allowed us to become the Oscar Madisons. Grandpa had been recently widowed, so he'd join us in Hampton Bays. Potato chips for dinner? Sure, why not? Make the bed? Why bother? We were just going to use it again tonight. Change clothes? What for? It was vacation, not a fashion show. The more times we could turn that T-shirt and underwear inside out, the less time we'd waste at a Laundromat when we could be at the beach, playing putt-putt, or seeing *Monty Python and The Holy Grail* or *The Rocky Horror Picture Show* for the fifth time.

By then it was understood in my family that we'd all fend for ourselves as far as food and clean clothes were concerned. As a result, I became very adept at making scrambled eggs and Kraft macaroni and cheese (the official foods of the seventies' latchkey child) and showing up at the homes of neighbors exactly at mealtimes.

I'd never starve, since, even in a snowstorm, I could walk the half mile to the Oh Thank Heaven for 7-Eleven and eat a microwave burrito with a plastic spork. And Mom bought the basics every week. She was covered if social services ever came to visit. There was a loaf of bread, a carton of milk, some eggs, and apples. A stick of butter was left out on the kitchen table. Over the years I noticed that one person in the family scraped the butter off the top, leaving a big uneven rut in the middle. I thought it was a silly way to get butter. I always cut a hunk off the end, like normal people. After my dad moved out, the butter was still being scraped off the top, and so I naturally assumed my mom was the knife skimmer. One day she said, "Why do you scrape the butter off the top? It makes such a mess." I replied that I didn't scrape the butter and that in fact she was doing it. (By this point, years had gone by—one can tell how often we ate together.) We examined the scrapes more closely and found tiny ridges in them, sort of like a serrated knife, but more like a cat's tongue. Looking down at Spaz, our cat, we realized who had been scraping the butter. Mom put a plastic cover over it.

Cooking held little interest for me, so eating at the neighbors was my first choice. I'd committed to memory the times every friend ate breakfast, lunch, and dinner. Depending on what day it was, I also had a good idea what the dinner menu would be—chicken, meatloaf, hamburgers and hotdogs, beef stew, a casserole, spaghetti (no one had heard of *pasta*) and meatballs, or something that involved "helper." Combine Hamburger Helper with Tuna Helper and you had surf and turf! Lunch was peanut butter and jelly, tuna fish, or a sandwich made with Oscar Mayer cold cuts. Another afternoon staple in my neighborhood was the grilled cheese sandwich. And everyone knew that those big, pale yellow bricks of government cheese made the *best* grilled cheese sandwiches in the world.

In order not to be viewed as a mooch ("What a coincidence! Once again Laura arrives right as the plates hit the table"), I created a code of conduct for myself in my capacity as a professional guest. There was a horse that used to run at the Fort Erie Racetrack across the Peace Bridge in Canada named Sing For Your Supper (before I knew it was a Rodgers and Hart song), and I felt there was a lesson in that. Thus, my first rule was to assist in whatever preparation or cleanup was necessary, and of which I was capable. Unfortunately, I was never an adept helper in the kitchen given my lack of culinary knowledge, my general clumsiness, and my shaky hands, so I did more harm than good. Instead, I decided that nobody liked a boring freeloader, and so I always tried to come prepared with a few jokes or stories. This was my introduction to the Rubber Chicken Circuit, or in my case, Shake 'n Bake chicken, where I received the training that would eventually land me the class-clown award, a spot at the Improv in New York City, and an appearance on David Letterman's show. (Though my act also got me barred from high school graduation, until I performed community service. I was *that* funny.)

Throughout my teenage years, I basically worked full time as a wandering fool, like Feste in *Twelfth Night*, traveling from house to house, exchanging comedy for food and air-conditioning.

❋ ❋ ❋

Mom and Dad both had an interesting habit of taking me aside and proclaiming that the other was crazy.

"Your father is out of his mind," Mom would state matter-of-factly.

"Then why did you marry him?" I'd ask.

"He looked like President Kennedy and he'd write me these amazing letters."

"Your mother is crazy," Dad gently broke the news to me. "I just think you should know that."

"So why did you marry her?" I'd ask.

"I didn't know she was crazy then. I only found out later."

Growing up, I spent a considerable amount of time guessing which one of them was *really* crazy; a parental shell game to determine under which cup sat the nut. On the other hand, in the seventies many people appeared to be three beads short of a headband, as compared to nowa-days, with prescription mood modifiers so readily available.

As a result, it was hard to know who to believe. Sometimes out of the blue, Dad would ask how old I was. Just for fun I'd tack on a few years. When I was fourteen I told him I was sixteen. I waited a moment to see if this raised any questions, but he just nodded, and so I asked to borrow the car and he said okay. Heather was laughing so hard in the backseat that I thought she was going to blow our new set of wheels. I once asked Dad to attend my final soccer game when I was a senior in high school. However, on game day I couldn't locate him on the sidelines. Was it possible that in the bright sunlight I'd missed the gray ghost, that he'd just melted into the bleachers? When I next saw him, Dad apologetically explained that he'd become lost and was unable to find the school. It was a small town, and we'd been in the same district my entire life.

The one sound I could always count on hearing late into the night at my house was not laughter or talking, but typing. Both of my parents are weapons-grade typists who back then had dueling Underwoods and backup Royalites. The old manual typewriters required a heavy touch, and at almost any hour, one could hear the clackety-clack followed by the zing of the thick metal carriage returning left, landing with a shudder, a smack, and the ding of an old-fashioned trolley car. This rhythm was occasionally punctuated by an "Oh bash!" (Dad) or "Fuck-ets buckets!" (Mom), followed by a short silence while correction fluid was applied and then blown upon until dry.

The century and a half between 1835 and 1985 should be known as the Carbon Age. At any given time, there was more carbon paper than toilet paper in our house. The major difference between the two was that toilet paper didn't leave black smudges all over everyone's hands that were easily transferred to the face, furniture, and countertop. If a person born during the epoch of the photocopy machine or word processor has had the occasion to cc folk, that's where those cryptic letters come from—carbon copy.

Once, I used a stopwatch to time Dad as he broke the typing record in the *Guinness Book of World Records*. Of course I wanted to call them immediately, but Dad wouldn't hear of such nonsense. Humorist Garrison Keillor likes to joke that Lutherans are such modest people that if you give them a gold trophy, they'll paint it bronze.

In elementary school, I was the only student who arrived with typewritten excuses. In fact, we're not entirely sure that Dad can write cursive at all, aside from signing his name. As for his printing, it's come to resemble his typing, the way dogs begin to look like their owners and older couples start to look like each other. I was the only first grader who brought in for show-and-tell a typed page reading, "The quick brown fox jumps over the lazy red dog." I proceeded to explain how the sentence used every letter of the alphabet and was a good way to test if all the keys on the Underwood were working.

Before I learned to type, in tenth grade, Dad was like something out of the fairy tale "The Elves and the Shoemaker." I placed the hand-written essay outside his door, and the next morning it was sitting on my dresser, perfectly typed. Although he never revised or rewrote, he couldn't help himself from correcting a few grammatical and punctuation errors.

Mom would comfortably make the transition to the electric type-writer and, later, to a computer keyboard. Dad, however, was to remain pounding away on an Underwood down at Erie County Hall until his retirement in 1985 and beyond; it was our own Smithsonian exhibit, and he was always on the prowl for typewriter ribbons and cleaning fluid. He actually tried a number of electric typewriters when the other court reporters made the switch, but his fingers were so strong by then, and conditioned for slamming those heavy metal keys, that he could hardly feel the dainty plastic buttons moving underneath his calloused fingertips, so he ended up with row upon row of the same letter after a single touch.

If Dad wasn't banging away at the typewriter keys, then I fell asleep to the constant grinding of his rock tumbler, which had two tin cans rotating twenty-four hours a day, like a brace of possum on a spit. Dad liked collecting rocks along the beach on Long Island for those two weeks during the summer and spent the rest of the year polishing them.

He said when he retired he wanted to become a beachcomber. *That would certainly please Mom*, I thought, with his cigarette smoke blowing out to sea rather than into the hallway.

❋ ❋ ❋

Show me a mother in college, and I'll show you a family that can cook. When my mom went back to school in 1974, she started simplifying. Until then, she had her kinky brown hair washed, set, and sprayed with hurricane-strength lacquer every week at Rocco's beauty parlor. Finding Mom asleep with pink tape on the sides of her face and a flannel cloth around her head, it was easy to think I'd walked in on an open casket. Either she had decided there was no longer time for such indulgences, or, more likely, her hairdresser finally wore out from the battle. Thus, Mom reverted to her natural 'fro and found she got the best cuts at salons that specialized in African American hair.

Her next act of emancipation was to close down the wash, dry, and fold laundry service. Dad came up with an innovative solution and just tossed his stuff away when it became unusable. Disintegration didn't take long with such a high concentration of trapped cigarette smoke. Meantime, I discovered that vacuuming my sheets could stave off a full wash cycle by at least several months.

In the kitchen, Mom declared that it was now every chef for himself. After warning us that letting the egg slicer and colander become rusty would no doubt result in lockjaw, we were left to our own devices.

Even before my mother halted the regular flow of food, cuisine was never a topic of much interest at our house. We needed gas for the car, paint for the house, salt for the driveway, and food for the body. Eating was just another job.

For dinner, Mom ate an apple, cheese, and some crackers, usually in the living room while catching up on the newspapers. She hadn't become a raw-fooder so much as a non-ovener.

My father had a different approach to meal preparation. In the seventies, our suburb didn't have any fast-food delivery services, no shrimp "flied lice" or Domino's, and it was still a few years before the grocer's freezer was stocked with latchkey child–friendly foods. It was premicrowave. In other words, one had to cook to eat. And because stuff in the freezer had to thaw out for hours, it was often necessary to plan ahead.

Dad's kitchen philosophy was simple: don't make anything dirty. That was it, the governing principle. The ideal meal was one where there was absolutely no cleanup. Therefore, one needed technique, a keen sense of planning, and resourcefulness.

Being of Scandinavian descent, my father comes by his utilitarianism honestly. After all, the Danes are the creators of Lego, the Eames chair, and half of Janet Reno. They also gave us physicist Niels Bohr, a father of the atomic bomb, which may explain why we never hear, "Come on over, we're having Danish food!"

The pragmatist's perfect food is the sandwich, Dad explained. The sandwich requires no plates, pots, pans, baking trays, whisks, ladles, tongs, or other utensils. It is the comestible equivalent of the Swiss Army knife—all in one, completely self-contained. And the perfect sandwich is the presliced meat and cheese variety, because it requires no spoon for mustard, no knife for spreading mayonnaise, no chopping of lettuce and tomato. However, Dad creatively extended the sandwich universe to include almost anything. Hankering for a banana split? Make it in a pita pocket! Want some chili? Dig out the inside of a hamburger bun and put it in there. If the menu required a saucepan, then we let that double as a plate or bowl.

There were a few situations that called for dirtying cutlery, but certainly none that would require more than one implement to consume a full meal. As the avocado is believed to be nature's perfect food, Dad believed the wooden spoon to be nature's perfect cooking instrument—stir with it, serve with it, eat with it. He was a model of foresight, the Nostradamus of noshing. If we could see that we were going to require a piece of flatware to eat our food, then we'd just stir the pot with that same table knife or else flip a burger with the necessary soup spoon. In other words, think outside of the box—the silverware box.

The last lesson Dad offered was that the secret weapon of no-cleanup cuisine is The Dish Towel. Before preparing any meal, Dad would gallantly fling a dish towel over his left shoulder so it'd be at the ready. If the wooden spoon was his sword, then the checked dish towel was his shield. It is to cooking what the Stetson is to the cowboy, explained Dad. It can act as a cutting board, place mat, salad spinner, trivet, spaghetti strainer, or napkin, and we could dry our wooden spoon with it after finishing the meal. In short, a properly used dish towel can save a life.

Finally, it was time to eat. Dad topped off the coffee cup he'd been refilling since the end of the Korean War, and I removed the milk carton that doubled as my glass from the refrigerator. We stood side by side over the sink, one of us munching a sandwich and the other spooning down macaroni or scrambled eggs directly from the pan, and perhaps a little salad or toast off the dish towel.

Sometimes there was *nothing* to clean (especially if Dad had covered the spatula with foil), and other times there was a pot and serving spoon or fork that needed to be rinsed. When I ate on my own, I soon realized that this was a task just as easily (and enthusiastically) accomplished by our dog. In science class I'd learned that dog saliva is cleaner than human saliva.

From our positions over the sink we could contentedly gaze up at the carefully organized rows of Waterford crystal drinking glasses and decanters. Across from us, through glass doors, we could enjoy the sight of Grandma's Royal Copenhagen china, complete with its eight-piece place settings and matching serving dishes. We felt secure knowing that directly behind us was a drawer chock-full of flatware, all lying clean, stacked, and dust free in plastic organizers. Everything was untouched and in its place; another perfect meal in our perfectly unsoiled kitchen. Mom would never even know we'd been there.

Okay, so maybe Dad's cooking lessons didn't prepare me for hosting dinner parties. But it did equip me for my first five years in Manhattan—living on low-budget fare made in closet-sized dwellings where the speck of a kitchen served as a storage area for boots and bikes.

Manhattan was on the cutting edge of the prepared-foods revolü-tion. Food in paper cartons with disposable wooden chopsticks? Abso-lutely brilliant! And what about burritos? The ultimate sandwich—a complete meal served in its own disposable wrapper, no utensils necessary. They'd improved upon Dad's system! And he hasn't missed the innova-tion. Last time I visited him in Truth or Consequences, New Mexico, my dinner was—surprise—a burrito. Dad served this modern miracle with his 1,000-watt, no-cook, no-crumbs, no-cleanup, no-kidding smile.

Sixteen

The Birth of an Entrepreneur...
From Socks to Stocks...The Wizard of Odds

By the age of eleven, I always had money in my pocket, earned from a variety of endeavors. If I needed more there was always a way to make it. For instance, the candy-bar racket arose because there was no access to chocolate at school, and it was particularly in demand during study hall, after lunch, and before the athletic practices that immediately followed the last class. So I purchased candy in bulk at a warehouse on Main Street. This inventory was taken to school and sold at a markup equivalent to that charged by the neighborhood 7-Eleven.

I admit to getting a little carried away sometimes. Having read numerous books about famous industrialists and how they'd made their own opportunities, I purchased a stockpile of canned food with an eye toward a bad snowstorm. When the blizzard of '77 hit unexpectedly and closed the city down for almost a week, I sold my stash to my mom and a few neighbors at a 25 percent markup. In retrospect, I should have sold Mom the food at the wholesale cost since she was using some of it to feed me (and she made up for the loss by charging me a storage fee).

Storms were good money makers in other ways. They backed up traffic on the expressway that ran past the end of my street, so it was easy to walk from car to car and sell doughnuts from a box and coffee out of a big thermos. Though I didn't believe in gouging, I could pretty much charge whatever I wanted. Not only that, but this was way before cell phones, so people would write down phone numbers with messages and give me a dollar to make the calls when I returned home. I didn't feel guilty taking their money, even though the Good Samaritan would have performed such services for free, because such charitable souls were few and far between in blinding snowstorms with a twenty-below-zero windchill factor. Furthermore, I always delivered the messages, even if it meant trying the line twenty times. The best part was hearing, "Tell me again. *Who* are you?"

However my favorite job was working with animals. I love dogs, and so I enjoyed walking and grooming those owned by neighbors. For the females, I added little touches, such as fire-engine red toenail polish and matching ribbons, according to the seasons and holidays.

I also cared for pets while their owners were away. The exception was for Chester and Mary Ruth Kiser, who lived across the street; I watched their black poodle, Poupon, when Chester was actually still at home. When Mary Ruth went out of town, dog care apparently did not fall under his jurisdiction. Chet, as Mary Ruth called him, was smart and funny, and for a time ran the English Department at the University of Buffalo. He was perennially tan (no small accomplishment in upstate New York), handsome in a rugged way, and bore more than a passing resemblance to Ernest Hemingway.

Mr. Kiser kept late hours when Mrs. Kiser was off visiting their children and grandchildren down in Maryland. At seven in the morning I'd go across the street, walk around the car, which was parked a little bit on the lawn, and slip into the house as quietly as possible, but inevitably Poupon was nowhere to be found. This meant the dog was in the master bedroom, on the side of the bed farthest from the door, where Mrs. Kiser normally slept. I could hear Mr. Kiser snoring from the bottom of the stairs. I'd tiptoe to the bedroom door, get down on my hands and knees, and crawl around the bed on the floor to where Poupon was also snoring. The other thing that Poupon and Mr. Kiser had in common was that they both slept naked.

Just as I reached the dog, Mr. Kiser would awaken slightly and mumble, "Hello?" And I'd always say, "It's just me, Mr. Kiser, coming to get Poupon." And he'd go, "Hmmm," and pull the sheet over himself, and fall back to sleep as if it was perfectly normal to have the girl across the street crawling around the floor next to his bed with his wife's poodle under her arm.

Babysitting for a dollar an hour was always a good job because the families usually had some snacks in the cupboard. During the wintertime, their thermostat could be cranked up, so long as I didn't fall asleep and let the parents come home to find their house warm. Inevitably, babysitters did fall asleep after jacking up the heat, because our bodies were so unaccustomed to warmth that we went into a light coma. In such cases, when I heard the car pull into the driveway, I had to make a mad dash to the thermostat, and then explain how I'd just turned it up for a few minutes because I'd felt sick. It was common knowledge that the only Buffalonians under sixty-five who had a legal right to heat were the ill and infirm.

If Mary and I were both babysitting, we'd call each other's houses, let the kids pick up the phone, and then dictate incredibly long messages. These involved appointments for their mothers with lots of directions, recipes, and long lists of items to bring to fictitious meetings. After the kids went to bed we'd be sure to throw the notes away. We liked to think these exercises improved the comprehension and writing skills of our young charges.

When Mary and I babysat late at night, her brothers would often come over and set the pile of leaves out front on fire or bang garbage cans next to the garage so we thought the house was about to be robbed. Or else a serial killer was trying to trick us into coming outside.

I signed up for a paper route the day I turned eleven, the minimum age to apply. Back then, newspapers were delivered by kids pulling wagons or riding bicycles, with big satchels over their shoulders. Lots of dogs lived on my route, and I carried plenty of biscuits to feed them, not so much to avoid attack, but just because I like dogs. As my creaky wagon rattled down the street, the dogs didn't bark at me, but for me. And because people often saw a pack of panting and salivating hounds chasing me, sometimes even knocking me down, they often misunderstood the situation and boosted my tip, a type of canine-combat pay.

I had to deliver the paper every day after school and on weekend mornings, and then collect the subscription money once a week and turn it over to a local dispatcher. It was necessary to keep track of who was going on vacation and also to hunt down the bill dodgers by trying to get them during dinner. I loved the independence and also the incentive system—the better I performed, the more money I made. Sure, the weather was lousy a lot of the time, but being born and raised in Buffalo, it didn't occur to me that there was any other way to live—that elsewhere people walked around in November without a parka, hat, scarf, gloves, and boots.

The only complaint I received as a papergirl was for my squeaky wagon, especially when it rumbled down tranquil suburban streets at six in the morning on weekends. I tried oiling the wheels, but nothing seemed to work. How was I supposed keep a wagon from squeaking in a place where there's an inch of road salt on the streets and sidewalks? It's amazing our knees and ankles didn't rust out and start to squeak like the Tin Man in *The Wizard of Oz*. The salt disintegrated our shoes and pant bottoms. Mothers were constantly yelling, "Take off your shoes!" so that white pathways weren't melted into otherwise beige carpeting.

Canyonesque potholes wrought by the combination of freezing and plowing were enough to keep the roadside littered with hubcaps and the alignment shops in business year-round. Still, the greater fear was walkways that hadn't been salted and were therefore likely to contain a glassy layer of ice under a deceptive coating of snow or on the surface, so thin as to be almost invisible (with the appropriate horror film name: black ice!). We never walked with our hands in our pockets after learning the hard way that force really does equal mass times acceleration. And a person could not possibly appear more foolish than when performing the Dance of Death on ice without skates.

I gave up my route and most of my other entrepreneurial sidelines when I hit upon magic shows. This was an interest of my father's, and as a young child I was constantly learning coin, rope, and card tricks. So when I was thirteen and overheard an adult complain that she'd paid fifty dollars to have a thirty-minute magic show for a children's birthday party, I immediately hung out my shingle.

Or rather, I placed an ad in the local newspaper announcing I would perform at children's birthday parties for a mere forty dollars. Apparently children's birthday parties are arduous enough when kids are able to go outside, but for those eight months of winter when they were trapped indoors, the phone rang off the hook.

I purposely left my age out of the ad, and I must admit that clients were rather startled to discover that their Harriet Houdini was barely a teenager and had to be dropped off and picked up by her mother. But the show was satisfactory, and when the audience misbehaved I explained that I was very proficient at turning children into toads, yet hadn't mastered the art of reversing that spell—in my closet at home I had six cardboard boxes filled with wart-covered toads waiting to be turned back into kids. They were good after that, although several volunteered fellow partygoers for me to practice on.

Most of the children had never seen a female magician before, causing one precocious six-year-old to remark, "Hey, you're half boy and half girl!"

❋ ❋ ❋

With the money earned from all of my jobs and business ventures, I began to invest in stocks. People regularly ask how I became interested in the market in the first place.

Honestly, I can't remember not being fascinated by Wall Street. And shoveling driveways for two dollars apiece as a kid gave me a lot of time to think that there must be easier ways of making money. For those who've not had direct encounters with copious amounts of snow, after it hits the ground and starts to accumulate, snow is not light and fluffy, the way it appears on televised Christmas specials and romantic comedies, but hernia heavy. When you shovel enough of it, your back and shoulders began to ache. You can feel muscles that you didn't know you had and that don't seem to be necessary for anything else. In fact, with the advent of professional snow removal, in a few years these muscles will probably be vestigial organs, like the appendix and wisdom teeth—no longer necessary for modern living.

Shoveling is hard on the psyche too. As soon as I made it to the end of the driveway, the street plow would groan past and fill the bottom back in again. But not with sidewalk snow. Oh no, onto the end of the driveway the plow packed a three-foot-high wall of the hard, pollution gray crust-and-ice mixture it'd been scraping off the roads. For this reason I'd have to dig a big V in the snowbank before the driveway entrance so the plow muck would get dumped in there. Only, that's like boring through hardened cement. The other thing that inevitably happened was, as soon as I finished shoveling, it started snowing again—truly the Augean stables. There's a reason that Buffalonians put snowblowers in their wills.

Once, while doing some heavy-duty shoveling and feeling sad knowing I was probably too young to die from a heart attack or stroke and too old to be mercifully run over by the plow, I finally thought, *Why not just go directly to where they make the cash?* I remembered that when famous bank robber Willie Sutton was asked why he robbed banks, he replied, "Because that's where the money is."

My parents were friends with a stockbroker named George Gregory, who went to our church. He kindly set up an account for me and listed my mother as the custodian, because I was under twenty-one and needed an adult to make the actual transactions. It wasn't like today's online trading where someone can pretend to be twenty-one. Mr. Gregory then passed on his copies of *Forbes* as soon as he was finished with them.

My father's mother, the big stock trader in the family, had died the year before, so she wasn't a source of help on this project. Also, at that time I didn't know much about her adventures in the market. People have often said I must have inherited this interest from her somehow, but it would seem we both arrived at trading independently, unless the Dow Jones can be transferred through a chromosome.

My mom and dad knew nothing about the stock market. I made my own decisions, and then my mother called in the orders. These judgments were mostly formed by reading a government publication put out by the United States Bureau of Mines. It wasn't intended as a newsletter for investors so much as a research report on what was happening in the mining industry. When it looked as if an area was going to attract particular interest or government backing, I would try to find out the companies involved in that type of business and invest in them. This was way before the Internet, and even before the television ran a ticker tape, so I had to go to the library to research companies in the Standard & Poor guides. And to find out how my stocks were doing, it was necessary to look up the closing prices from the day before in the newspaper.

This strategy proved successful enough to earn a couple hundred dollars every few months—money for skiing and vacations to Florida and New York City. The rest of the profits I reinvested in the stock market or used to buy silver (bars, not jewelry), which I was also hoping would go up in value.

Eventually, I was so flush that I became somewhat of a gambler as a teenager. Holiday gatherings consisted of me and a small group of relatives in their forties. No one else had children. As a result, it didn't exactly occur to anyone to get a touch-football game going or a round of I spy.

I may have been the only kid to show up at the school bake sale with store-bought cookies (almost never done back then and a sign of domestic calamity), but I've always been grateful to my mom for teaching me to play poker when I was five.

It was from playing cards with Uncle Jim, who worked as a police reporter, that I learned Damon Runyon–style lingo such as *cut 'em deep and weep, cut 'em thin and win, cowboys* (2 kings), and *woolworths* (a five and a ten). Members of the maternal side were also marathon slingers of profanity—strings of exotic words not found in any dictionary, combinations rhyming so beautifully that they rolled off the tongue and sounded like lyric poetry to my youthful ears. Absorbing these verbal gems not only made me popular in study hall, they would later come in handy on Wall Street.

I don't believe anyone in my family thought it was the least bit odd that on Christmas Eve, while most of my young friends were at church, I was perched atop a phone book, ordering the players, "Ante up, one-eyed jacks are wild." And when the stakes rose they certainly didn't treat me as a child. I clearly remember my uncle admonishing me, "Hold your cards up properly or you'll spoil the hand!" in the way you tell a seven-year-old to stop flinging her peas. Uncle Jim also had a good system for teaching you to pay attention to your hand. If one of us dropped a card he'd say, "Whoops! Nobody saw that jack of spades," thereby announcing it to the whole table, even if it was quickly snatched up while the others were preoccupied arranging their hands. Needless to say, to this day I don't drop my cards, even if I'm just playing solitaire.

My holiday presents worked basically like this: Mom would tell my aunt something I wanted, such as the dune buggy for Malibu Barbie, so that Barbie, with her porn-star physique, and sexless Ken could go for chaste drives along the California coast. My aunt would dutifully go shopping, and then she and my uncle would have a drug-dealerlike transaction in the corner of the living room that resulted in his name being included on the card. As for gifts from my parents, I'd have ordered those from the J. C. Penney catalog back in November, using my dad's credit card. They'd be delivered to the house, where I'd wrap them and place everything under the tree. On Christmas morning, I would pretend to be surprised by what I received, while in actuality *they* were. This system also worked well for my birthday and buying prom dresses.

When I was eleven years old, Uncle Jim took me to the horse-racing track for the first time. It was in Fort Erie, Canada, just a few miles (excuse me, kilometers) from the Peace Bridge. Batavia Downs was in the opposite direction and featured harness racing rather than thoroughbreds, but we never went there. Back then, rumor had it that the jockeys were so crooked they had to screw their socks on in the morning and the owners would steal the dimes off a dead man's eyes.

Theoretically, one had to be eighteen to place a bet at the track, so I always found a grown-up to translate my wheels, exactas, and daily doubles from cash to racing tickets. However, I soon realized that the window tellers didn't care if I was twelve or twenty-two. I was never once asked for proof of age. Off-track betting, on the other hand, was another story altogether, and they almost always asked for identification. Thus, when I wanted to play the horses all day, I had to ride my bike over the Peace Bridge to Ontario in order to bet at the actual racetrack.

My only run-in with the law during those years was a citation from a University of Buffalo campus police officer for riding my bike no-handed. "You must have at least one hand on the steering mechanism at all times," I was informed, rather unsympathetically I might add. Obviously he'd never tried bike riding while suffering from unrelenting allergies. My hands were usually fully occupied with blowing my nose and trying to keep the tissues from flying away.

❄ ❄ ❄

If anything in addition to playing poker and handicapping the horses helped to develop my interest in stocks and trading, it was my love of games. In particular, those that employed numbers, strategy, and probability, such as gin rummy, chess, checkers, and backgammon. My father and uncle regularly played chess with me, and the rest I played with friends, neighbors, and babysitters. As it turns out, the skills used to succeed in these pursuits are all rigorously employed in trading on Wall Street, particularly probability—the science of determining the likeliness of one event happening over another. And my freewheeling libertarian lifestyle (a dearth of TV channels, and the Internet still twelve years off) afforded me unlimited opportunity to play games with odds and then translate that knowledge to gambling and investments and, equally useful, determining what questions would be asked on tests.

Of course, it seems that no matter what hand one is dealt in life, the pasture's always greener across the street. As a young person I was well aware that I was leading a Pippi Longstocking–like existence, especially compared to the routines of my suburban friends. I occasionally overheard people whispering about "the Pedersen child" in a tone that suggested dark forces at work in the universe, and I caught their sideways glances.

Almost all of my friends had rules, curfews, mealtimes, chores, rewards for good grades, and regular allowances. If I needed extra money, I simply said, "Dad, can I have a couple bucks?" It didn't matter what day of the week it was. I suppose he assumed that I didn't have a hundred-dollar-a-month Godiva chocolate habit, or that I wasn't just hoarding his money in numbered offshore bank accounts.

However, occasionally I'd gaze longingly at these well-regulated families surrounding me and find them all very appealing. I'd surrender to brief romances with "normal" life, perhaps inspired by afternoon reruns of *The Brady Bunch*.

Unlike such TV families, we were a nocturnal clan and could be found eating, working, reading, or watching television at all hours of the night, though not together. Dad was in the habit of taking a break from his typing around midnight and boiling franks and sauerkraut, or else making an open-faced sandwich. If my mother was in the middle of a good mystery, there was no stopping her until four in the morning. I often went on late-night bike rides or to the twenty-four-hour store for a sugar fix. Back then, most television stations stopped broadcasting around one in the morning and the best we could get was a striped pattern or sometimes the Canadian national anthem.

One day when I was about nine, I asked Mom, "What's my curfew?"

She was sitting in the living room reading the newspaper and glanced up with a perplexed look and replied, "What do you mean?"

I explained that all of my friends had curfews and also bedtimes. "What are mine?" I clearly remember my mother staring at me as if I'd been visiting with the fairies.

"Just come home when you're done and go to bed when you're tired," she replied matter-of-factly.

But on that particular day I was not to be satisfied by this laissez-faire answer. "I think we should agree on a curfew and a bedtime," I said. I explained how it worked with my friends. They negotiated these times. The parents tried for earlier, the child argued for later, and they eventually split the difference. However, my mother wanted to discuss something sensible or else go back to her newspaper.

"Fine," she eventually capitulated. "Tell me what time you want as a curfew and a bedtime and that's what they'll be." Of course, that defeated the whole purpose. I could have said one in the morning and she would have agreed.

Eventually, I abandoned my case. The few times I did stay up until two or three in the morning on school nights, I felt so exhausted the next day I could hardly move. As a result of those sleep-deprivation hangovers, I went to bed by eleven-thirty almost every school night, right into adulthood.

The next child-rearing issue I sunk my teeth into was monitoring academic performance. There was no doubt I'd been a slow starter when it came to education, aside from that period in kindergarten when I was a no starter. I have vivid recollections of cerebral chaos right through the end of elementary school. A good day for me would be to tell a knock-knock joke without screwing up the punch line.

In junior high school I finally began to locate my academic balance. By eighth grade, I was bringing home the kind of report cards that were earning my friends ice cream sundaes, money, kudos, and other positive reinforcements. One day in junior high school, I came home and posted my first straight-A report card on the refrigerator—not that this was exactly a thoroughfare since most nights my dad went to the diner for a late dinner and I ate at a neighbor's house. But they had to pass the fridge to get to the coffeepot and, thus, would eventually collide with my report card. It was the only thing up there, since we weren't a fridge-magnet family, didn't have a shopping list, and rarely left notes regarding our whereabouts.

After two weeks passed without a word, I couldn't stand it anymore. When Dad came out to refill his coffee mug, I pointed to the report card and said, "Look, I got straight As." Dad was always juggling several pairs of glasses, and it's doubtful he had the correct ones necessary to see anything but the coffeepot. "Don't you think that's good?" I asked.

"Well, it's *your* report card, and so it doesn't matter what I think. It's whether or not you're happy with it that counts." He disappeared with his coffee.

My parents were never subscribers to the popular child-rearing tools of threats and bribery. And I eventually realized that my dad was right. Although the report card presentation had not been the Norman Rockwell moment I thought I was craving, it was *my* report card and did not represent my worth as a human being. And it was mine alone, whether the card was good or bad. We had no family crest, and our accomplishments would not be published in a society register. It didn't make much sense to strive for academic achievement just to receive praise. In certain areas there's a need for self-validation and, likewise, self-redress.

That was the last of my parenting experiments. Otherwise, my childhood was filled with friends, activities, modest athletics, and interesting experiences. Life in Amherst was becoming particularly exciting as homes were starting to crumble and sink into the earth, the town having been built on an old lake bottom, which was turning out to be part clay and part primordial ooze. No bedtime story could compete with the prospect of going to sleep on the second floor with a teddy bear and waking up in the basement surrounded by silverfish.

Seventeen

Everyone Was Groovy...Stardate 1965

In the seventies, both of my parents enjoyed a certain amount of popular music. Dad liked Simon and Garfunkel, Gordon Lightfoot, and Harry Chapin. My father was a talented folksinger and often led rounds at our church, accompanying himself on guitar, and he also did sing-alongs with the Sunday school. These included a number of tunes written or popularized by fellow Unitarian Universalist Pete Seeger, such as "Where Have All the Flowers Gone," "We Shall Overcome," and "If I Had a Hammer."

Mom's tastes ran more toward Don McClean's "American Pie," the Moody Blues, Bette Midler, and Fleetwood Mac. They both liked Neil Diamond. Neither of them listened to Barry Manilow.

The seventies were the heyday of the eight-track cassette player, terrariums, mood rings, fruit-striped gum, and the Big Wheel. Pet Rocks—a regular gray stone weighing about a quarter pound in a cardboard box with some straw in it—were launched in 1975 and immediately 1.5 million were sold. In 1976, red M&Ms were discontinued for eleven long years because the FDA banned Red Dye number two (even though M&Ms didn't contain this dye). Fortunately, the candy maker left the green ones, which everyone knew worked as an aphrodisiac, or, in the parlance of the times, "made you horny."

Speaking of mood enhancers, on winter weekends we often spent hours making candles, using everything from sand to ice cubes for special effects. It's hard to explain so many decades later, but it was a that swept the nation on the magnitude of the hula hoop in the late fifties and reality TV shows in more recent years.

Otherwise, girls made latch-hook rugs, beaded jewelry, and string art, while boys had ant farms, chemistry sets, and baseball cards. Girls who weren't tomboys played the Mystery Date Game, wore Blue Jeans perfume, used "Gee, Your Hair Smells Terrific" shampoo, and accumulated Bonne Bell Lip Smackers in such tantalizing flavors as Good & Plenty, Tootsie Roll, Dr. Pepper, Hires Root Beer, 7-Up, Orange Crush, Bit-O-Honey, sour grapes, grape jelly, and sugar plum.

We all went ice-skating. And we all wore clogs, even throughout the winter.

Boys hung posters of sexy Farrah Fawcett from *Charlie's Angels* in their bedrooms, while girls had their hair cut and blow-dried to resemble her famous feathered blond locks with flipped sides. Those of us who slaved over this look cannot deny it—the curling iron burn scars remain on our necks, ears, and foreheads. The less boy crazy of the girls wore their hair in a wedge like Dorothy Hamill's, the 1976 Olympic gold-winning figure skater known as America's sweetheart. In theory, this short and sassy bob was supposed to gracefully float upward when the girl spun around quickly, creating a halo effect, and was rigorously put to the test on playgrounds and skating rinks across the country. As to color, girls under eighteen did not tint or highlight their hair back then, except for temporary streaks of green, purple, or neon pink created with Jell-O, which was sticky and would soon start to smell (and not necessarily like the flavor we'd used).

September 20, 1973, was the big day for girls and women in America, as the Battle of the Sexes was fought and handily won by the distaff half. This contest involved a court, but not the usual one, where women petitioned for equality. At a time when women's tennis was not nearly as prestigious as men's, male champ Bobby Riggs challenged female Billie Jean King in order to prove that men were better athletes. Meantime, it was a sore spot with King that professional women athletes were paid poorly compared to men.

I was in third grade, and this was all anyone at school talked about that week, the girls firmly lined up behind Billie Jean King and the boys backing Bobby Riggs. The match was held at the Houston Astrodome and drew what was the largest-ever live audience for tennis, and also merited prime-time TV coverage. Riggs egged on the crowd by entering the stadium in a carriage pulled by women. King arrived in a red velvet litter carried by University of Houston football players in short togas. Then King beat Riggs in three straight sets by wearing him down with long rallies (he was fifty-five and she was twenty-nine). The next morning the boys in my class mumbled excuses. However, by lunchtime they'd recovered their bravado and were back to lobbing spitballs at our necks.

When Bobby Riggs died in 1995, Rosie Casals, who had been a commentator for the famous match, said, "For a male chauvinist, he did a lot of good for us. We'll always remember him in the best possible way. I always said he did the most for women's tennis."

Favorite movies in the midseventies were *Young Frankenstein*, *The Godfather*, *Rocky*, and *Jaws*, which was the coolest thriller to come along since *The Exorcist* two years earlier and Alfred Hitchcock's *Psycho* fifteen years before that. I was nine when the sharkfest was released (in the summer!). For children my age, this marked the end of ocean swimming. For those under ten, the fear of sharks carried over to swimming pools and even the bathtub, where they now kept a close eye on the spout and drain at all times.

Laverne and Shirley was the top TV show throughout my junior high years (1977 to 1979). Dad liked *Monty Python's Flying Circus* and *The Carol Burnett Show*. Mom never missed *The Irish Rovers* or *All in the Family*. I remember watching one episode where Gloria forgets to take her birth control pill; for many years after that, I was convinced a woman became pregnant solely by not taking a pill every day.

The TVs in my friends' living rooms were often set to soap operas or game shows like *Password*, *Family Feud*, and *The Gong Show*. We were particularly fond of *The Incredible Hulk*, *The Six Million Dollar Man*, and *The Bionic Woman*. If we weren't going to be given the opportunity to make money on national television, then having superpowers was the next best thing.

For commercials, we had Tom Carvel droning away in that gravelly New York voice, hawking Fudgie the Whale and Cookie Puss. Poor beleaguered Mr. Whipple was spying on people in order to reprimand them for squeezing the Charmin. And, as always, the Maytag repairman was the loneliest guy in town.

My folks didn't care how much television I watched. Other than some requisite bedtime reading when I was younger, neither parent monitored my leisure activities. However, my father dumped tons of books on every subject imaginable onto my bed. Sometimes he'd go to the bookstore and buy whatever was on the teen shelf, and other times he'd go to a garage sale or the closing of a library and come home with tomes on wacky stuff like spelunking, treasury-bill auctions, gymnosophists, and reflexology. His explanation for this eclectic assortment was that a certain amount of overexposure was necessary to develop one's true interests. And to Dad's credit, I must say that although I wasn't much of a reader at the time (and I'm still not exactly sure what a gymnosophist does), those books on the bond market and real estate caught my eye, and I read them from cover to cover.

My mother is a lifelong bibliophile and had her nose in a novel whenever possible. One of the reasons no one was too upset when she threw in the spatula was that she had a tendency to remove dinner from the oven only upon completion of a chapter in whatever book she happened to be reading. Because Mom was very aware of the dangers of salmonella, and food poisoning in general, she always went for that extra chapter to rescue us all from an early and potentially painful demise. As a result, Mom finished books faster and dinner was usually not just well done, but in fact ready for carbon dating. The smoke alarm was our oven timer.

Which leads to the revelation that my mother didn't exactly *quit* being a housewife. She just started doing things extremely poorly that she'd been really good at up until I was eight years old. The new slogan in the kitchen became, "Where there's smoke, there's dinner." Food started to taste better before she cooked it rather than after. Not only were formerly white T-shirts coming back tie-dyed, but also in toddler sizes. So my dad and I just finally retired her, like a run-out racehorse, which I think is rather what she was aiming for in the first place.

Only, she didn't exactly head out to pasture. Mom went on to earn a bachelor's degree, an RN certification, and then, at age fifty-one, a master's degree from the University of Buffalo. From there she landed an excellent job as a psychiatric nurse for New York State and was able to resume the benefits she'd accrued while working at the unemployment office before I was born.

The only domestic area that continued to be of interest to her was that I regularly cracked open my head, eventually racking up five sets of stitches by age twelve.

❋ ❋ ❋

The cultural lingo was rapidly expanding. In the United States, we seem to have a penchant for categories and labels: Baby Boomer, Hippie, Yuppie, Generation X, Y, and so forth. Historical and cultural reference points are important in shaping our values and perspective. It matters if one is a child of the Depression, World War II, or Vietnam/Watergate.

My school class was born between December 1964 and November 1965. The Baby Boom Generation (1946 to 1964) included everyone flanked by our parents and us, while Generation X (1965 to 1980) was the group born right after us. However, we didn't fit into either category, numerically or characteristically. On the early end, we weren't around for the Kennedy administration, later referred to as Camelot, and can hardly remember Vietnam, also known as McNamara's War. As fourteen-year-olds, we had Rubik's Cubes rather than Sony PlayStations. We didn't participate in the hallmarks of Generation X—computers and coffee shops—at least until college or afterward. Likewise, we were slightly old for grunge rock (though most of us had worn flannel since childhood). Nor did we start any dot-com companies in our twenties.

My generation was so mired in recession that the mad men of Madison Avenue skipped bothering to name us (they probably realized we wouldn't be buying much) and went directly for our little brothers and sisters. I might dub people born between 1964 and 1966 the "Space

Invaders"—though too late for the assassination of JFK, we were around
to see NASA deliver on his 1962 promise to land a man on the moon
by the end of the decade. And just as our parents can remember where
they were when JFK was shot, we can recall where we first played the
video game *Space Invaders*. In 1977, when my friends and I were around
the impressionable age of twelve, the Atari Video Computer System hit
shelves in time for the Christmas holiday season. Nine game cartridges
were available with scratchy and primitive sound effects that are still
unlike anything to ever come out of a TV set—the rumbling tanks of
Combat, the bleep-bloop-bleep rhythm of *Breakout*, and the portentous
silence of *Adventure*. Only no one in my neighborhood could afford
such extravagance. We were riding high if our folks had finally replaced
the black-and-white television with a color set.

If that's not enough to convince the world that this passed-over
group should be labeled the Space Invaders, consider that Valium, the
now ubiquitous tranquilizer taken to remedy the stress and anxieties
that seem to have accompanied the development of the modern world,
was introduced in 1964.

Otherwise, who were we? The first generation of kids not to spend
half a day searching for a skate key since skates now fitted over our sneakers and had attached screws to tighten them. We wore smooth, normal-
looking Speedo swim caps while our mothers still sported textured
rubber turbans complete with chinstrap and 3-D floral arrangements
that made them resemble parade floats. We experienced near-fatal flip-
flop accidents while playing kickball in rubber shower shoes, since it was
a decade before the advent of the much safer Teva-style sandals. We were
the last to grow up without mountain bikes and telephone-answering
machines, and the first to wear designer jeans and sneakers. We were
post-thalidomide and pre–Agent Orange; post-polio and pre-AIDS (at
least we were too young to be born HIV positive or contract the disease
in our teens). We would turn eighteen just as scientists discovered what
they first dubbed "gay cancer," and watch with horror as it turned out to
be the most devastating sexually transmitted disease in history.

We were born too early to enjoy sports bras, fleece, twist-top bottle caps, and Rollerblades while in high school. None of us wore safety helmets for batting, biking, or skiing. In junior high we had to don ugly green-and-white-striped one-piece gym outfits that resembled prison jumpsuits and made husky girls look even huskier. (Had they not received the memo from the home economics teachers about horizontal stripes being unflattering?) By the time we arrived in high school, these were gone, and we were allowed to wear our own shorts and T-shirts. Actually, the gym teachers just finally gave up after kids started regularly showing up in shorts and T-shirts, insisting that the prison garb was in the wash, on a permanent spin cycle.

Eighteen

Sleet Happens: The Blizzard of '77

According to scripture, a component of Job's suffering, to be used for a higher purpose, was experiencing the cold. God even foretells what we refer to in modern times as the snow day: "So that all men he had made may know his work, he stops every man from his labor." Little could God have imagined at the time how his program for suffering would have the exact opposite effect on future schoolchildren, making the snow day the focal point of numerous prayers.

During the winter of 1976–77, it snowed for a biblical forty straight days. And then on Friday, January 28, 1977, a massive storm with ferocious winds struck, paralyzing rush-hour traffic and stranding twenty thousand people in Buffalo and surrounding towns. Southern portions of the Canadian province of Ontario and parts of western and northern New York State were besieged by what was quickly declared The Blizzard of the Century, the most severe in the history of Buffalo.

The mercury plunged toward zero as hurricane-force winds peaking at over seventy miles per hour roared across the surface of Lake Erie. Freezing temperatures combined with icy blasts made for a windchill of sixty below zero. Visibility was nonexistent at 11:30 AM on January 28 and remained so for the next twenty-four hours. For almost two days, the storm raged, with wind gusts up to seventy-three miles per hour. The city became a frozen parking lot, with motorists abandoning cars and attempting to reach the first door they could find.

Deep snow had built up on the surface of the lake so that ten thousand square miles of powder blew inland, burying people in their cars and homes. By Friday night, January 28, thousands were stranded in office buildings, schools, police stations, fire halls, bars, factories, cars, buses, and in the houses of strangers. Highways were impassable, train lines were blocked, and airports were closed. Paralysis set in during this unique winter hurricane, with 1.5 million people caught away from their homes.

Even some people safe inside their own houses were trapped, since the snow was higher than the door and it was necessary to tunnel out. If you visit a friend in Buffalo and wonder why there's a shovel in the front hall closet in addition to the five or six in the garage, that's the reason.

One woman called emergency services because her husband passed away in their apartment after a long illness. A police officer finally made it to her door, checked the dead body in the back, and then tried to break the news to her gently: it would be at least a day, maybe two, before the body could be removed. The woman said she'd been married to him for forty years and so a few more days of being together would be just fine. The police officer opened a window in the bedroom, and the woman made him something hot to drink.

Once hotel rooms were completely booked, marooned workers overflowed into the lobbies and restaurants. Hengerer's department store opened the housewares section so people could get blankets, pillows, and linens. On the roads, thirteen thousand cars were stranded, with passengers eventually abandoning them to avoid freezing to death. By the morning of the second day, there were shortages of food and lifesaving drugs. Power failures left seven thousand households without heat in subzero temperatures. Not even the National Guard could get in to the area to help.

In the city of Buffalo, one house caught fire and it quickly spread to others. Many of the homes are old, made of wood, and built close together. The fire trucks couldn't get through, and there was fear of an inferno—that the entire city would burn. One truck finally made it, and only five homes were completely lost. However, the residents were all successfully evacuated.

Mayor Stanley Makowski went on the radio and television to plead with people not to leave their homes or wherever they had found shelter. A driving ban went into effect. A person could attempt to travel if a baby was on the way or if they were going to a funeral (but not a wake). Others went on television and sang "Where are the Plows?" to the head of the transportation department, using the tune of the then-hit song "Send in the Clowns." But the plows could no longer get through the streets, which were overloaded with abandoned and buried cars. Though one plow driver claimed that the small cars weren't much of a problem because they go through the rotary blades.

Additionally, several plows had broken down and been quickly buried themselves, thus contributing to the clogged roads. One snow-plow driver became stranded out near Lake Erie and radioed for help. It was fifteen hours before he was found. Out of the city's six tow trucks, five were soon stuck or nonoperational because of the heavy ice. Eventually, earth-moving equipment had to be brought in to handle the huge accumulation of snow and cementlike drifts.

Volunteers from snowmobile clubs, citizens owning four-wheel-drive vehicles (not nearly as prevalent back then), the Red Cross, and the Salvation Army flocked to assist police, firefighters, and hospitals to deliver insulin and search for survivors. In the suburb of Depew, volunteer firemen used a trenching machine to help rescue a family that had been snowdrifted inside their own home. Although there was some looting and vandalism, overall the storm succeeded in pulling the community together. Stores, restaurants, and hotels all pitched in, some offering their services for free.

On Saturday, January 29, President Jimmy Carter issued a declaration of emergency that covered four western New York State counties, including Buffalo, which enabled the Federal Disaster Assistance Administration to help with rescue efforts.

My father was stuck downtown in the lobby of the Statler Hotel along with many other court reporters, lawyers, and judges. Mom and I were at home, where she was assuring me that the school janitor would feed my gerbils, which were stranded at school. There was no Weather

Channel back then, but if one had existed in Buffalo, it would have no doubt been called the Bad Weather Channel.

The blizzard hit during the *Roots* miniseries, and though the TV drama had captured the attention of the nation, it received much higher ratings in upstate New York with so many viewers housebound.

Once the wind finally died down, residents watched *Doctor Zhivago,* only it was playing outside the window. A mountain range stood where there used to be trees, sheds, and jungle gyms. The neighborhood had become an arctic landscape, everything covered with a pure white blanket of snow, including single-story houses. Meantime, we kids had a blast. The sledding was incredible and ubiquitous—climb on top of a roof and away we went. The reindeer at the zoo had a good time too. The snow made it possible for them to step over their fence and wander about the city to do some window shopping.

At first the moms and kids safe in their houses felt terrible for all the fathers stuck downtown. The television news said that no rooms were left anywhere in the city and soon they'd run out of food. But after several hours of being stranded in close quarters and bedding down in hallways and lobbies, a party atmosphere took hold, and what they were in danger of running out of first weren't foodstuffs or pillows, but booze. The news went from showing a guy being told no room at the inn to raucous scenes of music blaring and people dancing in conga lines atop tabletops in hotel ballrooms. The delivery boy at the liquor store across the street from the Rand building worked all night and declared he'd never collected so much in tips in his life—and probably never would again.

On Sunday, January 30, New York governor Hugh Carey arrived in a cargo plane that carried snow-removal equipment. The residents thought they were coming out of a two-day storm when the blizzard struck again, closing roads that had just been reopened. On Wednesday, a driving ban was back in effect, while crews worked round the clock to dig the city out for a second time. Forklifts accompanied the plows and tossed street-blocking cars up onto the nearest lawn. The National Guard arrived to help, only there was no place left to put the snow. Some of it was heaped into railroad cars and sent south to melt.

Eventually the storm abated, roads were cleared, schools reopened, and people who owned white cars had learned their lesson. The blizzard was a boon to CB-radio manufacturers. People realized these two-way, short-distance radios could save a life when they were without power. The storm had claimed a total of twenty-nine lives across the region.

On February 5, President Carter declared nine upstate counties a major disaster area, the first and last such declaration ever made for a snow emergency. Soldiers were dispatched from Fort Bragg in North Carolina to assist in the cleanup, which would last several weeks. The total damage of the blizzard exceeded 300 million dollars. And the Buffalo Winter Carnival had to be postponed three times as a result of too much wintry weather.

A week later, I finally returned to my sixth-grade classroom to find that my gerbils, Ping and Pong, had turned into the Donner party. Only the bones of one were ever recovered, over by the wheel. However, I was unable to identify the body.

Winters in Buffalo don't always feature blizzardlike conditions. And occasionally there's even a storm-free year. But one rarely hears about it because Buffalonians are afraid that their relatives in Florida and Arizona might return.

When it comes down to it, the citizens of Buffalo are a Calvinistic lot, and most have decided that suffering during the winter is good not only for the constitution, but also for the spirit. During the dark days of February, you can almost hear the chorus of elementary schoolteachers chanting: "That which doesn't kill you makes you stronger."

Fifteen years later the city would become home to a major-league soccer team, and it was appropriately named the Buffalo Blizzards.

Nineteen

Taking a Turn for the Nurse

It was really no surprise that my mother decided to go back to school. Around the time I was born, she installed a 2,000-watt overhead light above a wall-length mirror in our bathroom and essentially converted it into her own first-aid theater. Whenever I bashed a shoulder or cracked open my skull, she'd haul me in there for triage. Once, after examining my fractured head under the glare of these klieg lights, the woman not prone to understatement announced, "I can see right inside to your brain."

My father, anxiously waiting in the doorway, promptly passed out. But then, he'd once fainted in a barber's chair while reading about a paraplegic. "You need about twelve sutures," she'd cheerfully forecast, as if it was going to be an adventure to have a needle and thread poked through my scalp. Even before she officially became a nurse, my mother never said *stitches*; it was always *sutures*. Likewise, bumps were *hematomas* and bruises were *contusions*. (If she ever has her colors done I'm sure they'll be blue-purple.) Mom didn't just threaten you with pneumonia; she told you what kind you'd *contract*: viral, bacterial, streptococcal, and so forth. One might say she had an innate sense for medicine, the way successful politicians have a knack for lying.

Nursing was her destiny. If she were the mother of all things, I am quite certain that all things would wear sweaters. Everyone in the household was issued white socks and underwear so as not to be poisoned by dye. A person only had to twirl a paper clip to be reminded that her grandfather died of tetanus. When one is thinking *fun party*, she's thinking *fire hazard*. If I had a few friends over and someone started hacking, from the next room we'd immediately hear, "Who coughed?" And there was something about her tone that made us afraid to admit it, as if we had state secrets in our possession. When a person sneezed, she no less casually inquired about the color of the mucus. Mom reads snot the way others read tea leaves or check the sky for a weather forecast. Move over Florence Nightingale.

In her bathroom-cum-operating-theater, my mother could steril-ize needles for splinter extractions, pluck asphalt from an eyeball, and thoroughly examine cuts and assorted road rash (*wounds* and *abrasions*) for signs of infection (*sepsis*). Her nickname was Eagle-Eye Ellen, and there wasn't much chance of anything getting past her, whether that was the intention or not.

She removed Band-Aids stuck to scabs that others were terrified to peel off. She extracted loose teeth in danger of being swallowed. And she applied ice to sprains and gauze to scrapes, so that a child could get back on base as fast as possible.

Mom was an early advocate of abolishing table salt (the silent killer!), even though her brother and sister used the saltshaker to punctuate their sentences and continued salting throughout lengthy expositions. She for-bade me from drinking cola (it takes paint off a car!) and railed at anyone who would listen against homemade douches (too much vinegar destroys the ability to fight bacteria). Mom was raising warning flags about skin cancer in the days when people were still slathering baby oil over their bodies and wrapping record album covers with aluminum foil to reflect maximum ultraviolet rays onto their faces. She was hostile to grease, fat, and cooking oil (hardens the arteries) and went around slipping ice cubes into ashtrays back when people smoked in confined public places. (Why should the rest of us die from secondhand smoke?) When it came to carbohydrates, "The whiter the bread, the quicker you're dead" was her mantra. These things are all a matter of course now, but back then Mom was considered a radical, and probably a quack as well. On the back of the toilet tank she always kept a box of pitted prunes.

Dad, on the other hand, would use medical research to suit his needs and ignore whatever wasn't helpful, such as studies linking smoking to cancer. He doesn't wear a seat belt since "the steering wheel will protect me in an accident." He read that nicotine and coffee help to prevent Alzheimer's, and he swears by that one. Same with a report that says wine wards off heart disease. (I admit that, in similar fashion, I clip everything published on the health benefits of consuming large quantities of chocolate.) Dad won't let a dermatologist look at his skin cancer because "it will all burn off when I'm cremated." Once when he was gardening, I looked over and asked, "Are you wearing foundation garments?" He said, "Those are my trusses." Apparently Dad lets hernias stack up the way other people do unpaid bills.

Over the years, my mother developed a reputation in the neighborhood as a provider of low-cost (free), low-pain healthcare, and thereby had a devoted following among my friends. When a neighborhood child (hint: red hair) was temporarily relieved of her eyesight after chewing an entire pack of bubble gum and blowing a helium balloon–sized bubble that popped and sealed her eyelashes shut, her choice was Nurse Pedersen.

For one thing, my mother never softened the prognosis by saying something wouldn't hurt when indeed it would, as the school nurse often did. She told it like it was, and so we trusted her. If Mom said, "This is really going to sting for a minute," we figured it was going to hurt less than whatever the pediatrician with the hypodermic needles and big clunky hands had up the sleeve of his white lab coat. Also, her neighborhood clinic admitted unaccompanied minors, so my friends didn't have to report injuries to their parents, who would otherwise force them inside to "rest quietly" or worse, insist on knowing "who did it."

As long as we didn't need a doctor, her don't-ask-don't-tell policy afforded a welcome measure of nurse-patient privacy. Kids showed up at the door with black eyes, bloodied elbows, cold sores, and ingrown toenails as if our home was the local emergency room. And my mother welcomed these volunteer patients. Even after friends grew up and moved away, they'd still phone in their symptoms from college dorm rooms across the country, and she'd provide long-distance diagnoses.

I was thrilled when my mother returned to school. She brought home fun things to play with, like a dissecting kit and a stethoscope through which I could listen to the dog digest her food. However, we all had to serve our turn as laboratory animals. The cat had his abscess cleaned and rebandaged. Dad's blood pressure was checked. And late one night, I awoke thinking there was a strangler in my room, which was of course my mother with one ice-cold hand around my neck registering the pulse in my carotid artery and the other holding a flashlight trained on her nurse's watch. After I screamed and leapt from the bed, she dutifully scrawled something in her notebook and said, "I didn't want to wake you."

I complained, "You scared the heck out of me."

She said, "Your pulse is normal, and that's the main thing."

Friends thought it odd that, when they came over to play, my mother practiced her craft in the kitchen by giving injections to an orange or studying a sheep's brain. By the time she was student nursing, our house was like an episode of *The Addams Family*. If kids stared for any length of time, she'd eventually look up, hungrily eye their healthy young bodies, and ask, "Should we prick your finger and find out your blood type?"

When my mother began her math classes, I'd already passed algebra and was regularly awoken at one in the morning for assistance. I asked why she didn't just look up the answers in the back of her book. I mean, that was the whole *point* of being in college instead of junior high school—they *gave* you the solutions. Child of the forties that Mom is, she insisted it was cheating. So I'd have a swig of Orange Crush, plug in the solution, work the problem backward, show her how to do it, and then crawl back into bed.

Mom was completely honest. She wouldn't bluff in poker because she felt it was too much like lying. She wouldn't so much as forge a signature, even if the person had given his permission. There was only one law she broke. After she'd lived in our neighborhood twenty years, a traffic light was installed at the end of the street. Mom didn't obey it because she'd successfully navigated the intersection so long without one that she felt certain it was there for others. Or that she was somehow operating under a grandfather clause, or else had squatter rights, because she ran that light every single day and twice on Sundays.

Had my mother gotten an earlier start on college she could easily have been a doctor. There's something bold and confident about her demeanor that, no matter what the situation, clearly states: "I'm in charge and you're not." Over the years I've noticed that in a genuine medical emergency this is the kind of firm leadership most patients are seeking.

For instance, one Sunday my mother was sitting in church during a naming ceremony when the father just barely managed to hand off the infant to his wife like a football before passing out. The minister asked if there was a doctor in the sanctuary. My mother and a dentist simultaneously accepted the call to the altar. The dentist deferred to her. One could make a case that this is only as it should be since he fills cavities for a living and she was by this time a registered nurse. However, my mother is simply the kind of person that one defers to in a medical emergency. She instructed the dentist to go and call 9-1-1. Then she adroitly went into her routine—airway, breathing, circulation—and determined that no on-site heroics were necessary.

The paramedics arrived moments later, and she reported her findings as they hustled the man off into the ambulance with a relative. My mother turned to the wife, who was still standing at the altar, slack-jawed and clutching her child. "Did your husband clean the oven this morning?"

The distraught wife, now wide-eyed at this bit of ESP, said, "Yes, how did you know? We're having twenty for brunch."

My mother just bobbed her head in acknowledgment and suggested, "Next time, open a window." Another case solved.

Yet she isn't always so decisive. Once I arrived home from camp with a painful lump the size of a chestnut on the top of my head. She replied matter-of-factly that it was either a horsefly bite (I'm allergic) or else a brain tumor. I was eleven. I vividly recall being terrified that I was going to die from a brain tumor. In the meantime, she didn't appear to give more or less weight to either possibility. She simply said that if it went away in a few days then we could be sure it was a bite. It did. It was the same when someone had a stomachache. She'd say it could be something the person ate or else acute appendicitis, in which case, without an emergency appendectomy, they'd die. Even with me, her own child, her *only* child, Mom has the capacity for a certain detached professionalism—never ruling anything out just because it happens to be the most unpleasant outcome.

Like an evangelist takes his faith to heart, my mother takes her medicine seriously. And it's accurate to say that over the years she's been an aggressive community healthcare provider. Mom has no qualms about sweeping a ballroom, bathroom, courtroom, or any other public space for illegal smokers and summarily escorting them from the premises, not caring a whit if they're big-shot executives or high-ranking politicians. And they all go meekly and quietly because they mistake her self-assurance to mean that she's in charge, either operating as an undercover security guard or head of the Red Cross. Or the KGB. Lenin, Stalin, Ellen. And though it's not yet illegal to smoke while driving, Mom is prepared for the day when it is. She can determine when the people in the car in front of her are puffing, because the smoke goes out their window and in through her vent, and she changes lanes as soon as possible.

Embarrassment would be an understatement for what I've occasionally experienced while trailing along in the flotsam and jetsam of her bandages and defibrillators. My mother can spring into nursing action at a moment's notice, without any warning, because her medical radar is constantly operating. Even when it appears that she's working as a greeter at church or serving food at a picnic, in actuality she's surveying everyone's physical and mental health. After someone passes by she'll lean over and whisper, "Apparently he forgot to take his lithium this morning" or "That entire family is hearing voices, and she could go into group therapy all by herself." Before we arrive at a party, Mom will enthusiastically say, "Stay close and I'll introduce you to an undiagnosed borderline personality disorder," as if we're embarking on an African safari.

But that's nothing compared to her penchant for tackling potential patients. When one elderly parishioner arrived at church with a few bruises on her arms and face, my mother immediately insisted upon knowing what had happened. The woman, who's been in her seventies as long as anyone can remember, lived on her own and explained that she'd taken a fall but had since recovered. Little did this woman realize that she was playing right into my mother's blood-pressure cuff—because Mom already had her mental slide rule out and was calculating when each bruise occurred by how it looked, and she had already determined that there'd been more than one fall, possibly three or four. (Don't try to tell my mother that you cut yourself on a Saturday when you did it on a Wednesday, because that wound speaks to her the way elephant dung talks to a jungle tracker.)

Mom abandoned her post in the foyer and hunted the woman down in order to read the elusive patient her medical rights: "As a healthcare professional, I must insist by law on knowing the nature and cause of your injuries." My mother has a way of wording things to make it sound as if there are law-enforcement officials waiting outside to arrest and bring us to trial if we don't cooperate. It probably didn't hurt that they were in a chapel, but the woman quickly confessed: she'd been experiencing frequent dizzy spells, passing out, and falling down. That afternoon my mother made phone calls to make sure she was getting the appropriate assistance and medications. Meantime, I wrote the woman a note of apology and said that she should consider herself lucky since she only had to be inspected by my alleged biological mother on Sundays and was free to do as she pleased during the rest of the week.

Twenty

Bus Stop

On August 16, 1977, the King of Rock and Roll died. Elvis Presley was forty-two years old, about the same age as most of our parents. Though my friends and I were only around eleven, it was obvious that the circumstances surrounding his death were a bit sketchy, especially this business about "cardiac arrhythmia." At least enough so that we kids could make out that Elvis of the shag-carpeting-on-the-ceiling was poster king for why we shouldn't do drugs.

Aside from a few records owned by my parents, I knew nothing about Elvis and had never even seen him perform, live or on TV. But I remember that fateful August day because the radio played his music hour after hour, and weeping listeners phoned in to request their favorites.

By the time of Elvis's death, the political momentum of the sixties and early seventies had stagnated. Busing students from one district to another and racial quotas were opposed by the courts, as were rights for homosexuals, and the Equal Rights Amendment for women had also languished. (Usually known as ERA, this was a proposed constitutional amendment that would say, "Equality of rights under the law shall not be denied or abridged by the United States on account of sex.")

The Cold War was now at the forefront, along with the prospect of the United States losing its economic (and thus political) leadership in the world. Between 1967 and 1977, American manufacturing productivity was being heavily outpaced by West Germany, France, and particularly Japan. Suggested causes were the failure to control the money supply, excessive taxation, and overregulation by government. No matter, these declines hit the industrial cities of the North the hardest, and triggered the start of the migration to the South and West that would continue through the century.

Our Cold War nemesis, the Communist Soviets, dominated the Union of Soviet Socialist Republics (USSR), controlled Eastern Europe, and were well established in Cuba. Now they were moving into Ethiopia and also central and east Africa. By the end of the seventies, ten African states were under Soviet "protection" and proclaiming themselves to be Communist. The Berlin Wall would not come down for another twelve years, in November of 1989, after a massive military spending increase under President Ronald Reagan, and the Iron Curtain would finally slip from its rod.

In the fall of 1977, I started junior high school in another Sweet Home school-district building. This one was a rectangular brick fortification that looked so much like a prison we used to check behind the room-number signs to see if they covered cell-block numbers. On the first day of seventh grade, I fully expected a warden to be waiting inside the metal doors to toss me a striped jumpsuit and a pile of license plates and bark, "Start painting!" There was a banner high up on the wall that said "I am responsible for my day." I'm pretty sure it was created in conjunction with the local parole board.

Despite the correctional-facility feel, the guards, I mean teachers, were mostly pleasant. This was just before the era of school lawsuits, and so educators were much more willing to take the inmates on field trips and even invite the entire class to their homes for a picnic. It was just after the era of corporal punishment (our parents' generation), so our teachers weren't supposed to hit us. The one exception was the home economics teacher, Mrs. Tweed (aka Boss Tweed), who wasn't beyond commanding a girl's full attention by yanking on a chunk of her hair, which came to be known as the Tweed Twist.

Many teachers went out of their way to make learning fun, not because they were being prodded with incentives or put through all sorts of courses on new learning theories, but simply because they were kind and devoted. For instance, a social studies teacher claimed to have the only recorded copy of the Gettysburg Address. At the age of twelve, most of us weren't sure if tape recorders had been around for thirty years or a hundred and thirty. So he'd play the "only recording," and kids would listen to the scratchy presentation with rapt attention. He also managed to have in his possession the bullet used to assassinate President Kennedy, and this was two decades before eBay.

Mr. Krawczyk (another Mr. K.) played tic-tac-toe against his detention charges. If he won, they wrote an essay; if they won, he gave them a pass to escape for a half hour. A black belt in pencil-and-paper games, Mr. K. was a formidable opponent, and otherwise lackadaisical students ended up writing more in one day than they otherwise would have in an entire school year.

The only truly scary player was the school nurse. She had the emptiest clinic in the history of healthcare, sort of the Maytag repairman of the junior high, the loneliest nurse in town. Commissar might be more accurate. She took "I'm okay, you're okay" to a whole new level. Basically, we would vomit in the classroom, on the playing field, anywhere, before going to the nurse. If a girl went down to the clinic saying she had a stomachache, our nurse would be sure to ask if she was having her period, in a stentorian voice that was easily overheard by the captain of the football team who was wrapping a knee injury nearby. A student who had just lost her father was informed that she'd essentially killed him with all of her shenanigans. There was no doubt in any student's mind that this was exactly the kind of god that the writers of the Old Testament had in mind—plenty of rules, power over life and death, and no mercy.

Finally, she retired, or else was called back to the Kremlin, and the benevolent Nurse Sherry arrived as her replacement. Nurse Sherry was sweet and all smiles, and soon the place was packed with kids experiencing all sorts of ailments and needing passes to get out of classes, skip tests, and leave early. These needy patients would grow up to cost the government millions in healthcare while the stoics from the previous regime went for decades without so much as an aspirin.

One of Nurse Sherry's duties was dealing with blue-jean injuries.

Designer denims reached the Buffalo suburbs by way of a 1980 television commercial featuring a teenaged Brooke Shields insisting that nothing came between her and her Calvins. And suddenly girls were lying across benches in the locker room sucking in their breath and pulling on their jeans, sometimes with assists and rebounds from friends.

The formal dress code for public schools had gone by the wayside about ten years earlier, so we were allowed to wear jeans, overalls, T-shirts, sweatshirts, and sneakers. However, it's doubtful when the uniforms were dropped that administrators had in mind as their replacements skintight Jordache, Sassoon, Sergio Valente, and Gloria Vanderbilt jeans worn with lacy camisoles and cherry-blossom pink, high-heeled Candie's molded plastic slides.

Even gum chewing was allowed. Though we still couldn't chew gum in chorus and had to stick that big wad of Bubblicious to the top of a Smurf-themed notebook until the period was over.

It was around this time that the movie *Saturday Night Fever* delivered disco fever to our doorsteps. John Travolta played a working-class Italian guy who lived to shine on the dance floor. Growing up in an ethnically diverse industrial town that had just run out of opportunity, we identified with such escapist fantasies. Suddenly women were clothed in spandex unitards and wraparound skirts. In the school gym and converted basements, we jumped around to the Bee Gees, Commodores, and James Brown. Equally popular were Patti LaBelle's "New Attitude," "Born to Be Alive" by Patrick Hernandez, and Gloria Gaynor's "I Will Survive."

Up until then, the fashionable dances had been the Mashed Potato, the Monkey, the Twist, and the Watusi. They were quickly abandoned for the Bus Stop, the Bump, the Time Warp, and the Electric Slide. For hours we line danced, all facing forward in a military phalanx, to Van McCoy's "The Hustle," "A Fifth of Beethoven" by Walter Murphy, anything fast by disco diva Donna Summer, and then we performed groundbreaking calisthenics to the Village People's "YMCA."

This was about the extent of our rowdiness. It wasn't as if the radical sixties had been erased by the time the late seventies rolled around, but the economy was still abysmal, especially in Buffalo. Despite the decline of heavy industry, it remained a blue-collar city populated largely by first- and second-generation Americans. Most of us knew from life at home and stories around the dinner table that times were tough, and we were concerned about the survival of our families, so many kids had after-school or weekend jobs.

In my neighborhood, most parents worked in factories, schools, local businesses, or government jobs. There were plenty of teachers and civil servants, along with a few doctors and lawyers and a dozen or so nurses, the main job available to women back then if they didn't become teachers or secretaries. Yet, our mothers thought they were doing pretty well, because when they graduated from high school in the Nifty Fifties, classified ads divided men's work and women's work, a practice that ended in the early sixties. Also phased out was the policy of firing airline stewardesses on their thirty-second birthday.

Many people, like my parents, had moved a few miles away from the city because the suburban schools were thought to be better and, after the unrest of the sixties, were considered safer. Most of us kids were expected to do slightly or substantially better than our parents. If they'd left high school early, then we were at least supposed to finish high school, and perhaps go on to college. If they labored with their hands and their backs, then we were expected to work with our minds.

In the seventies and early eighties, girls obtained their sex infor-mation from Judy Blume books, and mothers got their laughs from Erma Bombeck's syndicated newspaper column about the perils of homemaking. Men were busy hiding copies of *Playboy*, and boys were busy digging them out. (This was before the *Sports Illustrated* swimsuit edition.) If kids couldn't find copies of *Playboy* or *Hustler*, they searched for bare-breasted tribeswomen in *National Geographic*. It's possible that when these boys finally encountered actual naked women they were perplexed not to find their anatomy more pendulous and ornamented with gold rings, henna designs, or pieces of ivory.

Nothing demented my junior high experience quite like the release of *National Lampoon's Animal House*. Arrested development firmly set in as the world suddenly became our frat house. Though food fights had always been a staple at Sweet Home, especially at the peak of overcrowding, the movie brought the cry of "Food fight!" roaring back to the cafeteria. Likewise, it led to a resurgence of toga parties ("Toga! Toga! Toga!"), a revival of the song "Shout," neighborhood trees filled with underwear, and exploding toilets. "Double-secret probation" became a code word among teenagers, though for what I still don't know.

Surprisingly, the largest fashion shift in the seventies affected the geezer set. Oldsters who'd spent a lifetime imprisoned by starched collars, tight neckties, binding foundation garments, and bunion-generating footwear suddenly embraced function. As opposed to yelling at us kids, "Is that what you're going to wear?" and "Put some decent shoes on!" senior citizens were loading their closets with sweat suits and sneakers. Every wedding had at least one grandma in a flowered dress, pearls, and a pair of Reeboks along with a grandpa in a wheelchair, sporting an Adidas tracksuit (it was still a "suit") with racing stripes down the side and a zipper up the front of the jacket. Flights to Florida carried enough appliquéd sweatshirts to locate the passengers by satellite photograph, should the plane nosedive into the Atlantic.

When compared with the district norm, my high school class was considered particularly disposed to academics and athletics. A local journalist would later write a story about the strange anomaly and remark that there appeared to have been something in the water that year. Dozens headed to Ivy League schools and Big Ten universities and then earned graduate degrees, which was rather remarkable for this middle-class suburb at the time.

The class one year ahead of us was, for the most part, a rather hard-bitten, antiestablishment group of back-of-the-bus smokers; at least the ones in my neighborhood were. They wore jean jackets, rarely carried books, usually left school early in the day, and never checked to see how the chess club was doing.

My friends and I gave a wide berth to these suave rebels without folders as we huddled at the front of the big yellow school bus while clouds of cigarette smoke and the dissonant chords of Black Sabbath's

"Children of the Grave" blasted in the back. The driver would often stop the bus and threaten them. The cult of Judas Priest just laughed and sneered. We'd been told that these disaffected youth were headed for a bad end, but we were slightly envious and worshipful all the same. As each day in seventh grade passed, it was hard not to fantasize about the following year, when we would rule the back of the bus and jostle and tease the lowly seventh graders.

That day finally arrived in the fall of 1978. My friends and I excitedly boarded the bus prepared to take our rightful place in the cool back seats. However, we were still nonsmokers, carrying books instead of boom boxes, and our favorite song wasn't "Highway to Hell," but the popular Dr. Pepper jingle.

Much to our dismay, a large group of seventh graders had boarded the bus at an earlier stop and taken over the backseats. My eighth-grade friends and I conferred about this, and I volunteered to be the spokesperson for our disgruntled group. As the bus lurched around the corner, we moved toward the back of the bus, me in the front. This particular lot of seventh graders was unsavory looking—dressed more for a concert than school, the girls wearing halter tops, heavy layers of makeup, and pants so tight it was possible to see the imprint from their days-of-the-week underwear, the boys in black rock-band T-shirts with metal chains attaching their wallets to the belt loops of acid-washed jeans.

"Get out of the backseats," I said.

"No," said one scowling preteenager.

"Make us," snarled another of Satan's helpers and casually lit up a cigarette.

I couldn't think of a way to accomplish our mission aside from challenging them to a spelling bee. My friends and I returned to our old seats up front, huddled around the bus driver, and had the pleasure of being the first ones off for yet another year, along with enjoying close proximity to the emergency kit. At least we kept custody of the fire ax.

Twenty-One

Enter, Stage Left...O.B. (Order Big)...
A Decent Docent Doesn't Doze

It was at the start of eighth grade that I met an extraordinary individual, assigned to be my social studies teacher for that year. Peter Heffley looked like a combination of Gandhi and a Keebler elf, acted like Mary Poppins and Peter Pan rolled into one, and dressed as if coming from one of Jay Gatsby's parties. He would become my mentor and lifelong friend.

What Gertrude Stein said turned out to be true: "It is inevitable when one has a great need of something, one finds it." At the time, I felt certain there was a phenomenally happy person trapped inside of me who didn't quite know how to get out. Pete shared his love of books, music, art, theater, and, most importantly, he gave me a tremendous amount of his time.

Pete is an incredibly joyous human being, overflowing with energy (and musical numbers). Born in 1945, he was a laughter enthusiast long before I came along, based on reports of Pete swinging out across his high school auditorium on the curtains and riding around in a sports car flinging thousands of buttons into crowds and fountains.

Pete brought his joie de vivre and je ne sais quoi to the classroom, incorporating all the latest movies and *Saturday Night Live* skits into his lectures. For a lesson on World War I, he pretended to be the great-aunt of Roseanne Roseannadanna, a popular character from the show in the late seventies. A wealth of interesting and unusual historical information,

Pete would offer such tidbits as how the White House bathrooms had to be enlarged for the corpulent President Taft, and that F. Scott Fitzgerald became addicted to Coca-Cola back when one of the ingredients was actual cocaine. Pete revealed that FDR had carried on an affair with his wife Eleanor's private secretary, Lucy Mercer, and that First Lady Eleanor and journalist Lorena Hickok appear to have shared an especially close friendship as well. Our all-time favorite historical footnote is how Hickok, known to her friends and colleagues as Hick, was given the nickname Hickey Doodle by a previous girlfriend.

Pete rarely came to my house, but I distinctly remember the first time he did and the exchange that took place between him and my mother, since it was so characteristic of them both. My parents were having some church friends over, and Pete was going to be in the neighborhood for another party, so I told him to stop by. When he arrived, I introduced him to my mother. She offered him a gin and tonic. Pete said he'd like that very much, but could she leave out the tonic. Then he asked if she minded if he used the bathroom, since he had "horrible diarrhea." She pointed Pete in the right direction and yelled after him, "Be sure to open the window!"

After most introductions, Pete's next line is usually, "Where's the bathroom?"

Between bad nerves and irritable bowel syndrome, or perhaps a spastic colon, Pete is no stranger to the lavatory. When friends return from vacation and tell him about Milan's La Scala Opera House, the Tuileries Garden, or the castle at Rothenberg, Pete will describe the bizarre restroom he used at each location.

It wasn't long before Pete asked me to be his assistant for the musicals he directed at the high school. There was always a lot of laughter, and it was clear that the aspiring young drama students loved to be in his presence. Pete was a natural for center stage, as long as the appearance was informal. He claimed not to have the nerve to perform professionally. In fact, when scheduled to make a speech at his parents' fiftieth wedding anniversary, Pete had a few substantial Manhattans beforehand and collapsed into a potted palm, leaving an uncle to improvise the toast.

After several years of working on musicals at Sweet Home, Pete was invited to direct at a nearby Catholic girls' school, complete with an attached barracks full of nuns. Pete directed the musical *Sweet Charity,* and the nuns were oblivious to the fact that the dance girls were actually hookers. Because the nuns were hard to tell apart, and so many were called Mary, we usually just referred to them by their job title or some other distinguishing feature. For instance, there was Sister Mary Attendance, Sister Mary Basketball Coach, Sister Mary Janitor, and Sister Mary Wheelchair. Pete could get the otherwise somber Sister Mary Wheelchair to burst into high-pitched giggles by asking her to pop wheelies and jump garbage cans.

While Pete was working onstage with one or two individual cast members, I'd often sneak back into the nuns' private residence to perform an experiment. I had a theory that nuns would never flush a live goldfish if they found it swimming in their toilet. Sure enough, every time I left a goldfish, it could be found in a bowl on the counter the following afternoon. By opening night, they had enough to stock a pond.

Outside of Sister Mary Librarian's office, I'd happened upon a box of books that were being discarded, and one from the early fifties caught my eye. It was essentially a manual on how a good Catholic teenaged girl should behave. At the back was a quiz with questions such as:

What should you do if a boy comes over and your parents aren't home?
A) Invite him inside for something to drink.
B) Go for a ride with him in his car.
C) Tell him to come back when your parents are home.

I loved the retro-ness of this handbook, and every free moment I'd climb the ladder to where Sister Lois worked the lights and have an in-depth discussion of each situation with her, as if these could be actual circumstances facing a teenager in the eighties. Lois treated the questions with extreme seriousness, and for the one about a boy coming over she suggested that it might be okay to sit on the front porch with him and drink lemonade, so long as he didn't come inside the house and provided you told your parents about it later. Meantime, as we were speaking, the girls in the show were slipping away from rehearsal and out to the parking lot with the boys (who had been brought in from another nearby Catholic school) and racing toward home plate. The phrase *good Catholic girl* oftentimes best served as an example of an oxymoron.

It was once said about President Teddy Roosevelt that he wanted to be the bride at every wedding, the baby at every christening, and the corpse at every funeral. I think the same thing might be said about Pete, so long as the show was spontaneous. When we walked into the shops on Buffalo's artsy Elmwood Avenue, Pete would give impromptu performances for the customers and sales staff.

One bit that always got a laugh centered on Pete's baldness. His hair had bolted for the exits in his twenties, leaving behind a two-inch corona of fringe along with a neatly trimmed beard and mustache. We'd be standing in line at a store and I'd suddenly shout, "Pete, your toupee!" Everyone's head would whip around to stare at Pete, while a look of abject horror crossed his face. He'd throw his hand on top of his head and go, "Oh no, my hair!" We'd both search the floor the way people do when they lose a contact lens.

When strangers ran into us on the street and confused Pete for someone else, he'd immediately assume that identity, and a bizarre and usually hilarious conversation would follow. The person would frequently refer to someone totally unknown to Pete, an Aunt Gladys, for instance, and Pete would do a wonderful conspiratorial aside and whisper, "I always thought she was a secret drinker." Whether the person smiled knowingly and confirmed or vehemently denied, the accusation made the encounter equally funny.

Pete certainly didn't inherit his theatricality from his mother, Mildred. The tagline for her was adapted from the title song of the musical *Mame* to "You put the *dread* in Mildred." The town where she lived, Angola, I quickly renamed Angina. Mildred was very astute when it came to people and business matters, but such a pessimist that she was actually a source of great amusement. Not only did she see the glass as half empty, but as having cracks in it and providing a breeding ground for germs that were likely to kill us.

The three of us were having a lovely brunch at a restaurant called the Old Orchard Inn, and, after Pete and I battled it out over the basket of sticky buns, Pete remarked what a gorgeous day it was and pointed to the stunning blue jays right outside the window. "They're mean bastards," Mildred immediately chimed in. "They steal the eggs from the nests of other birds." If we said that her flowers were nice, she said, "They're about to go on the turn." If we said the weather was beautiful, she shot back, "It's supposed to get real bad tomorrow." And my all-time favorite: If we said that it's so much warmer than it was yesterday, she announced, "This is the kind of weather that makes people sick!"

Unlike his mom, Pete can find humor in almost any situation. During a Mexican-themed party given for members of my church, over burritos and gazpacho a woman was telling Pete and our friend Russ how she'd attended all the church functions, including a beaver party. That was all he needed to start asking her as many questions about the beaver party as possible, in an effort to coax her into saying things like, "We had nice, hot beaver. They roasted it on a spit."

When not a slave to his unpredictable bowels, Pete gathered friends to attend plays, concerts, dance performances, and musicals. Not just in Buffalo, but at the Shaw Festival in Niagara-on-the-Lake, the Shakespeare Festival in Stratford, Ontario, and others in Toronto, New York, and even at the National Theatre in London. Once, when tickets to *Amadeus* were sold out, we ended up seeing the bawdy Broadway musical *Oh! Calcutta!,* where the performers were naked throughout most of the show. It became a running gag that Pete took me to my first blue musical at age fourteen while he was supposed to be acting in the capacity of teacher and chaperone. I'd create skits in which the board of education finds out about *Oh! Calcutta!* and Pete is forced to clarify in what ways the experience was highly educational.

During the day, we traipsed through antique stores, museums, and galleries; Pete would explain what we were looking at, unable to help himself when it came to elaborating on whatever the nearest docent was saying. However, his attention span was slightly shorter than mine, which was about a minute, and so we spun through life at a pace that courted tetanus in rust-prone upstate New York.

Summer afternoons were often spent in lawn chairs reading aloud from *The New Yorker* about Martha Graham, Rudolf Nureyev, or Josephine Baker and her Rainbow Tribe. We waded through enormous biographies and delighted in finding hilarious anecdotes, like when Dwight Eisenhower was asked if he knew General Douglas MacArthur, and he replied, "Yes, I studied dramatics under him for seven years."

❀ ❀ ❀

Pete was a solid meal ticket from eighth grade on. Rarely did we go any-place expensive, but he was always good for a stop at Burger King, the soda fountain, or a hot-dog stand. When it came to food preferences my motto was "If it's free, then it's for me." Pete's motto: "Lunch means never having to say you're hungry."

Early on, I learned that Pete rarely ordered enough food for him-self and counted upon eating everyone else's meal, even when he was paying for it. Pete believes that food has fewer calories when a person doesn't order it himself or if it's consumed while cooking or standing around. So if I wanted a small then I ordered a medium, and if I wanted a medium I had to order a large.

I'd try and persuade Pete to order first, as a way of gauging the potential for shrinkage. For instance, when Pete insisted he wasn't hun-gry and didn't order anything, I knew to order big across the board. He'd look aghast, mostly for the benefit of the counter person, "A large? You must be *awfully* hungry!" And I'd think, *I'm not, you are!* As soon as the fries hit the tray, before I'd so much as salted them, before he'd even paid, before we'd moved away from the counter, Pete would stuff a quarter of them in his mouth while saying, "That's way too much. You'll never finish all that."

However, if Pete ordered a chicken sandwich or even just a small french fries, I'd have a couple minutes head start as he polished off his own food first. Otherwise, he struck like lightning and could scrape all the whipped cream and hot fudge off a sundae before I set the tray down on the table. Once, and only once, I made the mistake of being in the restroom when the food arrived.

In addition to assisting with the school play, I also worked at Pete's frequent parties. His apartment was the entire upstairs of a large house on Gates Circle in the Silk Stocking District of Buffalo, crammed with antique furniture, lamps with ornate bases or hand-painted shades, gilded mirrors, stunning old clocks, elaborately decorated porcelain vases, and oil paintings with fancy frames. Brilliant red kimonos festooned with intricate embroidery were mounted on the walls, and the floors and shelves were home to statuary of all shapes and sizes. Our friend Suzy Benzinger, a Broadway costume designer, dubbed the apartment Versailles-in-Buffalo. Indeed, the Louis XIV–interiors were photographed for several magazines. One could make a case that between the maroon moiré silk window treatments, matching couches covered in turquoise shantung, white marble clock inlaid with onyx, oil paintings of voluptuous women, and the life-size statue of a naked Venus, only Toulouse-Lautrec, busily capturing the scene for posterity, was missing.

Thus the scene was set for Pete's soirees—candlelit dinners with classical music playing in the background. There'd be shrimp cocktail, usually some sort of chicken with rice and vegetables, and a fancy dessert from the bakery. My job was to take coats, serve cocktails, get the food heated and on the table, then clear and clean up afterward.

Although Pete paid me for my Felix Ungering, the best part about these dinner parties was the free food. When I cleared the appetizers and later the dinner table, I spirited the dishes off to the kitchen and ate every last bite that remained. Not even teeth marks could stop me. Quite the contrary, they were an indication of freshness. Therefore, the strategic part of the night for me was not making sure the food came out at the right time, but sizing up guests upon arrival, trying to determine the clean-plate club from those who might leave me a meal, perhaps even a full dessert. I lived for the lactose intolerant, the dieters, and those with sugar problems.

I never told Pete exactly how I was cleaning the plates, and when he'd stop in the kitchen to instruct me on storing the leftovers, I'd always say, "They ate every bite." He'd look a bit puzzled, as if he could have sworn there should have been extra food. "It must have been really good," I'd say. Then he seemed pleased that the guests had enjoyed everything so much.

❋ ❋ ❋

When not serving at parties and assisting on school plays, I helped Pete study to become a guide at the nearby Albright-Knox Art Gallery. While we ate at Burger King, I'd hold up homemade flash cards of all the works of art so he could tell me about them while I checked the information against what was written on the back. Pete gave the best art gallery and museum tours, second to none. He passed the test with flying colors, one of the highest scores they'd ever had.

However, Pete was soon asked to leave under a Tiepolo-colored cloud for giving too much information about certain objets d'art. For instance, there was a painting of a young boy who'd guide the upper classes home through dark alleyways from the theater, lighting the way with a torch. Pete added that it was possible the artist intended the boy to have a slightly sinister rather than angelic expression on his face, since occasionally these street urchins would club their wealthy customers over the head with their torches and rob them. To appreciate another painting, Pete felt it was necessary for gallerygoers to understand that the artist, Amedeo Modigliani, had embarked on an affair with South African writer Beatrice Hastings and on one occasion threw her out of a window. And that another Modigliani mistress, Jeanne Hébuterne, walked backward out of a window a day after the artist died, killing herself and their unborn child with whom she was almost nine months pregnant.

So ended Pete's short time as a docent. On the bright side, I learned the meaning of the word *defenestration* and could actually use it in a sentence.

One adventure led to another, and my teenage years were like those of Mary Poppins's young charges, who arrive at Uncle Albert's to enjoy a tea party on the ceiling and then follow Bert the chimney sweep and jack-of-all trades through a magical cartoon paradise, complete with dancing penguins. Years later, when a reporter asked Pete if he'd been my mentor, he replied that, like Athena from Zeus, I'd sprung from his head fully formed.

Throughout Pete's forty years of teaching, thousands of students stopped back to tell him he was their favorite teacher of all time. Then one day we were having lunch at a diner when the owner, a former student, came over and exclaimed, "Mr. Heffley, we all just loved you!" Pete smiled and graciously thanked the woman. He was very used to this. She continued, "You were one of my...(long pause)...top five favorite teachers!" Pete looked as if he'd been hit with a stun gun. To help him process the remark, I quickly added, "I guess if you'd been her fourth favorite teacher she would have said top four, huh?"

Twenty-Two

Down on the Farm...Doing Time...Beat It

The result of Irish and Scandinavian skin combined, my pallor is that of someone who has been living under the basement stairs for several decades. On my mom's side of the family, tanning means four minutes the first day, seven minutes the second day, and so forth, until we're the dark pink color of a medium-rare steak. By the end of every summer, I looked like Heidi, if she were half Cherokee. Especially since sunblock wasn't waterproof during my pool, pond, and sprinkler years.

No amount of bug spray could keep the bees, mosquitoes, fleas, and deerflies from administering chomps and stings that instantly swelled to the size of communion wafers. At the end of a day, other kids would have one or two bites, and I'd have two dozen, as if the insects understood that with me they were getting the most bang for their bite. Sure, I knew what poison ivy looked like, and I remembered the popular adage "Leaves of three, let it be." But I didn't have to touch poison ivy to have my arms and legs turn bright red with welts; I only had to see it through a window.

I'm the first to admit that I never did a lick of housework throughout my childhood. I never turned on the vacuum cleaner, loaded the dishwasher, or ran the lawn mower, not once. My mother never asked me to clean anything. As best as I can tell, she was rather obsessive about cleanliness and felt that anything my father or I touched would only be made messier and she'd have to rewash it anyway. After a day of playing outside, she made me hose off in the backyard before even entering the garage. And there was no way my mother the nurse was going to let me chop off my fingers and toes with a lawn mower (she'd memorized the statistics on yard-work injuries, and they were right up there with riding a motorcycle). Besides, every time I was outside when the grass was being mowed, I started sneezing, my eyes swelled shut, and my lungs shuddered.

Though I may have enjoyed a chore-free domestic life, I worked outside the home, as many females began doing in the seventies. I can't remember a week when I didn't have some job or another, and usually I had two or three. I've been paying Social Security since age eleven. It was taken out of my first real paycheck, for being a camp counselor, which offered an unpretentious two-digit salary. Although my constitution rejects the ungreat outdoors, there weren't many full-time jobs for a preteen girl to pursue, and so, as with most career trajectories, I had to make sacrifices to get started. Sometimes one must dig down to climb up.

It's true that in Buffalo we joke about having three seasons—almost winter, winter, and construction. But it's also true that we have the best summers in the world. Summer usually hits around June 30, so we didn't want to sleep late or else we might miss it. The gray clouds suddenly clear, the snow melts, and we actually have to fill the gas tanks in our cars, rather than just shift into neutral and hydroplane on the ice.

During the summer, I worked at a children's day camp called Acadian Farm, located twenty minutes outside of the suburb where I lived. When I was a child, we only had to drive fifteen minutes from the heart of downtown Buffalo to be in the burbs. Fifteen minutes farther out and we were in farmland. A few miles more, and we were in *The Shining*. By the time the tank ran out of gas, we'd reached *Deliverance*.

The small farm where I worked boarded horses year-round and operated as a children's day camp in the summer. Kids learned to ride and care for horses, played games like capture the flag and crack the whip, had chicken fights in the pool, and set up tugs-of-war across a man-made pond with a horse-manure bottom. We entertained each other with skits, rowed boats in the pond, went on hayrides, and made the standard camp crafts—boondoggle, god's eyes, macramé belts and bracelets, and macaroni picture frames.

In the mornings and late afternoons, we performed chores—haying the horses, weeding the garden, sweeping out the tack room, and tending to the smaller animals, such as pigs, goats, rabbits, and guinea pigs. I was in charge of giving the pigs their water and slop. Campers would regularly throw into the slop bucket perfectly good sandwiches, apples, and bananas, and so, lazy about bringing my own lunch, I'd share with the pigs.

Once a month, the blacksmith arrived in his specially outfitted van filled with peculiar objects. We all gathered around, fascinated as he trimmed the horses' hooves and banged away at their shoes atop the metal anvil. After he nailed on the new shoes, we were given the old ones to hang over our beds for good luck. More than once a horseshoe fell off its nail in the middle of the night and bonked someone on the head.

A number of the riding horses had previously belonged to circuses. However, we didn't know the commands to make them perform their routines, and we didn't have a list of the tricks they knew. So sometimes we'd yawn and stretch our arms in the riding ring and suddenly one of the horses would kneel down as if praying, and a surprised six-year-old camper would slide down the horse's neck to the ground.

One scorcher of an August day, I was bringing a horse around for a bath when an eight-foot black rat snake slithered out from underneath the barn. There's only one mammal that hates snakes more than I do, and that would be a horse. The mare reared and came down on my toes. Sadly, counselors didn't carry disability insurance in those days.

Aside from the constant rope of snot hanging from my nose and swollen silver-dollar-sized insect bites covering my arms and legs, the farm was lots of fun. It was the place where I learned that puking and crying are contagious among children, just like the giggles. And that the words *booger* and *fart* should be used as a main source of inspiration when trying to amuse bored campers through a long, rainy day.

For several years I had the youngest children, aged five and six, while my friend Debbie had the oldest kids, eleven and twelve. People would occasionally slip four-year-olds into my group, especially if they had older brothers and sisters and the parents wanted to get rid of the whole brood at once. Sort of a reverse Little League, lying to make your kids older.

One summer I received a quiet and slightly peculiar child. The first few days he kept wandering off. And I mean wandering off—a half mile away. Terrified that he'd get lost for good and I'd be held responsible, I took some baling twine from the barn and attached the rambling camper to my belt. He now had a circle with an eight-foot radius in which to operate. That worked fine for the first week. I could keep a close eye on him, and he didn't seem to mind being my little prisoner, I mean shadow. I'd untie him for riding, games, and swimming, or if we were in an enclosed area such as the indoor ring. However, in the middle of the second week he began to cry. I untied him, and within an hour he'd disappeared again. I panicked because this time I couldn't find him and was running all sorts of scenarios through my head about how to explain this one to the camp director, not to mention the boy's parents. I finally located him in the hayloft, communing with the pigeons. I brought the twine back out, tied it around me, and gave him the other end of the leash so he could pretend I was his dog. That got us through the rest of the summer. It was only when a friend of his parents came to visit on the last day that I found out he was a year underage and also autistic.

When Debbie and I grew bored, we'd organize a troll hunt. My little campers would be taken on a hike in the woods and instructed to watch out for trolls. They were told that if they carried a purple flower, then no evil could befall them, and we even issued purple flowers, which they held in front of them like Olympic torches while tiptoeing through the woods. As I worked my little guys into a full lather about the possibility of trolls—by now every branch that snapped or bird that flew out of the brush caused them to scream and practically wet themselves—Debbie's twelve-year-olds were in the art room painting themselves brown and green to resemble trolls. They took a shortcut to our designated meeting place in the woods and more or less ambushed us. Most of the kids loved it, just like they wanted to hear ghost stories, even though they knew full well they would end up peeing their pants and not sleeping.

There was always one kid who had nightmares, and a concerned parent would phone the next morning. If we didn't get at least one call we figured we really weren't doing our jobs as counselors, and it was probably time to organize a vampire hunt—didn't the kids know that the entire camp was once a graveyard and that some pretty grisly murders took place in this area, and those who escaped the murderer often fell into the waiting jaws of wild animals? In fact, there was once a child just about their age who became lost from the group...

❊ ❊ ❊

Junior high ended after eighth grade, and it was off to Sweet Home Senior High, another brick building with turd brown accent panels and turquoise trim executed in the school of Soviet construction known as functionalism. It made the Bauhaus architects look like designers of Las Vegas hotels.

One winter, the snow on the roof was so heavy that there was danger of a collapse, and anyone on a varsity sports team was asked to arrive armed with a shovel. The reward was doughnuts and pizza. We thought it was a great deal.

The school was experiencing a transformation from the loosey-goosiness of the swinging sixties and seventies, complete with student lounges, back to a more conservative environment. When we arrived in the fall of 1979, smoking on school property had once again been banned, though we could see burn marks in the burnt-orange carpets covering the deconstructed learning spaces. These good-karma areas, filled with modular tables and chairs, had supposedly been more conducive to information flowing into the mind than traditional classrooms, with their rows of individual metal desks and attached chairs facing a teacher. The free-range learning spaces were being divided back into regulation-style classrooms with blackboards, while the faculty were putting down their bullhorns and breathing a collective sigh of relief.

Apparently they felt there had been a little too much openness employed throughout the sixties and seventies, when students would light joints in the hall, wear unisex fishnet tops, attend lectures according to their bio-rhythms, walk out of class whenever they pleased to set up lawn chairs in front of the school to catch rays, hand-tool leather wallets, strum Neil Young songs on a guitar, and practice free love rather, well, freely.

Yes, the students from those earlier years had done all the heavy lifting when it came to breaking the rules, boundaries, and barriers, not to mention the wills, of their teachers. The dress code had been whittled down to exactly that: be dressed. There was no more "yes, sir," "no, ma'am," or corporal punishment, just the beginning of students threatening to call lawyers if they felt browbeaten, damage to their self-esteem, or deprived of their constitutional rights.

Gone were classes in civics, geography, and grammar. We'd learn about politics from jokes on late-night television shows and become versed in geography by seeing maps on TV whenever the United States government decided to bomb some faraway country. Apostrophes were forevermore destined to pop up in inappropriate places, if at all; colons would only be dealt with much later in life—in hospitals, with proctologists. Our parents, with their forties' public-school educations, were the last generation to correctly use *whom* and not end their sentences with prepositions. They knew their verb types well enough to properly state that people were "lying on the beach" as opposed to "laying on the beach," though when it came to the hedonistic sixties and seventies, in most cases the latter was probably also correct.

Our teachers had been firsthand witnesses to the collapse of syntax during their careers, and by the time we arrived, they were immune to double negatives and hearing "ain't." Misuse of the English language no longer jarred their ears, jangled their nerves, and made them cringe. After weathering the hippies, they were too physically, mentally, emotionally, and grammatically exhausted to go around correcting anyone about anything. Our teachers were suffering from PSSSD, post–sixties-and-seventies stress disorder, along with a severe case of chronic student fatigue syndrome. These tired survivors were counting the days until retirement, when the hard-earned pension checks would start arriving.

Our predecessors, with their platform shoes, pink-tinted sunglasses, puka-shell necklaces (consult seventies' photo of teen idol David Cassidy in *Tiger Beat* magazine), and hip-hugger jeans had worn these once idealistic educators into the academic ground. The favorite phrases of those students had been "You can't make me" "So what?" and "Who cares?" Well, they got their wish, because a lot of teachers did stop caring, and you couldn't exactly blame them. Sure, they may have been old-fashioned and square with their short, thin neckties, *Life* magazines, and Dean Martin albums, handing out boring written assignments on colonialism and saying the pledge with hands placed firmly over their hearts, but they certainly hadn't gone into teaching for the money. If you think the pay is bad now, it was a pittance back then.

Most eventually lost interest in trying to force-teach long-haired kids reading copies of *Rolling Stone* and listening to Jimi Hendrix—not so much because of how their students looked, or what they read, or what music they liked, but because their young charges would no longer pay attention to the Man. It's understandable that students were disgruntled by society, and some may have effected change through protesting and petitioning, but their high school teachers weren't drafting boys or refusing jobs to minorities. On the receiving end of so much abuse, more than a few teachers probably took secret pleasure in reading that emergency rooms were overflowing with teenaged girls who'd broken their ankles tumbling off six-inch rainbow-colored wedgies. Maybe disapproving instructors even chuckled about the bad acid circulating at Woodstock and wondered if a groupie could drown in bong water.

A handful of teachers took the can't-beat-'em-join-'em attitude toward the hippies. Mr. Russell told us how he used to leave the door to his house open and students would hold drum circles in the living room to raise group consciousness. Sometimes he would eye meditate on his front lawn, and once a high school senior thought he was Jesus Christ. With his patchy beard and doleful eyes, Mr. Russell indeed looked as if he'd raised some serious consciousness. He told us to call him by his first name, Phil, because it meant "love" in Greek.

Then we'd get a few holdouts, the Mrs. Minivers of education, unfazed and unflustered by tear gas, bomb threats, and debauchery. These were most often women in prim dresses and sensible shoes, policing the aisles while smacking rulers in their hands, scowling at gum chewers, and making everyone recite their prepositions by rote, pretending that nothing at all had changed since FDR declared the New Deal.

My typing teacher was right out of a fifties' steno pool, the fabric of her life being mainly stretch polyester, fashioned into skirtsuits from Simplicity patterns using a Singer pedal sewing machine with a bullet bobbin. She had a teased bottle-blond updo and a strict bearing based on a line out of Euclidian geometry. If you looked up the word *efficiency* in the dictionary, she'd be there looking right back at you through rhinestone-studded cat's-eye glasses attached to a matching chain. Her typing classes, by the way, were filled to the max with girls; the secretarial track for women was still alive and well.

One civic-minded social studies teacher was so entranced by the Cold War that she insisted Communists were hiding in our sewers and waiting for a signal to attack us. As part of a World War II lesson, she explained how her father had once attempted to shoot Adolph Hitler in a U-boat off the coast of Seattle, using a hunting rifle. My high school was in a rural area, and one day, when a black garden snake dropped down from between the ceiling panels of the classroom, her eyes took on a fevered brightness as she insisted it was a plot by the Chinese to overthrow the government (though no one noticed the reptile to be wearing any sort of armband or insignia). The Chinese, she was fond of relating, had a secret cave that could house the entire population of their country in the event of an invasion. Her true-blue students dutifully used red folders and book covers to keep things interesting.

For sheer entertainment value, my hands-down favorite was the school gym teacher/football coach/health instructor, who encouraged "walking off" all injuries, including slipped disks and collapsed lungs. He was a 250-pound former linebacker with bad knees whom the kids secretly called Franken Berry after the breakfast-cereal cartoon monster. Pacing at the front of the classroom, pitched forward as if battling a mighty headwind, he'd rail at us that "douching does not stop pregnancy," while pounding on Resuscitative Annie's chest for emphasis. How is it possible that he was never tapped to appear on an STD telethon?

Best in Show went to a posture-perfect peroxide-blond history teacher who sewed enough of her own brightly hued ultrasuede pantsuits to have a different one for every day of the week. Patriotic to the seams, she was fond of explaining the flag to her students as follows: "Blue is for the oceans on both sides of our great nation, the Atlantic and the Pacific; red is for the blood spilled by our brave boys on the battlefield; and white is for virginity, which you girls know nothing about anymore!" Impervious to the civil rights movement, she determined in what order students should present their book reports by employing "eenie meenie miny, moe, catch a nigger by the toe." The sherry-sipping widow confided to Pete and Russ that some nights she'd sit at the organ wearing baby-doll pajamas, fire up one of her beloved Winston cigarettes, and play "Embraceable You."

Like our hippie predecessors, we wore jeans (not so flared) and T-shirts (not so loud), but unlike them, we did our homework and did not talk back. When administrators threatened that bad behavior would go on our "permanent record," we imagined a dossier that would compromise every college application and job interview and follow us right up to the pearly gates. If we talked back at home, we'd be talking to the back of a hand. Our fathers had fought in World War II and Korea, and our mothers had grown up being seen and not heard, and eating what was put in front of them. The result was a finely honed appreciation for the fruits of democracy, a solid work ethic, and a strong legal system. Furthermore, our parents believed in time travel, to the extent that they regularly threatened to "knock us into next week" for any type of misbehavior.

The mischief we kids got into was mere pranks and basic rebelliousness, as opposed to the rejection of any system or status quo. For instance, one of our science teachers wore a rug on which you could fly to Morocco. When he'd show a movie in class, he'd sit slightly in front of the projector. Inevitably one of the kids would inch the turning wheel toward the back of his head until it sucked up his entire toupee.

And there was the German-language teacher who was so over-weight that her car permanently tilted to the left because the suspension on the driver's side was completely shot, possibly the result of an overload of Black Forest cake. Early on, a group of students nicknamed her Frau Cow. The moniker was passed down from one generation to the next, and students who didn't take her class never even knew her real name.

I like to think our teachers revived slightly when the bright yellow smiley decals came off and were replaced by stolid green Izod alligators, and the dashikis gave way to button-down-collared shirts with straight-leg jeans, making kids unable to sit cross-legged for long periods of time. Ponchos with fringe (thankfully) disappeared and Windbreakers appeared. Okay, a number of us sported Mork-inspired rainbow-colored suspenders, but this represented a slavish devotion to a sitcom alien, not a call for revolution. Pop tart Madonna, the Material Girl, would not begin to fuel the fashion of underwear-as-outerwear until the year after we graduated. Likewise, multiriveted body parts were still on some silver miner's drawing board and butt-crack tattoos had not yet become widespread

Survivors liked to tell stories about life back when the flower children had taken over. Mr. Hardy, a French teacher shaped like a bottle of Shalimar who perspired at the very mention of physical activity, had been in charge of one particularly raucous hallway where all the juniors and seniors were assigned lockers. It was his job to ensure that none of the pot-slinging hipsters left their classrooms before the bell rang to signify the end of the final period of the day. He told us how marauding gangs of the discipline-challenged used to mow him right down. The tales were so vivid in the retelling that potbellied Mr. Hardy would break into a flop sweat and take out a handkerchief to mop his brow.

Finally, in the late seventies, the school's administrators were able to reinstate the ban on smoking and dropping acid in Cafeteria B and, to a large extent, restore law and order to a postapocalyptic public-education wasteland. The end of the Vietnam War, a drop in horoscope enthusiasm and Ouija board–driven career choices, and a slightly reduced student population greatly assisted in this crackdown. Jazzercise would be permitted, but only in the gymnasium. Yet the new regime was unable to do much about the practice of free love, other than to ensure that students remain clothed. Dry humping was tolerated in my school system, whereas the parochial schools and some nearby public-school districts banned such displays of unfettered passion. At any given time, walking down the halls was like threading our way through porn-movie auditions, with couples clinching up against lockers and huddled in doorways and corners, darkened or not, having peak physical experiences under an almost visible cloud of hormones, while facing the despair of spending the next forty-five minutes apart.

The faculty at the senior high had for the most part been hired the year the school was opened, in 1963; therefore, by the time my class came along in 1979, almost all were in their forties, about the same age as our parents. When they attended teachers college in the late fifties and early sixties, our future instructors surely believed their days would be spent standing nobly at the front of a classroom and imparting knowledge to eager, obedient, and appropriately dressed students. They graduated, found jobs, and after that came the tie-dye deluge.

Granted, a number of them had enrolled in teachers college during the Vietnam War. And with regard to the dozen or so immensely lazy teachers, a student couldn't help but wonder if becoming an educator had not been a lifelong dream and dignified calling so much as a way to avoid the draft.

The hippies who had gone through the decade before were just then starting to become parents and professionals. Our parents, like our teachers, were people of the fifties. And not the fifties that happened in New York City, San Francisco, and New Orleans, but the fifties in Detroit, Pittsburgh, and Cleveland.

Parents in my neighborhood were the Beat Generation only insofar as they'd spent the decade working their way through college, traveling to the United States from someplace that held no opportunity for them, or in the military. Thus, they were just plain *beat*. Still, they'd been taught to consider themselves incredibly fortunate because most of *their* parents had worked on factory floors and loading docks, in steel plants and grain elevators. Many were the children of immigrants who'd fled war-torn Europe, poverty, religious persecution, and even death camps. And for those who had been too young to clearly remember the Depression, their parents (our grandparents) had reminded them of it at least once a day, so they now felt as if they had experienced it directly.

As a result, our parents greatly appreciated the tranquility of a leafy suburban neighborhood, job security, health insurance, indoor plumbing, the public library, decent schools, and the arrival of such fabrics as nylon that replaced itchy wool socks. If they had to travel during the week because of a sales job, then when the weekend came they were thrilled to be off the road. The only howl they emitted was not about jazz musicians, political radicals, and psychiatric patients, but about the sky-high heating bills that started arriving in October. The only acid dropped was sulfuric, and that was to unclog the drain in the kitchen.

Tom Wolfe's paean to the Beats, *The Kandy-Kolored Tangerine-Flake Streamline Baby*, arrived in 1965, the year I was born. However, bedside tables in my neighborhood were more likely to hold copies of *Reader's Digest* and Dr. Benjamin Spock's best seller on raising babies. By the middle of 1967, dubbed "The Summer of Love," sex was the last thing on our parents' minds as they ushered squalling toddlers through potty training and spent nights trying to put colicky babies to sleep.

As for the Age of Aquarius, with the economic slowdown that began in the late sixties and carried through the seventies, for our parents it was the Age of Financial Precariousness. There were children to feed and clothe, while Detroit continued to produce station wagons that not only guzzled gas but were in constant need of repair. American automakers were about to realize that *planned obsolescence*, a manufacturer's decision that the product will become nonfunctional within a defined time period, would soon translate into carloads of consumers singing, "I think I'm turning Japanese"; lemon laws would not go on the books until 1984. Most moms weren't in the workforce, and, unlike today's shoppers armed with never-ending rounds of credit cards, when our parents ran out of money, they simply stopped spending it.

Throughout the seventies, Bethlehem Steel continued to lay off workers while other factories closed entirely. It grew harder and harder to find a job in Buffalo. If a person had one, salaries stayed put or decreased due to hours being cut back, while prices continued to spiral upward. One joke went that things were so bad, a local guy decided to drown himself in Lake Erie. Another fellow spotted him from shore and swam out. The drowning man shouted, "Don't save me! I don't want to live!" The guy swimming out to him replied, "Don't worry, I won't. I just want to know where you work."

Those of us attending high school in the early eighties were able to escape some of the seriousness through the usual teen pastimes: tunes, TV, and movies. *B-52s* didn't conjure up images of the Boeing jet bombers that had been used extensively in the Vietnam War. No indeed, the B-52s were an adventurous New-Wave indie-rock band with songs like "Rock Lobster" that we could freestyle dance to while our parents, who leaned more toward Frank Sinatra and Lawrence Welk, shouted, "Turn down that racket!"

Pink Floyd's chart topper "Another Brick in the Wall" debuted in 1979 and was to rule the airwaves for many months, essentially morphing into our class anthem. Particular emphasis was placed on the chorus, regularly chanted in school hallways and on the bus: "We don't need no education...Hey, teacher, leave those kids alone!" We shouted it from the bleachers in the gym, but we also dutifully went to class, did our homework, and competed for grades and prizes.

Just after I started high school, disco adopted a thumping funk bass with Kool & the Gang's "Celebration." And every teen knew the words to Rick James's 1981 "Super Freak." Not many people knew that Rick James was born in Buffalo as James Johnson Jr. in 1948. Apparently he had no great love affair with the city, as he ran away at the age of fifteen.

It wasn't long before disco was dead, with the necessary bumper stickers and Disco Sucks T-shirts to prove it. Ready to take its place and become the sound track of our adolescence were rock groups like The Police, Devo, Talking Heads, Michael Jackson gone solo, and a bubblegum girl group called the Go-Go's, with their smash single, "We Got the Beat." My friends covered their lockers with stickers for the bands Styx, Aerosmith, Queen, the Eagles, and spacey Led Zeppelin, and the more artsy among us transferred their names to our blue denim-covered three-ring binders. For the studded-leather-and-Dodge-Charger crowd, whom we referred to as *burnouts*, there was satanic Iron Maiden, the garishly costumed Kiss, and AC/DC's *Back in Black*, which sounded to most adults as if all the household appliances had been turned on at the same time and someone was screaming because his arm was caught in the disposal (this album is now available in cell-phone ringtones!). The coolest thing in the world was to attend a concert and wear the T-shirt to school the next day.

Singing antiestablishment rock songs, drinking beer, and wearing T-shirts that adults didn't approve of (featuring marijuana leaves, skulls, and anything suggestive of Satan) was about the scope of our rebellion. Few kids in my neighborhood had money for drugs. Most parents were killing themselves to save enough for us to attend college if we could earn the grades to get in. We knew this. Even the burnouts worked hard in their shop classes so they could become auto mechanics and car thieves after high school.

When *Saturday Night Live* began in 1975, it left its mark. The impact was heightened because the cast was largely made up of midwesterners and Canadians, and their brand of humor spoke directly to us. All week long kids would reenact sketches and pretend to be favorite cast members. We worshipped the characters created by Bill Murray, John Belushi, Chevy Chase, Dan Ackroyd, and Gilda Radner. Especially beloved were the Loopners in the nerds sketch and Dan Ackroyd arriving as the refrigerator repairman with six inches of butt crack exposed. Things got even more boffo when Eddie Murphy joined the show and riffed on Mr. Rogers and Buckwheat. Don Novello played Father Guido Sarducci, giving updates on the tricky road to sainthood and taking aim at education with the "Five-Minute University" sketch. To this day, friends still do the Land Shark dialogue whenever speaking into an intercom.

In 1979, Steve Martin was a wild 'n' crazy guy on *Saturday Night Live* and the star of a wacky full-length feature film called *The Jerk*. It was the time of cult classics such as Bob and Doug MacKenzie's *Great White North*, Cheech and Chong's *Up in Smoke*, *Meatballs*, and of course, *Caddyshack*. We learned about the Dalai Lama not from history class, local Buddhists, or enlightened movie stars, but through Bill Murray as Carl the groundskeeper: "Gunga galunga."

In truth, these depraved characters appealed more to the boys. Teenage girls had fallen under the strong influence of a recently released movie and homage to the fifties called *Grease*. Girly girls knew all the lyrics, were pros at doing the hand jive, and on Halloween dressed as bobby-soxers by raiding the back of Mom's closet for a poodle skirt, cardigan, and chiffon scarf to tie around the ponytail and neck.

The humor of 1980's *Hollywood Knights* cast its sophomoric spell, resulting in such copycat antics as placing a brown bag of dog crap on someone's front porch, setting it on fire, and ringing the bell. The object was for them to answer the door and stomp it out, while we laughed ourselves silly behind a nearby hedge. Also popular was climbing fences to skinny-dip in neighbors' pools and then steal each other's clothing. At the induction ceremony for the national honor society and also on parents' night, we spiked the punch. There was endless mooning out of car and bus windows. And if we wanted to brave the downtown scene, the motorhead crowd held Friday and Saturday night drag races on Buffalo's Ontario Street.

The following year, the Canadians gave us the movie *Porkies*, which inspired juvenilia such as paging Mike Hunt over the loudspeaker at the rec center and trying to get the name worked into the high school announcements, along with our own creations, such as Hugh Janus. Boys would go to any length to see girls naked, whether this involved power tools or periscopes. And Chinese fire drills while driving to and from school were popular, where everyone hopped out at a red light, raced around the car, and quickly climbed back in before it changed to green.

Inspired by movie mischief, late one night in the dead of winter, Mary and I cut up several dozen sherbet-colored Styrofoam egg cartons and went through the neighborhood attaching them to tree branches. When we walked around the next morning to view our handiwork in the daylight, we decided they actually looked pretty—pastel pink, yellow, blue, and purple "flowers" on otherwise bare, dark branches against a cold, gray vault of sky. Apparently the "vandalized" neighbors were of the same opinion, and almost all left them up until spring (that Styrofoam can survive a Buffalo winter makes it obvious why this material is a major problem in landfills). And so it happened that our big attempt at a prank turned into a public service.

Twenty-Three

Real World 101

On November 4, 1979, sixty-six Americans were taken hostage at the American embassy in Tehran, Iran, by militant student followers of the Ayatollah Khomeini. (On TV, some of the student activists appeared to be slightly older than my parents.) Khomeini demanded the return of former shah Mohammad Reza Pahlavi, who was undergoing medical treatment in New York City (where I'm certain that all sick Iranians were dispatched, regardless of economic standing).

A few weeks before the holiday break of my sophomore year, on December 8, 1980, John Lennon was shot outside his apartment building in New York City. The Beatles didn't mean much to my friends and me, the final album *Let It Be* having arrived in 1971, when we were fully occupied playing duck, duck, goose and musical chairs. But it turned out that the Fab Four were significant to many of our parents and teachers, and for several days afterward these adults appeared hollow-eyed, stumbling around, and wondering aloud what had gone wrong. They couldn't understand how it was that we'd finally finished fighting all these wars and made it through two decades of social unrest only to live in a country where people assassinated rock stars.

Following Christmas vacation, Ronald Reagan took office as the fortieth president of the United States, having beaten Jimmy Carter in a landslide by asking Americans if they were better off than they were four years before. Minutes after the inauguration on January 20, 1981, the Americans held hostage in Iran for 444 days were flown to freedom, following a deal in which the United States agreed to return 8 billion dollars in frozen assets to Iran. Jimmy Carter had demonstrated that the presidency was essentially an impossible job, and yet Ronald Reagan would continue to prove that basically anyone could do it.

The murder of John Lennon and the hostage crisis began true political awareness for me and most of my classmates. My memory of President Reagan being shot in the chest on March 30, 1981, by a would-be assassin in Washington is quite clear. As he entered surgery, the former actor joked, asking if his doctors were all Republicans. And when his wife, Nancy, arrived at the hospital, he is reported to have said, "Honey, I forgot to duck."

Five months later, Pope John Paul II was shot while blessing an audience at Saint Peter's in Rome. He survived after five hours of surgery to treat massive blood loss and abdominal wounds. Rather than cracking wise about the matter, the pope credited Our Lady of Fatima with helping to keep him alive through the ordeal.

I recall how elated women were when, in September of that year, President Reagan appointed the first woman, Sandra Day O'Connor, to the United States Supreme Court. Finally, it seemed as if all vocations really were opening up to women. People started to speculate for the first time whether they'd see a woman president in their lifetimes. And it was a good thing, as far as I was concerned, to have all that excitement and adventure finally available to the sisterhood. Because there's no doubt in my mind that, had I been born a hundred years earlier, there'd be only two words for the situation: Calamity Jane. I'd have thrown on a hat and trousers, hopped on a horse, and lived my life as a man. And with my figure, it's pretty safe to say I'd have pulled it off.

The Reagan Revolution meant slashing government spending (purportedly), increasing the military budget (definitely), and cutting taxes (at least early on). This was supposed to create a trickle-down effect that would in turn boost the economy (one of his critics deemed it "voodoo economics"). In actuality, the result of these measures was a terrible recession in 1981. Yet, they eventually gave way to boom years of high technology and productivity that would last through the rest of the eighties, despite the spectacular but brief stock market crash in 1987.

However, these good times were accompanied by the largest federal budget deficit in history, along with numerous huddled figures on the streets, the likes of which hadn't been seen since the Depression. And former factory towns like Buffalo saw no hope for replacing all the lost jobs.

Whatever our mothers felt about his fiscal policies, Reagan certainly caught their attention in 1981 when the Department of Agriculture proposed that ketchup be considered a vegetable when calculating the nutritional value of school lunches. The suggestion caused such uproar that the rule was never instituted. Meantime, we kids were working the opposite end of the food chain, attempting to employ the Twinkie Defense when called out for bad behavior. The era of personal responsibility was crumbling, and, going forward, it would be possible to blame most blunders on external factors or medical conditions.

Prior to 1980, aside from the bad economy, the real world hadn't directly impacted our lives. We took our time transitioning to adulthood. In elementary school, we girls despised the opposite sex. They were the hair pullers, stone throwers, mud lovers, and worm cutters. In junior high, we progressed to playing touch football with boys and embarking upon such risqué games as spin the bottle and pass the frozen orange. It was the job of the girls to organize the parties and kissing games. It fell to the boys to play the role of victim, often making us drag them away from shooting baskets in the driveway. But once it was on the record that they'd been forced into such compromising circumstances, no attempts were made to shirk their duties.

By high school, we no longer needed games to start a make-out party—just a place. After an hour or so, the lights were dimmed and kids paired off in corners to the sound of Meat Loaf's hard-charging, hormone-stoking *Bat Out of Hell* blasting from a stereo with heavy bass, followed by the Cars album *Panorama*, which contained the fabulous hit single "Touch and Go." If kids wore braces, they tried not to get stuck together, which usually involved calling someone's father and the appearance of a flashlight and needle-nose pliers. Total embarrassment.

A seriously committed couple was more likely to spray paint the news of their devotion on a highway overpass than have sex. Among my girlfriends, few drank or even smoked. And First Lady Nancy Reagan was warning us teenagers not to do drugs (while she needed to be warned not to listen to astrologers).

I learned that drugs can kill brain cells from my mother's nursing books and Mr. Wyatt's health class. Anyway, that was all I needed to know; no need to repeat it, thank you. It wasn't necessary to sit me down in front of the public service announcement that showed an egg frying on a hot stove with the ominous voice-over: "This is your brain on drugs!" Obviously I was going to need every brain cell in my possession. I didn't have the test scores of a person in possession of a mind that could afford to play fast and loose with its gray matter. Thus, I decided it was best not to take any drugs, including alcohol, allergy medicine, and aspirin, just to be safe. The closest I ever came to a drug trip was in the form of an excursion to Quebec with my high school French class, during which I was swigging codeine cough medicine to beat back a bad case of bronchitis. I arrived home with a new boyfriend and photos that looked as if they'd been snapped from the top of the Château de Frontenac.

Reinforcing this antidrug stance was the fact that at the start of high school, the academic fog, which had until then cast a long shadow over my life, could be declared permanently lifted. I clearly recall the amazing feeling of finally understanding what was being taught in social studies, math, science, and English. It was also at this moment that I realized I had little or no interest in most of it. Sure, I enjoyed a good book, but certainly not *Beowulf* or "The Fall of the House of Usher." However, I continued to attend school because that's where my friends were, and so that's where the fun was.

Throughout my four years of high school, I played on the soccer team every spring. I was an enthusiastic player more than a talented one. Coach Radka kindly described me as "a bull moose in a china shop." He had all those great coach sayings like "hustle your bustle," "you gotta want it," "drop the piano when you're running," "they caught you napping," "the ball won't kill you," and "now you got a piece of it, it's time to get the whole pie." His cheeks turned slightly red when he suggested that the girls who were experiencing chafing from their thighs rubbing together should try a bit of Vaseline.

Coach Radka was a born-again Christian and believed in the inherent worth and athletic ability of every player. He played us all. We almost always lost. I was no help here. As sweeper, I'm not even sure what color the net was on the other end of the field or how someone got there. But the good thing about being on a bad team was that I had the chance to play a lot more than I would have if we were winners. After all was lost, usually shortly following halftime, Coach Radka turned the field into an aerobics class and put in the second, third, and fourth strings.

Soccer was strictly an after-school sport, thus participation didn't exempt one from the state-mandated three days a week of physical education. Usually it was fun to take twenty minutes to play softball, bounce on a trampoline, or perform group calisthenics designed for gulag prisoners, but classes were large enough that it was easy to slip away on the days we weren't in a sit-up state of mind. Candy and soda machines couldn't be found for a mile in any direction, so not many of us actually needed more exercise than we were already getting. (Translation: Still no good video games.)

My most vivid memory of gym class is an eleventh-grade badminton course where, for about six weeks, I was teamed with another girl for doubles. Through some random matching system, my partner was severely anorexic, weighing about eighty pounds. She was positively skeletal, as if she'd just hopped down off the rack in the science room. When class began, she'd only recently arrived back from a monthlong stint at a clinic in Rochester.

At the time, I was five foot nine and almost 150 pounds. My main objective was to not accidentally collide with my frail partner, thereby instantly killing her. I could only hope that when it came to badminton, size didn't matter, and we'd be able to pass the time without injury or embarrassment. There wouldn't be any real competition, of course, since nobody took public-school gym class seriously.

While waiting to play our season opener, we got to talking and my partner, who happened to be extremely bright, told me about her experiences at the clinic. It transpired that the doctors had given her a weight target she had to meet in order to be released. They put her on the scale every day for several months. So one morning, she drank an unbelievable amount of water before the weigh-in and just barely managed to get sprung.

Okay, now I was wondering if I had some sort of duty to tell a gym teacher or guidance counselor that she shouldn't have been released. Worse, I was afraid that a blow to the eyebrow from a birdie would take her out, or that moving three steps to the left on a badminton court might melt off the six ounces between her and certain death. I decided not to rat her out, assuming that if a person spends a few months flirting with anorexia, there must be some follow-up from doctors. However, I did manage to make sure that we did not play badminton by feigning some sort of a thrombosis every time a court opened up.

Twenty-Four

Earl and Me...The Sewing Circle Turns Square

Although western New York is the birthplace of some of North America's wackiest religions, God never spoke to me. However, another person did: Earl Nightingale.

The name is probably not ringing a bell among those who admire great thinkers like Nietzsche, Kierkegaard, and Emerson, especially if you're under fifty. But Nightingale became the portable tent I would carry through life.

My dad's best childhood friend still lived on Long Island, so we'd visit him when traveling there in the summertime. Rich held various jobs for the Carnation Company, most having to do with managing a sales staff. He gave my father a box of motivational tapes by Earl Nightingale. I don't know how much impact they could have in the field of court reporting, but Dad found the messages worthwhile with regard to life in general, and so he passed the tapes on to me.

A series of motivational tapes is probably an odd item to have given an eight-year-old girl back in the seventies, especially when *self-help* meant transcendental meditation or heading to an ashram. Dad didn't label a person according to age or gender and was liable to turn up with absolutely *anything* he found interesting, whether it was an abacus, boomerang, zither, Lawn Jarts, or box kite (all real examples). Dad was the king of strange stuff. Let's not forget the blowtorch.

Earl Nightingale was a Depression-era child, like my father, and had a wonderful broadcaster's voice, also like my father. Nightingale had been in the marines, hosted some radio shows, and then went on to speak and write full time on the subject of achievement. His first full-length recording, *The Strangest Secret*, sold over a million copies back in the sixties. Nightingale partnered with businessman Lloyd Conant, and together they tackled the infant self-help market. The best-selling *Lead the Field* and *The Essence of Success* soon followed. I would later find the material was similar to that of Dale Carnegie, Napoleon Hill, and the Reverend Dr. Norman Vincent Peale.

However, it was Nightingale I stumbled upon first. Indeed, he borrowed from, and sometimes reworked, the best material of the time, but he always credited those individuals attached to the original information. Today, his equivalents would be Tony Robbins, Ken Blanchard, and Dr. Arthur Caliandro at the Marble Collegiate Church in Manhattan (Norman Vincent Peale's successor). But most of the motivational work being done nowadays has too much cheerleaderlike enthusiasm for my taste. And much as I liked Dr. Norman Vincent Peale and admire his successor Dr. Caliandro, at the end of the day these pastors of the Dutch Reformed Church toss it all up to God. Having someone else in charge doesn't work for me, even a project manager with the Almighty's credentials.

Earl was calm, thoughtful, measured, and sensible. I'm willing to admit that because he was my first motivational romance; it's like a first love, and therefore I'm not capable of being objective. After all these years, he's still the one for me. (Earl died on March 28, 1989.)

First and foremost, Earl offered concrete thoughts about achievement, highlighting the fact that *you don't have to be too smart*. I was immediately hooked.

He talked about starting from scratch with no particular advantages, working hard, working honest, and working smart. It made sense the way he told it and explained exactly how to proceed, often by using engaging anecdotes and real-life examples. Earl kept breaking down concepts to make sure the listener understood. He talked about where to get ideas and how to be observant. One story he recounted focused on looking for fortune all over the world when it was right in front of your nose at home—diamonds in your own backyard. Another featured a prisoner of war who used his jail time to teach himself to play a better game of golf by thinking about all the rounds he'd played in the past, visualizing and then improving upon each shot.

Earl spoke of leadership, problem solving, passion, a sense of urgency, the importance of focus, and determination. If a person listened long enough, Earl taught him how to think.

In the meantime, Earl kept reminding his listeners that they didn't have to be the best and the brightest, just ambitious, and then to learn to make the most out of what they already had. He provided great hope and inspiration for the underdog.

Is it trite? Is it all just common sense? Was it merely commentary from a guy who didn't make the A-list broadcast team? For me, Earl offered a way to view everything from my education, goals, and plan for the future to how I wanted to live my life and the kind of person I wanted to be. He urged me to learn, plan, organize, and focus. Earl told me to get out there and make mistakes.

Top 10 Earls of Wisdom

- Our attitude in life determines life's attitude toward us.
- We can let circumstances rule us, or we can take charge and rule our lives from within.
- What's going on inside shows on the outside.
- Whenever we're afraid, it's because we don't know enough. If we understood enough, we would never be afraid.
- People with goals succeed because they know where they're going.
- Your world is a living expression of how you are using your mind.
- Wherever there is danger, there lurks opportunity; wherever there is opportunity, there lurks danger. The two are inseparable.
- Creativity is a natural extension of our enthusiasm.
- You can help others by making the most of yourself more than in any other way.
- You become what you think about.

✳ ✳ ✳

Two decades before Google and Wikipedia, learning came where you found it. Classroom grammar and civics lessons may have been a thing of the past, but we had ABC's animated *Schoolhouse Rock!* every Saturday morning. Anyone born between 1965 and 1975 can liberally quote from these educational shorts, such as "I'm Just a Bill," where a dejected scroll of paper is dragged through our labyrinthine legislative process to become a law. Similarly, "Conjunction Junction" explained how to hook up words and phrases and clauses using *and*, *but*, and *or*. However the list clearly did not include *like* and *you know*.

The early eighties were when the repetition of *like* and *you know* permanently entered the vernacular. Prior to that, they were employed in similes the way Robert Burns wrote, "My love is like a red, red rose," or else as a question or statement during introductions, for instance, "You know the Smiths."

My friends and I entered high school not saying *like* and *you know* several times in every sentence, and four years later we departed as the carriers of a sloppy new speech pattern. It spread like head lice. Teachers and parents attempted to fend off the invasion, but most eventually fell victim to the dialectical disease themselves. Soon it was a staple in movie and television dialogue.

When I was young, most homes had a TV antenna on the roof, operated by a dial inside the house. Viewers quickly determined that the best reception was achieved by having a person stand next to the TV, touching it with one hand and holding a wire hanger above his head with the other. Or if we had rabbit ears (a ten-inch-high antenna that resembled, well, yes, the head of a bunny) atop the set, then we wrapped tinfoil extensions around the tips and attached ourselves to those. This was usually a job for the youngest child, especially in a large family like the Pynes. At our home, when Dad ran his electric razor in the bathroom, the TV became a test pattern of fuzz and stripes. This happened when almost any electric appliance was activated, similar to the way flushing the toilet caused the person in the shower to get scalded.

At the start of high school we had only four channels, and by graduation there were cable channels, VCRs, and satellite dishes. Without those and the as-yet-in-the-future DVDs, TiVo, and pay-per-view, we had to watch the Christmas specials—*Rudolph the Red-Nosed Reindeer, Frosty the Snowman, Dr. Seuss' How the Grinch Stole Christmas!*, and *A Charlie Brown Christmas*—the one night a year that they came on, or wait another twelve months. The news was on the three network channels four times a day, and we either saw it or we missed it.

This was also the time when remote controls arrived. Prior to that we had to drag ourselves up off the couch and crouch in front of the set while clicking around to decide what to watch. The knobs were mostly broken, so we left pliers on top of the set. The TV remote control appeared around the same time as electric car windows and garage-door openers. They are the main reasons people had to start joining gyms and using Nautilus machines, although the automatic garage opener did provide one quick wind sprint to the car before the eighty-pound wooden door squashed them like a bug.

The advent of increased home technology brought with it the beginning of a major power shift from adults to teens, and even children. With ATMs, microwave ovens, security-alarm systems, VCRs, and PCs, kids had increasing supremacy over their adult handlers. Need the stereo set up? Talk to a twelve-year-old. Want to stop the clock from blinking on the new VCR and tape your favorite shows? Hope your teenager isn't away for the weekend.

Our parents were the last of a lot of things. Even if they'd grown up in low-income households, they possessed good manners and used proper grammar. The women had almost all learned how to cook, sew, and lay a proper table when they were young. Many of our mothers had walked with books on their heads as teenagers to develop good posture, and they practiced penmanship until theirs was first-rate. Fathers held doors for ladies and knew how to fix things around the house, including the family car.

Corporal punishment was still acceptable when our parents went to school. They didn't dare tell their parents that a teacher had hit them, because their fathers would hit them even harder, especially if they'd crossed rulers with a nun; parents were not very interested in the child's side of a story. Our parents were raised to respect their elders and not ask questions. There was no such thing as quality time with their parents, just chore time.

In the fifties and sixties, parochial schools required a girl's skirt to hang to the knee (a yardstick would be used for surprise checks the way random drug testing is sprung on workers and athletes today). Our fathers were expected to keep clean handkerchiefs in their pockets, not wear caps indoors, and carry packages for women.

This was BC: Before Cablevision. It all went out the window with my generation. As for not training the girls to be perfect young ladies, it's safe to say that many of the mothers were in on it. They started taking jobs outside the home, though usually only after we were launched into junior high school, and most did not bother teaching us homemaking skills. My mother and I are a good example of this divide. When Mom married, she had only a public-school education from Lafayette High in Buffalo. But from her mother and grandmother she'd learned how to do needlework and cook from scratch without measuring cups. For the most part, my girlfriends and I aren't proficient at these things.

My mother did make a feeble attempt at teaching me to knit, but I'm a lefty and she's a righty, and so one of us always had to stand on her head. And quite frankly, neither of us was as interested in domesticity as we were in playing poker, so we ended up doing that instead.

Twenty-Five

Will Work for AC...Mom Turns Pro...
The Mosquito Coast

While working outdoors all day as a camp counselor, I assumed it was my lot in life to forever shower with Solarcain and suffer itchy bug bites. It quickly became apparent that I was not only allergic to grass, leaves, pollen, and insect bites, particularly bee stings, but also to animal hair, flowers, ragweed, barn dust, and hay. Summer was a constant carnival of itchy eyes, coughing, sneezing, and nosebleeds. About thirty minutes of direct sunlight produced second-degree burns. Jumping into a pool or lake was a radiation accident in the making. Scandinavian Creed: Outdoors from ten 'til two is not for you!

We didn't have air-conditioning in my school or house, so I wasn't aware that sitting inside a climate-controlled building could remedy most of these complaints. It wasn't until I was fifteen and went from sneezing and scratching and scorching outside into the centrally air-conditioned home of the Kohnstamms that I discovered there was a cure. Having finally found my drug (Freon), I promptly quit camp and took a job at my godmother's Mexican restaurant.

I loved being a short-order cook. The fast action, multitasking, and making change for both Canadian and American money was akin to playing fifteen hands of blackjack at once. The manager was more often than not knee-walking drunk from Dos Equis beer, on the phone sobbing and fighting with her boyfriend throughout the entire shift. So I'd race between the cash register, enchilada steamer, deep fryer, and

226

soda machine, and then perform a quick mop job out front and in the bathrooms. During breaks I was also allowed to eat my fill of Mexican food, which I did with alacrity. When the midnight movie at the Wehrle Drive-in across the street let out at 2:00 AM, we had our rush hour. Afterward was the long but sunless bike ride home. One particular month, the distributor for our ground chuck had a recall and it turned out I'd been serving kangaroo meat. Did I just imagine feeling that extra spring in my step as I bounced from freezer to fryer? No matter, that ended beef burritos for me, but I still enjoyed the beans, rice, and vegetables.

Eventually I decided to show off my talent for making Mexican food. At the church auction, Mom offered a party at our place with a south-of-the-border theme. We allowed for twenty people, but an enthusiastic auctioneer signed up sixty amigos. The night before the soiree, I went skiing at Holiday Valley, followed by dancing and a diner breakfast, and arrived home at seven in the morning. At three in the afternoon I awoke to my mother hollering, "The guests will be here in two hours, and there's no food!" I roused myself and began chopping, slicing, and sautéing. The food came out a bit late, but all went well.

A few years later, after my parents divorced, a Mexican dinner I prepared at the home of my father's girlfriend was not as successful. Without a deep fryer on hand, I thought it would be fine to fill a saucepan with oil and boil that. Shortly thereafter, the fire department arrived. Betty graciously said that she'd been planning to repaint the kitchen anyway.

The Mexican restaurant was a lengthy bike ride away, especially in the rain. As soon as I turned fifteen and could get my working papers, I took a job closer to home, at a truck stop near the entrance to the 641-mile-long New York State Thruway. There wasn't a hot grill, just several coffeemakers and racks of fresh baked goods, mostly doughnuts, delivered daily from a large Buffalo bakery that operated several satellite locations.

Having already worked in a restaurant, I found some of the business practices at the new establishment to be highly unusual. For instance, I was instructed to put the money in a brown paper bag and stow it in the freezer at the end of each day. About six o'clock every evening, a short man with an Italian last name came by to collect it. (At the time, the only place with a bigger Mafia influence over local business than Buffalo was probably Youngstown, Ohio.) When I asked where to put the register tape in order to save it for the accountant, I was told to throw it away. And when I questioned how they'd like me to keep track of what was sold so inventory could be regulated, I was informed that there was no need to keep track of anything. When I asked what to do with the leftover baked goods, and some days there were a lot, they said to throw them away. Well, I wasn't about to follow that procedure. Neither of my parents ever threw away food. After closing up shop I disbursed the remaining stock on my way home. It was fun going down the street like Robin Hood on a bicycle, piled high with bags of fresh bread and boxes of doughnuts, stopping at houses with large families to feed.

In that particular job I met a lot of truck drivers. They were very kind, always tipped big, and regularly invited me out to see their cabs. A couple of them called me Girlie Girl, which was funny and made me want to tease my hair and apply lots of frosted blue eye shadow. Many years later, when I had .to hitchhike from Dallas to New York after September 11, 2001, I headed out to the highway, confident that my old friends would get me home. Of course, that didn't stop me from taking the hotel room Bible just in case it was necessary to read some scripture as a way of sidestepping the topic of dating. Truckers can be very friendly folk indeed.

❀ ❀ ❀

Over the years, no matter where my mother took an entry-level nursing job, she ended up in charge of the floor, wing, or department within a few weeks, and then the entire place inside of six months.

On one evaluation a coworker went so far as to write that my mom was "intimidating." She was actually shocked by this and asked me if I thought she was intimidating. I said that it was surely meant as a compliment. After all, there was the time when her office building caught

228

fire, the furniture was moved onto the front lawn, and two athletic-looking local citizens tried to steal the couches. My five-foot-six, sixty-something mother came out of the building, which happens to be in an economically challenged section of Buffalo, and with no one else in sight she formally addressed the two sturdy neighbors performing the removal: "Excuse me, gentlemen, but those couches are the property of New York State, and I'm going to have to ask you to put them down." They were stunned. They obliged. In fact, they hauled them back into the building for her.

Mom's job held many dangers: working in the inner city, driving on streets that were rarely plowed, and embarking on home visits where nearby drug dealers operated freely. I knew she was in an unusual line of work when I received an insurance policy from Albany detailing what I should do in the event she was taken hostage. She never was, that I know of (or else they decided to give her back in a hurry), but Mom had a few of her own safety guidelines: always sit in a wooden chair (who knows what's in the upholstery), don't drive a state-issued vehicle (good way to get shot at), and never enter a home where there's a pit bull or a boa constrictor in the window (used in urban debt-collection proceedings).

The only time I've found my mother unenthusiastic about plying her trade as a nurse is in winter by the roadside. If we're driving together and she spots an accident she murmurs, "Oh please, let someone be there." Apparently there is a law or code stating that a medical professional must stop if there's been an injury. She slows the car and when she sees the flashing lights of an ambulance says, "Oh, thank God. I'm off duty."

The rest of the time she's ready and eager for a crisis. Mom particularly embraces an opportunity to brush up on her Heimlich maneuver. This is because it's one of those procedures someone can't really practice unless a person is actually choking, for fear of sending their spleen up into their nostrils. And to my mother, a first-aid dummy just isn't the same as getting her hands on a real chest cavity.

My family lives in fear of the Heimlich maneuver. This is an area where we take precautionary measures—cutting meat into small bites, chewing food carefully—because, quite frankly, having one's guts smashed in is not a particularly pleasant way to conclude Thanksgiving dinner. Once, as I started to cough and sputter at the table when some water went down the wrong way, I immediately became alarmed after I saw my mother put on her Heimlich face, equal parts concern and delight.

"Can you speak?" she shouted across the table. (Inability to speak is the first sign of a choking victim, according to the first-aid books.) Yet I could have spoken if I'd only had a second to swallow and relax. Instead, I saw her rising from her chair, eyes gleaming, drawing her hands together. Then I went into a full panic. I definitely did *not* want my ribs jacked up into my throat, and so I tried to talk but, amidst the growing dread, just couldn't manage to catch my breath. By then she was moving fast, a predator closing in on its prey. In the nick of time I managed to push my chair back and flee from the table. (Second sign of a choking victim: running from the table.) She chased me into the living room. The rest of the family froze as if watching the final few minutes of a tied Super Bowl. They were probably alarmed by the thought that it could just as easily have been one of them.

By the time I took flight, I was not only convulsed with terror, but also with laughter, and my face was turning purple (third sign of a choking victim) from simultaneously coughing and gagging. My mother threw her arms around my chest. "No!" I finally managed to yell out. I was released onto the floor in a heap of gasps and giggles.

"Why didn't you speak up in the first place?" she asked in her no-nonsense tone, though I sensed a distinct note of disappointment in her voice. "I thought you were choking to death."

To Mom, the light at the end of the tunnel is usually an oncoming train. Or as she prefers to say, "It's just that I know too much."

Fortunately everyone in the family rotates being the target of the matriarchal medical reactionary. One Easter, my uncle passed my mother the potatoes and she noticed a dark spot on his arm. "Have you had a doctor look at that?" Nurse Doom inquired with more than a slight hint that there was a dramatic revelation to follow. He said no.

She announced that it looked like a malignant melanoma and should be removed and sent for a biopsy as soon as possible. And if it was indeed a melanoma, then he'd be dead within six to eight weeks and there wasn't anything that anyone could do about it. Then she passed him the roast beef. He was no longer hungry. Instead he asked me, "How come every time we invite your mother to dinner we end up wanting to land a medevac chopper on the roof?"

The only real problem with her diagnoses is that she's usually right. My uncle did have a form of treatable skin cancer.

My aunt has found a novel use for my mother's nursing skills. She's very intelligent and knows that there are times that she should go to a doctor, but, like many of us, she needs that extra push. So she calls my mother. The phone calls are pretty much the same:

Nurse Ellen: Hi Susie, how are you?

Aunt Sue (in the midst of an embolism, but completely calm): Fine, thanks. What a gorgeous day we're having.

Nurse Ellen: Yes, I thought I'd go for a walk later. Perhaps you'd like to join me.

Aunt Sue: No, thanks. I've been feeling a bit tired.

Nurse Ellen (radar goes on alert): Oh, really? Have you been getting enough rest? Is it allergies? Are you taking any meds?

Aunt Sue: No, no, it's just that I passed out a little while ago.

Nurse Ellen: You passed out?! You have to see a doctor immediately! How's your pulse?

Aunt Sue: It's hard to tell because I'm experiencing shortness of breath and have these shooting pains down my right arm...

Nurse Ellen: I'M CALLING AN AMBULANCE NOW!

Aunt Sue loves to call with dizziness, gaping wounds from kitchen accidents, and chest pains and act as if nothing is wrong. She knows she should go to the hospital, but for some reason she requires the additional impetus of my mother screaming into the receiver: "Call 9-1-1 because you're going to die!"

My mom can pretty much tell what's wrong with a single glance. As a kid, I'd arrive home from school and she'd take one look at me and instantly declare scarlet fever, bronchitis, or walking pneumonia. A few hours later, the doctor would confirm and prescribe.

More recently, a neighbor was ailing with cancer, and as my mother and I were bringing in some groceries, we saw the woman from about thirty yards away and my mother leaned in and whispered, "Looks like pneumonia." A week later the woman died. My mother asked a relative the cause of death and was told an autopsy was being performed. The following week she reported back to my mother: pneumonia.

In her own emergencies, my mother is equally efficient and not known for depending on the kindness of strangers, or even family members, for that matter. Healthcare isn't a two-way stretcher. It's no secret that she views the rest of us as medical incompetents. When I was thirteen, my father and I arrived in the kitchen one morning to find my mother with ten stitches above her right eye. She'd risen in the middle of the night and accidentally hit the corner of her dresser, driven herself to the emergency room and then back home again.

"Why the heck didn't you wake us up?" My father asked in astonishment.

"Because you're both useless," my mother calmly replied. "You," she pointed at my father, "pass out at the sight of blood, and you," she turned to me, "can't drive anyway." Okay, she had a point. Two points, actually.

Once we were in high school, my friends and I had fewer bumps and bruises that needed treatment. Our teeth had come and gone and come in again for good. However, we developed a new appreciation for my mother's bathroom operating room. It was the only place in town a teenager could really examine his or her skin for pimples. It also came in handy for applying makeup. My friend Mary quite accurately dubbed the full-wall mirror under the blazing lights the Truth Mirror. Mary was in the habit of fixing her hair and face at her house and then stopping by our bathroom for the finishing touches before heading out on a date. She insisted she just couldn't be sure of how she really looked until she consulted the Truth Mirror. She said it was easy to think that you looked pretty good and then glance at it and be completely horrified. The Truth

Mirror could make a teenager feel so zit faced, frizzy haired, and plug ugly that they didn't want to go out again until they were twenty-one. Some friends wouldn't even enter my mom's bathroom, or if they did, they'd strike a match rather than switch on the high-powered searchlights.

Though it can be hard to pinpoint the exact causes of a divorce, I'd say that my folks split on grounds of irreconcilable healthcare and sanitation differences. For my mother, there seems to be a divide between having a man in her life and having a man in her house, a chasm that cannot be bridged with Lysol. Whereas she has no interest in anything that can't be thoroughly vacuumed, my father's going to be cremated wearing a T-shirt depicting the surgeon general with a big red line through his face.

Dad's a marathon smoker, champion caffeine consumer, and hasn't seen a hospital bed in over forty years. It's probably not an exaggeration to say that if he were to modify his habits, the stock prices of companies that sell coffee and tobacco would plummet. If he ever gets his cholesterol checked, I'm sure that instead of numbers there'll be just one word: pastrami. In fact, when Dad is cremated they'll have to secure the area just so no one dies from secondhand-smoke inhalation.

Dad's philosophy about doctors is, essentially, that if he doesn't go, then there's no chance they can find anything wrong with him. His theory on cleansing agents might be called the Ganges Principle, referring to the fact that people who bathe in the Ganges River every day, amongst the detritus of garbage and dead bodies, experience no ill effects, because their immune systems are accustomed to it. And that the best way to build a formidable immune system is to surround oneself with a certain amount of pollution and let it build up over time. At the end of the day I suspect that Dad doesn't really believe in germs at all, for the same reason he doesn't believe in ghosts and gods: because he's never seen one.

No matter his reasoning, it turns out that Dad really *was* ahead of his time. Just recently medical science has given us the hygiene hypothesis to explain the rise in asthma and allergies. This theory states that households in developed countries have become so clean and sanitized that our bodies' immune systems aren't receiving the early training they need to fend off allergens later in life. While Mom displayed guest towels that the family wasn't supposed to get dirty (I perfected wiping my toothpaste-covered mouth on the inside where she wouldn't find the evidence), Dad saw total disintegration as the only sign that a towel needed replacing.

Dad is the kind of guy who, when his shoes start to wear out, wraps them a couple times with duct tape. He's convinced that the spick-and-span crowd, with all that constant scrubbing at mold and dirt and dust, is just asking to get struck down with the first viral infection that comes along. Next stop, polio. He'll tell people that it's not wearing clothes that ruins them, but all the washing and drying in between. Dad believes good health stems from living in harmony with the natural world, and therefore spiders have as much right to live in a person's bedroom as a person does. In fact, they may be the only thing between the person and a fatal case of malaria. Once, when I asked why he didn't remove the cobwebs taking up a full third of his wall and ceiling, Dad said that they helped to control the mosquito population. (Apparently he was just short a water table of having his own private ecosystem in there.)

If I had a truly untenable entomological situation in my room as a child, such as a cigar-sized centipede, the most I was going to get Dad to do was perform a shoe-box capture and then relocate the creature to a nearby forest. I think bumblebees and carpenter ants must have pictures of him hanging in their hives and entrances to their hills, the way Buffalo Democrats used to have photos of JFK and the pope in their front hallways, framed by enough decaying palm fronds to start a bonfire.

People said that Dad was never the same after the Korean War. People said he was never the same after the brain aneurysm. As I got older, I realized what they actually meant was that Dad had always been an interplanetary traveler who communicated with the stars and possibly other galaxies. Dad could go out for the mail and nine times out of ten come back without it. And we're not talking about walking to the post office. The mailbox was right across the street.

He is so forgetful that he'll often say, "I think I'm going senile—I walk into a room and can't remember what I went in there for."

I'll reply, "Going senile? You couldn't remember anything forty years ago."

And he'll say, "Really? I don't remember that."

It's obvious that Dad was not meant for war. In retirement, he spends a good portion of his time capturing animals in Havahart traps and returning them to the wild. Dad is looking for a catch-and-release flyswatter. Now, if Attila the Mom had been sent to the Korean peninsula instead, it's doubtful there'd be any of this 38th parallel inanity dividing the haves and have-nots. Everyone would own a bar of soap, scrub brush, and vacuum, and be expected to use them with regularity. There'd be three vegetables a day, laundry detergent with bleach, and a dry, white cotton sock on every foot. Arms akimbo, she would have told Kim Il Sung, "Stop all the nonsense, mister."

By the time the eighties arrived, the hippies had gone to law school and there was little tolerance for people communing with nature. Only the quick and the cleansed survived in Nurse Ellen's ward. As a preemptive strike, she had already said no to secondhand smoke by quarantining Dad's room, which looked like the place where pawnbrokers go to die. This was achieved by taping up the door—so effectively that when Dad managed to pry it open, there was a tremendous sucking sound, as if a tornado was ripping through the hallway.

Now in fairness to Dad, part of the problem (I like to think) was that he'd lost his sense of smell after a brain aneurysm in his late thirties. Okay, he's not what one would call extremely observant to begin with. His was the car coming around the corner with the briefcase on the roof and the coffee cup on the hood. And my mother loves to tell the story of Dad lying unconscious in the hospital and how he'd get out of bed and roam the hallways searching for cigarettes, sort of like a smokewalker. Now *there's* a spokesperson for big tobacco—right on death's doorstep, his only concern a final puff. Dad was rewarded, though not in the heavenly way. The only permanent affliction from the aneurysm was a loss of smell—smoke away. And since scent is somehow connected to taste, he no longer had that either, for food or clothing.

One afternoon, I was standing in the kitchen with my mother when she poked her head up like an alert prairie dog and barked, "Smoke! There's a fire!" She ran to the taped-up door and saw smoke wriggling through the crack where the shag carpet had interfered with her plastic barrier. Mom quickly unstuck the door and barged in to find my father calmly puffing away and typing while his curtains blazed orange and blue directly above him. Though I'm sure Dad determined that the fire was good for his ecosystem...more like a controlled burn.

Twenty-Six

Home at Sweet Home...
Class Clown...Dressing Down

On a typical school morning, Mary would arrive at seven and let herself in using the key we cleverly kept hidden under the doormat. She knew to be very quiet because my mom worked all night and we never wanted to wake her up, for a lot of reasons.

As the youngest of nine children, Mary had been assigned the bathroom slot of 6:10 to 6:20 AM. If for any reason she missed it, or if an older brother or sister went into sudden shower overtime, Mary was basically soap out of luck. Sometimes she'd arrive before seven to shower and wash her hair at my house. Mary was also guaranteed hot water at my place, which was another big attraction, especially in the wintertime. In fact, that's why I took a bath the night before, because I couldn't face the cold in the morning. When it was really frigid outside, my hair would freeze into long icicles.

I allowed twelve minutes every morning to go from being in a complete coma to having my body on the bus. This involved choosing an outfit (whatever was on top), changing into the clothes (if I hadn't slept in them as another step to avoid the cold), and then wrestling my hair into some sort of braid. However, it looked as if I'd spent only five minutes. I've always been a fashion fatality, usually resembling someone rescued from a flood and dressed in donations from kindly villagers.

A copy of *Vogue* never made it into our home. Mom's fashion philosophy was as follows: If it needs to be ironed or dry-cleaned, don't buy it. If she liked a sweater, she bought it in every color. Dad's personal style statement is any shirt with two pockets, one for each pair of glasses with room left over for his cigarettes and lighter.

The way I timed my morning routine throughout all four years of high school was by switching on a record player in my room the moment I awoke. Gordon Lightfoot's album *Don Quixote* was on the turntable, and I knew that by the time he finished the title song, I had to have my face washed, teeth brushed, and be dressed. When "Christian Island" began I'd better be working on hair and then grabbing any stuff I needed for school. Quick glance in the mirror: bad-human day, good-cockatiel day. When the third track, "Alberta Bound," came on, it was time for breakfast. As that ended I should have been heading out the door. If "Looking at the Rain" started, then I'd probably missed the bus.

Mary fixed her hair and makeup in the Truth Mirror and then made breakfast while I went through my Gordon Lightfoot regimen. She must have learned to cook from her mom, because Mary was a regular one-woman Denny's and could make any breakfast item, but chocolate-chip pancakes and cinnamon French toast were her specialties.

I threw back some of whatever Mary had cooked while we listened for the big yellow bus to chug down the street like clattering thunder. One could hear the old double-clutch dinosaurs with a top speed of forty miles per hour from the next state.

Mrs. Thompson, the bus driver, would honk if we weren't at the bus stop. If Mary and I came flying out the door, she'd wait for us to run the hundred yards from my house to the corner. If we were too far behind schedule, I'd step onto the front porch and wave, signaling that we'd take the shortcut and meet her at the last stop before she left our neighborhood. In this situation, we had to dash a quarter mile at top speed in clogs on a full stomach.

If only one of us caught the bus, Mrs. Thompson always asked, "Where's your sister?" The first two years of high school we insisted that we were not sisters. We told Mrs. Thompson the entire story: only child and youngest of nine, coming over to shower and cook, and so on. She didn't buy one word of it, thought we were lying through our syrup-covered teeth. After a while we forgot about it and just said the other one was sick or playing hooky, or whatever the case was. Inevitably someone would overhear the conversation and give us a hard time, saying, "You shouldn't lie and tell Mrs. Thompson that you're sisters. One day she'll find out the truth!"

Mary continued to be popular with the boys. As we dashed toward the bus, young guys driving Mazda RX-7s would go into a skid while yelling stupid nothings out of their car windows at her. I was still being mistaken for a boy, and I'm sure my wardrobe didn't help on that front.

Mary was generous in giving me her used boyfriends. Oftentimes her current beau would have a brother or a friend who needed fixing up, so I never had a strong incentive to get myself all gussied up in order to attract guys. Mary was also a fount of relationship knowledge. Between having eight older brothers and sisters and a steady stream of admirers, she knew everything.

Mary used to switch boyfriends the way other girls changed their outfits, leaving me a nice selection of sloppy seconds. Whatever Mary was casting off was better than anything I could have reeled in on my own, even with a makeover by Elizabeth Arden herself. She'd find someone more interesting, and we'd have a quick summit in the restroom. A transfer time and place would be decided, the bowling alley or a local bar. (In the Buffalo of the early eighties, a thirteen-year-old girl with a bit of makeup could stroll into any bar and order a drink. The owners wanted women for the guys to spend their paychecks on. As for underage guys, forget it; they still got carded into their twenties.)

We never explained to the guys that a switcheroo was in progress. Mary would just say she was going to make a phone call and never come back. I'd remain with the castoff, not exactly telling him that Mary was the past and I was the future, but after a few hours and a few beers he got the drift. They didn't seem to mind all that much. I suppose they never really imagined that a beauty like Mary would be their girlfriend in the first place. At the end of the evening, she'd stop by with her new man, and the old one seemed happy enough that by being with me he'd still get to hang around with her. In addition to being attractive, Mary was always a lot of fun.

Occasionally we decided that both guys were yesterday's news. Then we'd head for the ladies' room, mindful to bring along our purses and jackets, climb out the window, and head for happier hunting grounds altogether.

Mary had access to her oldest sister's CB radio, which was basically the AOL Instant Messenger of its day. It was where people met and even married, the way Mary's oldest sister had. On the flip side, I imagine there was an amount of misrepresentation on the CB similar to what one gets with Internet dating, especially since we couldn't send photos.

As teenagers we'd sit in her sister's car, which was parked in the street out in front of the house, put our "ears" on, and use the radio to flirt with truckers. Mary knew some of the lingo from her sister, and I knew a bit from my dad, who had a CB radio in his cave, and the rest we picked up from listening. Buffalo was *Nickel City*, a reference to Indian nickels, the pre-1938 five-cent coins with a buffalo on the back. A *bear in the air* was a state patrolman in a helicopter or a light plane that spots and clocks speeders. A *bear bite* was a speeding ticket from a cop who may have been a *Smoky the Bear* in a *brown wrapper* (unmarked car) until he stuck his *disco ball* on the roof. We made up handles and after signing on were quickly asked if we were *YLs* (young ladies) with nice *seat covers* (legs). The truckers wanted to know what *cash register* (toll booth) we were near on the thruway, what *panty-hose junction* (coffee shop or truck stop) was near the *chicken coop* (weigh station for trucks), and if we were going to stop for *motion lotion* (gas or diesel fuel) soon. We'd be asked to meet for *black water* (coffee) or *barley pop* (beer) in order to eyeball each other.

We didn't have cars, but if Mary wanted a ride all she had to do was walk down the road in whatever direction she was going and one would magically appear. She rarely had a bike, though when she did she hardly used it. If we were walking to the mall, it would only be five minutes before some guy would pull over and offer us a ride. However, Mary knew that I wouldn't get into a car with strangers. Like any other city with high unemployment, the Buffalo area had its share of psychos, bunco artists, and disgruntled former factory workers cruising around. So when a car pulled up Mary would say, "It's a friend of my brother." With as many siblings as she had, and the fact that the area was not that big, this was entirely possible. We'd get in the car with a couple of guys. Mary would start talking, and I'd suddenly realize that she didn't know them from *anywhere*. But they'd seem nice enough and usually asked us out later, and we'd go. Afterwards I'd complain, "You told me you knew them!" She'd always say that she thought it was so-and-so but she'd been mistaken, that it was hard to tell from the side of the road.

Another thing I once caught Mary doing during our walk to the mall on a very cold day was hitchhiking without my knowing it, her thumb down near her waist and trailing slightly behind us where I couldn't see it. That's when it dawned on me that she must have been doing it for years. I suddenly recalled all the snowy days when cars had screeched to a halt beside us and a guy leaned out and said, "Hey, girls, need a lift?" Mary would just look at me as if to say, "Well, there's a happy coincidence!" In frigid weather, a teenage girl can't exactly strut her stuff wearing a ski jacket, boots, ski mittens, and a Buffalo Sabres cap. It was a challenge to attract drive-by pickups dressed like a hazmat worker with snot frozen to the upper lip. And quite frankly, when the windchill factor made the temperature ten below zero, I was just as interested in finding a ride, even if I suspected that Mary's "friend of her brother" might be a new acquaintance.

Mary always seemed to know of a party, or could find a party, or find some people who knew of a party. She's the only person I know who belonged to a ski club and rarely brought along skis; she'd usually spend the night drinking mulled cider and socializing in the lodge or on the bus.

The ski club had a good system for returning everyone alive. They put a tag around our necks and drove us in a Greyhound bus to Kissing Bridge, Bluemont, or Holiday Valley, the local resorts, where we could get as drunk or break as many bones as we wished. At 11:00 PM the lights were turned up and ski patrols whizzed around on snowmobiles, digging the bodies out of ravines and gullies. They looked at the ID tags and dumped people onto the correct buses, which were by now veritable honky-tonks on wheels.

People often ask if I ski. I'm from Buffalo. Of course I can ski. In fact, I learned back in the days of runaway straps, heavy metal skis, and wool outerwear. For those of us who grew up with mailboxes across the street, on some days we had to cross-country ski just to reach them. Maybe that's why I now view skiing as a job I should get paid for. Sort of like my friend who loved radios—after becoming an electrical engineer, he complained that he'd ruined a perfectly good hobby.

If a person can ski the areas south of Buffalo, then she can ski anywhere. We're talking nights of about twenty below with the windchill factor and sliding down a mountain of sheer ice. We sharpened our skis the way other people sharpen their skates. When Buffalonians first attempt Colorado powder, they topple over face-first.

However, most Buffalonians have a terrific time skiing. Resorts are not far from where we live, there's usually plenty of man-made snow (translation: ice), and there are good mountains. At first I belonged to my high school ski club, but then Mary and I discovered that because we both had family members at the University of Buffalo, we were eligible for its ski club. It was less expensive and went out three times a week, instead of just once, like the one at our high school.

The university ski club provided a whole new supply of boyfriends with good balance and chapped lips. As usual, Mary was in charge of procurement. She was still more of a lodge bunny, the toast of the chili-con-carne crowd, and so by the time I'd made a few runs and come in for a snack, Mary had several possibilities lined up. Usually some guy would be flirting with her, and because most people ski in pairs, his friend would be getting antsy to go back out and do a few more runs. Mary would conveniently send me off to ski with the friend. He'd have had a few beers by then and not be feeling too particular. We'd talk going up on the chairlift. By the time we arrived back at the bus, I had a new boyfriend.

✳ ✳ ✳

In high school I had a battery pack of extra energy, and if it wasn't going to be put to use masterminding bank robberies and bookmaking, there needed to be another outlet.

Humor has been part of my life as far back as I can remember. Dad used to play the social parody songs by Allan Sherman and Tom Lehrer on his guitar. Though I couldn't seem to remember much that was taught in school, by the age of eight I knew all the lyrics to not only Sherman's "Hello Muddah, Hello Fadduh," but also Lehrer's "Poisoning Pigeons in the Park," "The Old Dope Peddler," and "We Will All Go Together When We Go." This last number was about a nuclear holocaust and included such inspired lines as "No one will have the endurance to collect on their insurance." I also took to heart what Lehrer said in his introduction to that song: "Life is like a sewer—what you get out of it depends on what you put into it."

My early material consisted mostly of telling jokes about teachers, mimicking teachers, drawing cartoons lampooning teachers, and writing poems and songs making fun of teachers. Additionally, I had a number of props—rubber animal noses, headbands with attached wings, and a nun's habit.

My high school class was fortunate to get in under the wire before mimeographed dittos became photocopied pages. Dittos had bright purple ink and when fresh off the machine they radiated an intoxicating smell of ink, alcohol, and chemicals. We'd press them to our faces as if getting high on airplane glue. When students walked into a classroom and saw a batch of them that had just been run off, they gleefully shouted, "Dittos!" and like a bunch of crackheads we'd fight to get them under our noses.

I specialized in laying my hands on the dittos before they were run off and making a few alterations. For instance, I'd write fun (but true) facts around the edges, such as this gem: While Henry David Thoreau was supposedly living off the land in solitary confinement at Walden Pond, outlining his philosophy of self-reliance, he was going home to have dinner with Mom practically every night and probably bringing along his laundry.

The teachers always knew who was behind such mischief, but they never actually caught me, and it was just silly stuff anyway. If we were studying an author or historical figure in school, I'd look them up beforehand to find some inappropriate detail that wouldn't be served up in school, such as Edgar Allen Poe having married his fourteen-year-old cousin, and then ask the teacher about it. While studying the French Symbolists, I asked about Paul Verlaine leaving his wife for Arthur Rimbaud and then shooting Rimbaud and being imprisoned for two years. As we read *Main Street,* I inquired about Sinclair Lewis's alcoholism and how he finished several of his novels in rehab clinics. Had this in any way been a result of Lewis having suffered from bad acne as a teenager and being terribly pockmarked?

For livening up the school bus, I was fond of any sort of pig para-phernalia, whether it was attachable ears or glasses with a snout. On the soccer field I usually wore a pig T-shirt and a headband with wings stitched to the sides that I'd crafted myself (about as far as home eco-nomics took me). My purse had a moose on one side and a photo of Elea-nor Roosevelt on the other. I usually had some ridiculous drawing inside my notebook that I could flash to crack up a friend at the exact moment a teacher was delivering some important piece of information.

Aside from the soccer team and helping Pete with the musicals, I wasn't much of a joiner, though I liked to drop in on events according to my own schedule. For instance, Mary and Heather both volunteered at Millard Fillmore Hospital in downtown Buffalo. They were registered, and they had name tags, uniforms, training, and schedules. I'd often accompany them and grab a candy-striper smock out of the laundry room, wheel the gift cart around, tell a few jokes, and do coin tricks for some of the kids. After an hour or so, my attention span would be exhausted and I'd wander around the city until it was time to meet them and leave. The only telltale sign that I wasn't supposed to be in the hos-pital was that I didn't have a name tag. Heather and Mary referred to me as "the unknown volunteer," because whenever the gift-shop manager or volunteer coordinator would ask about their blond friend, they'd pretend not to have seen any blond girl. We did this for many months, and eventually the staff probably volunteered themselves for psychiatric testing.

No one had heard of anything called attention deficit disorder when I was growing up (forget restless legs syndrome). If ADHD had been part of the lingo, I imagine my name would have easily made the Ten Most Wanted list. I had such a case of disco arms and ankles that my fingers could drum out the entire "Star-Spangled Banner" while my shoes wore down two spots on the linoleum floor. It was impossible to pay attention to anything for more than a minute unless I was extremely interested, and then the limit was five. In photographs from these years I am the blurred spot.

It's safe to say that the only area where I distinguished myself throughout a decadelong academic and sports career was in playing Boggle, a game where you see who can make the most words out of sixteen random letters. I searched to see if a college scholarship existed for strong Boggle players, and though there seemed to be ones for everything else, including welding, knitting, and aquatic entomology, I found nothing.

❊ ❊ ❊

The student body at my school was less financially gifted and more casual than that of the nearby Amherst and Williamsville districts. Where we leaned more toward sneakers, jeans, T-shirts, and sweatshirts, they preferred Shetland-wool sweaters, Dockers-style khaki pants, loafers, and Pappagallo purses. Along with the requisite preps, burnouts, brains, geeks, and musicians, we specialized in towel-snapping jocks and vivacious cheerleaders.

But the lines were not drawn as strictly as in a Hollywood movie. Neighborhoods were small, and most of us had known each other since childhood, so once we became teenagers it was difficult to forge a whole new identity on a low budget. Few kids owned cars in high school. About the most we could do to claim a clique was buy a shirt with a little whale on it, smoke, attach a chain between our jeans and wallet, join the mathletes, or carry a lacrosse stick.

The other problem with creating a particular look was, of course, the weather. There were a number of items in which we would simply freeze to death—leather jacket as outerwear, any revealing top, a short skirt. Likewise, certain footwear was prone to land us prone in a snowbank, particularly high-heeled shoes. Even Bastad clogs, all the rage when I started high school, posed a challenge when navigating more than a few inches of snow and slick patches of ice. In order to traverse towering drifts, one developed a kick-shuffle step that used the closed toe as a shovel to keep wet snow out of the open back. Tattoos and piercings? Better put them on your eyelids if people are supposed to see them more than four months out of the year.

No matter what social group one was in, everybody avoided hats, mittens, scarves, and boots. These items were decidedly uncool, except for baseball caps. Teenagers with vigilant bathrobe-clad mothers (who watched from the window as their charges left the house in the morning and were ready to leap into highly embarrassing action) tossed the offensive items behind a neighbor's bushes before arriving at the bus stop, and then retrieved them after school. Similarly, girls who attended Catholic school wiped their lipstick and eye shadow off before entering the building, and then reapplied it at the end of the day before being seen by the boys.

In the early eighties, my high school was about 5 percent black, and, though the black kids tended to hang out in a certain place between classes and do the secret handshake, everything was integrated and I don't remember any tension. There were a few interracial couples, which was okay with us, but usually not with our parents.

Ninth grade was the first time I ever heard rap music. In September 1979, Sugarhill Gang's song "Rapper's Delight" was the first rap song to hit the top-forty charts. It was the precursor to hip-hop and, with assistance from the by-now-ubiquitous boom box (aka ghetto blaster), spread like rock and roll had in the 1950s. Soon all the kids, black and white, could recite the lyrics with the "rock it to the bang

bang boogie" chorus. And the boys taunted girls with: "If your girl starts actin' up, then you take her friend."

Hip-hop's diverse expressions—dance, music, and visual art—may have been going strong in the Bronx for several years, but this was the first we'd heard of it in the Midwest. Subsequently, boom boxes grew in size, weight, woofer, and effectiveness, along with other characteristics heretofore associated with the arms race. They reigned supreme in every park and parking lot, spreading communal music until the mideighties, when the Walkman (and noise laws) made such blasting obsolete.

Tenth-grade biology class was the first time I ever heard a full rap song recited a cappella as a form of recreation, instead of being played at a dance, complete with cutting and scratching. While our teacher, Mrs. DiCenzo, was out of the room, Sam Nixon sat on one of the granite islands we used for lab experiments and rapped "8th Wonder" for twenty straight minutes. Only, Mrs. Dicenzo had been in the doorway, and she gave him hell about memorizing such a litany of song lyrics while being unable to recite the first two steps in the photosynthesis process. So much for his shot at most-improved student.

The punk rock scene was jarring big cities between 1979 and 1985, but mostly passed Amherst by. No spiked hair and tight black T-shirts for us, unless it was at the high school's production of the musical *Grease*. One night after skiing, I tagged along with some University of Buffalo students to the venerable, but shadowy, Buffalo dinner-theater-turned-downtown-nightclub called the Continental (which later launched the Goo Goo Dolls) and experienced my first punk band, along with fans who appeared to have landed facedown in a tackle box over at the bait shop. It left no lasting impression aside from a lingering deafness, and I certainly had no urge to hurry home, steal safety pins from my mother's sewing basket, and thread them through my cheeks.

My most enjoyable high school experience had to be escorting a blind student from one class to another in the afternoon. This journey was particularly entertaining because he used his complete lack of sight as an opportunity to grope every girl in school, profusely apologizing as he made his way through crowded halls while landing all the breasts he could lay his outstretched hands upon.

Home economics was fast becoming anachronistic in a school where tiny computer labs were taking over storage rooms, the first tutorials in this new discipline being patched together by math teachers and taught during their free periods. Meantime, calico-aproned home-ec teachers were assigning projects that we couldn't undertake because we didn't have the basics in cooking and sewing. Former bake-off champions now in their late fifties were training us to be homemakers, envisioning a world that only existed in *The Adventures of Ozzie & Harriet* reruns. One educational filmstrip (before movie reels, filmstrips were akin to slide shows, but with a bulb that would overheat every five minutes, catch fire, and melt the celluloid) instructed us how to be ladies: arrive fashionably late, blend foundation makeup into the neck so there wasn't an orange fault line, and appear slender—wear the color black, vertical stripes, and A-line dresses. We sat there in overalls, holding field-hockey sticks, and laughed our heads off. By then, a Burger King, 7-Eleven, KFC, Wendy's, or McDonald's was within walking distance of all our homes. Mother-daughter dresses had gone the way of the bouffant hairdo. Clothes could be bought at nearby Kmart for less than what we'd pay to purchase the fabric and sew them. Bye-bye, Butterick, bye-bye.

Twenty-Seven

Can't We All Get a Lawn?...
Pedersen v. Pedersen...Telling It to the Judge...
The Play within the Play

Dad first announced that he was planning to divorce my mother when I was twelve. He said he hadn't wanted to leave until I was old enough to take care of myself, so that's why he'd waited the extra ten years. He reminded me again that my mother was crazy, while my mother never missed an opportunity to remind me that my father was the crazy one. Just as my father liked to say that my mother drove like a maniac, my mother insisted that my father drove so slow that we'd be killed by traveling under the speed limit.

I was actually rather stunned by the news because, yes, we were without a doubt an odd family, but then we'd always been so. What had changed?

During the seventies and early eighties, divorced couples went from being statistical outliers to commonplace. Still, none of my friends' parents were divorced. The word had unpleasant connotations, and even kids knew that. People whispered, "broken home" as the child walked past. A small town outside Buffalo wasn't exactly Berkeley. My neighborhood didn't have a reputation as a hotbed of wife swapping and transcendental meditation. It was better known for bowling night, bingo night, and Time-Life books.

Furthermore, no one on TV was divorced, just widowed, like in *The Courtship of Eddie's Father*. The opening song to *The Brady Bunch* didn't make it clear what had happened to the original spouses, though one assumed it wasn't divorce, but cancer or, from a Buffalonian's point of view, hypothermia, or perhaps an industrial accident.

So in the middle of a summer day, I climbed into bed with my dog, Fifi, to cry because I was soon to be The Child of Divorce. After a few minutes of being sad, I realized that my parents probably couldn't be more miserable than they'd been up until then, and that they'd been staying together to try and make my life a happy one. Furthermore, my situation wouldn't change much, unless someone suddenly decided to start cooking. My main concern was that I wouldn't have to move. I went back to my dad's room and asked if I'd have to move. He said no.

Little did we know at the time that Dad wasn't going to be moving either, at least not for several long years. According to New York State property laws, if one spouse leaves, the other can claim abandonment and will most likely gain possession of the house. This turns homes into war zones, forcing years of bitter cohabitation as divorce cases slowly grind their way through the courts. Over the next four years, we continued living together, my parents' lawyers both advising them to hold their ground.

Everyone came and went as usual. Dad lived in his bedroom/office in the back of the house, but he'd always done that, since he wasn't allowed to smoke anywhere else. Mom used the garage for her car and came and went through the back door; Dad used the driveway and the front door. I like to think of it as one of the first reality shows—a couple locked in a court battle and forced to live together in the hopes of getting a fair settlement.

Thus, the divorce started when I was twelve, and by the time it went to trial and the appellate division, I was almost sixteen. While reading *The Odyssey* during that time, I remember thinking that the Pedersens might just beat old Homer when it came to tales of dragged-out misery and adventure.

Divorce was especially difficult in New York State for additional reasons. There wasn't anything like a no-fault provision (which it so happens the Catholic Church opposes), thus one had to have grounds for divorce. One party had to allege cruel and inhuman treatment, adultery, or abandonment.

Dad installed a lock on his door. Mom could open it with a credit card, but he didn't know that. This was a safety issue rather than an espionage tactic, because she worried about the room catching fire and burning the rest of the house down. It seemed to me that the lawyers worked overtime to create a sense of paranoia, suggesting that my parents were maneuvering and hiding money. They weren't. They're not tricky people.

After the proceedings got under way, things had a weird way of happening on holidays. My parents had married on Saint Valentine's Day. Now my mother was served with divorce papers the Friday before Labor Day weekend. Heather and I were sitting in the living room playing the board game Masterpiece (still no video games) when the doorbell rang and a woman with an envelope wanted to see my mom *in person*. After the woman left, my mother was visibly upset. Though we knew this was coming, I guess it didn't seem real until that moment.

I said, "I thought you said that Dad is crazy." She said that was true, but it didn't mean she wanted a divorce. This was my first glimpse into the human psychology of preferring the known, even if it was known to be crazy, over the unknown.

Mom soon came to terms with what was happening and said, "I could never be married to anyone who voted for Nixon anyway."

❋ ❋ ❋

My parents' divorce was the only shadow to cross my otherwise enjoyable and easygoing high school career. Perhaps one reason we didn't do much together as a family and the entire "dorm" living situation arose in the first place was because my parents hardly did anything with each other. I tend to think they landed in one of those fifties marriages that seemed like a good idea at the time, and then later realized they weren't very well suited to each other. Complicating matters was the fact that much of the thinking in the sixties and seventies suggested that unhappy couples should have a child, and when that didn't work, they should stay together for the sake of the child.

Soon both lawyers began asking me if I would meet with them, as my parents were fighting for custody. I had a little insight into how the court system worked, since my father had worked on numerous matrimonial cases over the years. I remembered him regularly saying that judges were old-fashioned and tended to award children to the mother unless some charge of neglect could be proven, and even then, the claims had to be awfully strong.

The idea of a custody battle seemed rather silly, since I was an extremely independent teenager by this point. On weekends, Pete and I would go to the Laundromat together. My next-door neighbor was the librarian at school, and I can only imagine what she thought of a teacher pulling into my driveway and me dashing out with a bag of clothes.

After the Laundromat, Pete and I would return to his apartment where he'd fire up his deluxe steam iron while we watched *Grey Gardens* for the umpteenth time. It's the true story of the crumbling mansion that was home to the reclusive aunt and cousin of Jackie Onassis, Edith Bouvier Beale, and her daughter, Little Edie. The two women camp in a single bedroom of a twenty-eight-room East Hampton estate gone to ruin while accusatorily rehashing memories of opportunities and lost chances. Little Edie does some unusual things with turbans fashioned out of sweaters, and they have quite a few cats and raccoons. Pete loved how the mother keeps telling the daughter that she isn't talented, and the daughter argues how she would have made it in show business if it hadn't been for the mother.

As best I could figure it, the lawyers were using me as a pawn in their battle. The only thing we had of value was our house, originally purchased for $20,000 in the early sixties and worth about $65,000 in the early eighties. The down payment of $2,000 had belonged to Mom, which she'd saved from working at the unemployment office. But typical of the times, the house was put in my father's name alone, as were the cars and the credit cards (thus, she had no credit history and had difficulty applying for new cards—take a lesson, women). It stood to reason that whoever landed the child automatically won the house.

Though Mom and Dad weren't exactly hands-on parents, they loved me like crazy. I'm not saying that I was any great prize as a child, because I was as energetic, strong willed, and annoying as any sugared-up kid could be, probably more so. I'd make a mess, aggravate, and remain vigilant for logic traps and double standards. I was a wiseass. Mom and I would have fights. I'd pick up the phone and threaten to check myself into Gateway, the group home for troubled adolescents. I assumed they'd have food there, maybe even a cafeteria. My mother would tell me not to be ridiculous—the court had to sentence a teenager to live there.

But I was the only game in town. It wasn't *Star Trek*; there was no next generation, no nieces, nephews, cousins. If all went as nature intended, I would be selecting their respective twilight homes. In the meantime, I knew that they'd take a bullet for me, exchange themselves as prisoners to secure my freedom, and if I needed a vital organ, one of them would hop on the table. In fact, I was confident that if I needed a heart one of them would give me theirs, and life along with it. (A sweet thought even though it's obvious that Dad is never going to be an approved organ donor, unless it's to science fiction.)

I called for a conference and announced that I wasn't taking sides. The lawyers told me that eventually I'd have to testify in court, and the reason for meeting beforehand was to make sure I'd be comfortable with that. In other words, they wanted to influence my testimony.

At the end of the day, I didn't care much whom I lived with, since we all did our own thing anyway. Neither of my parents ever asked where I was going or what I was doing. Having custody of me as a teenager would have been like having custody of an escaped chimpanzee. I was everywhere at once and always one step ahead of the zookeepers.

That said, I didn't want to go on record as selecting one parent over the other and have Laura's Choice hanging in the air for the rest of my days. Being asked to choose between parents, both good people, knowing they would be informed of the decision, and that it would be a matter of public record was incredibly icky, to say the least. The message I sent back to the lawyers was that I wasn't singing, not to them, and not to a judge.

By doing this I was, by default, agreeing to stay with my mother, based on precedent at the time. But at least it was the law making the decision, not me. My refusal to caucus only set into motion another round of attempted talks by lawyers.

Otherwise, the holiday curse continued. Mom's credit cards were cut off that Thanksgiving. When her time in the house came to an end, it was put up for sale the afternoon of Christmas Eve. Best of all, the final divorce decree was granted on April Fool's Day.

After resisting the entreaties of lawyers from both sides for almost two years, I was finally summoned to the courtroom. By now I was fifteen. The jingle-jangle morning of my court appearance, I sat on the end of my bed and stared in the mirror and promised myself that no matter what happened I wouldn't cry. We'd learned in school that Native Americans used to train young braves to be strong by making them stand in a freezing cold stream for hours at a time without flinching or complaining.

It didn't help that before the courtroom appearance I had an early morning appointment at the orthodontist to have my braces tightened. By the time I arrived downtown, my teeth and gums were aching so much that I could barely speak properly. Since I only needed to be in court for an hour, my parents had arranged for my godmother to pick me up at half past eleven and bring me from the courthouse in downtown Buffalo to my high school out in the suburbs.

The judge decided I'd be questioned in her chambers rather than sit in the courtroom where my parents had been testifying. However, when Mom and Dad came out for a break, I peered inside the spacious wood-paneled courtroom that was nicknamed the Crystal Ballroom because of its palatial chandelier. As I walked toward the judge's chambers, I saw my father racing toward the men's room. He was pale and looked very ill. My mother's lawyer was taking her over to his office to lie down because she had a headache.

254

The judge presiding over the case was named Delores Denman. At the time, she was in her midfifties, had a bleached-blond helmet coiffure, sported a reverberating red, double-knit, permanent-press pantsuit, and had a throaty voice that could probably find a smoke and a drink if they were buried underneath the county jail. When I entered her office, she greeted me with a handshake that I mistook for a karate move and then introduced me to the court reporter who'd be documenting our conversation. I already knew him from skateboarding up in the reporters' common room.

In her raspy, authoritative baritone, Judge Denman explained the purpose of the court reporter and said that whatever we spoke of would be confidential. I replied that I knew what he did since my dad was also a court reporter. And I'd been around the corrupt city of Buffalo long enough to know that anyone else who wanted access to this "confidential" conversation could easily find a way to get it.

Judge Denman cut to the chase pretty fast. Whom did I want to live with—my mom or my dad? Which translates to any child as: whom do you love more—your mom or your dad? I had a prepared statement ready, but the morning's orthodontic procedure, my parents' unglued states, and the specter of a tomato-red Delores Denman shooting questions like machine-gun fire in that whiskey-and-soda voice unhinged me. My answers were evasive.

Judge Denman was not about to be put off her mission by a fifteen-year-old with a mouth full of taut metal. "You must like one of your parents better than the other," she continued.

I felt tears behind my eyes and made them recede by envisioning that freezing cold stream and defiantly crossed my arms in front of me. "No. I'd just like to stay in my house." This last line was to become my refrain.

She looked through some notes on her desk. "It says here that your mother was a Brownie leader." She looked up at me like the child catcher in *Chitty Chitty Bang Bang*, trying to lure me into her net with a delicious-looking lollipop.

"I just want to stay in my house."

Laura Pedersen

Judge Denman returned to her secret files. "It says here that your father played chess with you."

Guilty as charged. I confessed. We had indeed played chess together. He usually let me go first.

After a few more rounds, she looked up and said it was her opinion that I was blocking out my parents' divorce, that I needed psychological help, and she was going to recommend that I receive it.

I guess I should have been relieved. After all these years of my father saying my mother was crazy and vice versa, it had finally been confirmed by a professional that they'd raised a perfectly crazy child.

I was dismissed. In the marble hallway, Dad was sitting on a bench looking very upset. It's pretty hard to imagine him shooting people in the Korean War when he tears up at the opening of a salad bar. My mother was already back in the courtroom, where they were about to resume battle. It was a quarter to twelve, and my godmother was nowhere to be found. She showed up an hour and a half late. It was pouring outside, or raining cats and dogs, as she liked to say.

I should have just gone home, but I wasn't thinking straight. Originally the plan had been to arrive at school before noon. Betty dropped me off at ten minutes to two, right before the final period of the day. My last class was biology, and we were dissecting a perch (a truly disgusting fish). My lab partner was terrific, one of those smart pocket-protector guys, so all I had to do was show up and make jokes while he did all the work. However, if I missed the class I'd have to take the revolting thing apart on my own one day after school.

If I'd had my wits about me I *never* would have gone to the front office. As an expert on truancy, I knew full well that we couldn't sign in after noon. This was because the school could no longer claim state aid for us (their daily government payment), and we weren't covered by their insurance. Had I been thinking clearly, I would have gone directly to the biology lab where my filleted perch awaited me. Mrs. DiCenzo, the bio teacher, wouldn't have noticed that I'd already been marked absent for the day.

But I was in a trance with the song "One (Is the Loneliest Number)"

256

clogging my brain, accidentally used the front door, and was spotted from command central. I drifted into the office with a note saying I'd been to the orthodontist. I didn't think it was any of the office ladies' business that I'd been taking part in the judicial process. The clock on the wall said two. The attendance czars gave me the business: "Why did you come at all? Why didn't you make the orthodontist appointment for after school?" Finally, I grabbed my note from the counter, took off, and snuck up the stairs to the science wing.

By the end of class, we'd finished slicing and dicing the ugly fish and Mrs. DiCenzo tested us individually. I somehow managed to name a gizzard here and a stomach there, thanks to coaching by my partner, who is most likely the head of a billion-dollar biotech company today.

It had stopped raining by the time school let out. My parents arrived home much later. I released a statement explaining that I'd stuck to my party line and didn't choose between the two of them. Aside from that, no one said anything else about the day. Dad went into his office, and my mother went out.

❋ ❋ ❋

The Saturday morning after the divorce proceedings was the start of a glorious Indian summer weekend. It was the kind of day where it seemed impossible that the brilliantly colored landscape would soon be gray and white.

Rising early, I rode my bike the six miles down to Pete's apartment on Gates Circle in the city of Buffalo. He was aware that I'd had my day in court and wanted all the details. Even though I normally told Pete everything, I knew I'd cry if I told him the story and replied, "It was so horrible I can't talk about it."

However, Pete is nosier than any kid is stubborn. He kept grilling me. I started with Delores Denman, and he loved the bit about the spray-starched hair and the flame-red pantsuit. Pete made me demonstrate the gravelly voice and jujitsu handshake. I told him about the judge's use of esoteric details regarding my parents' involvement in my life to prompt me into choosing one over the other.

Like most theater directors, Pete had a particular affinity for blowsy grande dame characters. As soon as he'd worked up the script, voice, and attitude, he had me play myself and he assumed the starring role of the judge.

Pete played Judge Denman splendidly, better than she did herself. And this made me laugh like crazy. He was having so much fun with his new routine that we did it over and over until he started ad-libbing funny activities from my distant past when I had no details left to offer. Pete couldn't resist adding a fake cigarillo, pretending he was smoking during the interview.

We went for our usual walk, had something to eat, and went shopping. Pete was breaking into his Judge Denman character when talking to waitresses and salespeople. Soon he was Delores to shoppers in the aisle of the grocery store, the cashiers, and even strangers on the street.

In the afternoon, we went over to Russ's house, as we did most weekends, since he'd just be arriving home from the tag sales. Russ would show us the array of jewelry, paintings, lamps, and hats he'd picked up that morning, tell us how much he paid and what he thought he could sell each one for. Though he worked full time as an art teacher at my school and was a well-known local collagist, Russ ran a booth out at Hickey's flea market on Sunday. He had hilarious stories about the other "pickers" fighting over items and haggling over a lamp priced two dollars that he knew was worth more than a hundred. There were often unusual brooches or feather boas that he'd unearthed, and Pete would model these and do some characters and we'd all laugh. Or Russ might perform the opening of *The Glass Menagerie*, where Amanda Wingfield is desperate to sell magazine subscriptions and people fob her off or else hang up the phone. The two also specialized in a lively rendition of the opening song to *The Patty Duke Show*.

Russ would make lemonade, and we'd sit on his front porch discussing all the funny things that people had said and done that week. We'd fight over the butterfly chair, since it was considered to be the most comfortable. Russ had some wacky neighbors, and he'd tell us hilarious stories about his encounters with them, such as the woman who managed to burn her middle finger while taking a casserole out of the oven, and every time she showed it to Russ she'd accidentally give him the finger.

Once we were all settled, Pete unveiled the Delores Denman routine, which by now we had down to a one-act play. I was supposed to act more girlish and innocent than I really am, and Delores would coax and wheedle and then break into this horrible smoker's cough and ask for a shot of whiskey or some bizarre drink like a Grasshopper or Pink Squirrel. Russ laughed so hard that his chair almost toppled off the porch. We had plenty of sketches in our repertoire that we'd built up and enhanced over the years, but this one, although brand new, was already a favorite.

That evening the three of us went to a local restaurant we enjoyed, largely because in the summer the proprietor claimed to have air-conditioning but said it was broken, and in the winter she said the heat was being repaired. Only it had been like that since opening five years before. Pete and Russ and I didn't believe they had either a cooling or heating system, but we'd always politely inquire how the repair work was going and nod understandingly, as if we empathized with the difficulty of finding a good handyman.

Pete broke into his Delores Denman character with the waitress and continued cracking us up. We went down to the waterfront, walked along the pier, and ate ice cream cones while talking and laughing about school and some of the teachers we all knew. A favorite was the home economics instructor, who fancied herself a part-time clairvoyant; she'd invited Pete and Russ to a séance the week before, during which she experienced tremendous flatulence and insisted it was the spirits calling to her.

Finally, I rode my bike home. It had been the most perfect day. It struck me that there are some situations where we have to be responsible for our own happiness. My parents were depressed and upset, and there didn't appear to be anything I could do to remedy that. I tried not to think about the divorce anymore. Same with red pantsuits.

Twenty-Eight

Disappearing Act...The Walkway Less Traveled

Accompanying the conclusion of the trial came a recommenda-
tion that I undergo a full psychiatric evaluation at a local mental
institute known for specializing in the treatment of the criminally
insane. It didn't seem very crazy to me to avoid going on record as preferring one of my parents over the other. However, a receptionist began
calling the house with telemarketer regularity in order to schedule an
appointment. Because this was something proposed by the court, I
feared that if I didn't go, it was grounds for packing me off to reform
school or maybe even jail, since I was now sixteen. Did they not realize
how stressful it would be for an only child to have to join a gang?

I queried Dad about the possibility of getting charged with con-
tempt if I dodged the funny farmers. He asked, "Do you want to go?"

"No way."

"Then tell them to go to hell," he said. It was the only time I'd ever
heard him swear.

Amazingly, all that time my parents spent in the courtroom didn't
result in a divorce, but rather a decision—a decision that slightly favored
my mother, and so my father's lawyer immediately appealed. The case
was now sent to the appellate division in Rochester, New York. And so
we all continued to live together!

However, I was not summoned to testify again. And by this time the
custody battle was asinine. I roamed about like a fox, wherever and whenever I pleased. In less than two years I'd move out and live on my own.

The final divorce decree is dated April 1, 1982. My mother had done okay in the first settlement, but this one largely favored my father. The proceedings took place before the enactment of the equitable-distribution law in New York State, which would make settlements more favorable to long-married women by awarding them closer to half the marital assets in a divorce.

After being married a little more than twenty-three years, there'd be no silver anniversary for the Pedersens. We couldn't have afforded it anyway.

A few days after the divorce was final, I woke to find an empty cave at the end of the hallway. In the same manner that political enemies in totalitarian states disappear in the middle of the night, the movers (or possibly the EPA) had taken Dad at dawn.

The house had always been quiet except for the two typewriters clacking away and the dog barking at passersby. Now it was eerily silent, with Dad gone and Mom working until midnight.

It took four coats of primer and three coats of yellow paint to cover the telltale stains from decades of smoking. While Heather and I painted, the radio played "Summer, Highland Falls," from Billy Joel's new album *Songs in the Attic*. As I slopped paint across the walls the piano man crooned, "These are not the best of times, but they're the only times I've ever known." By the end of the second week, the nicotine had seeped through all the layers of paint.

Dad transplanted himself to a small apartment a few blocks away, where he never bothered to unpack. The silver lining in all this was that as soon as my father had a new address, I was presented with a golden opportunity to end all contact between parents and school under my own version of the Privacy Act, though I preferred to think of it as saving my folks from undue stress and unnecessary paperwork. Not that they'd become overly involved in my education to begin with, but I just didn't care for the idea that particulars about my life might be freely circulating between parents, teachers, and administrators without my approval.

As soon as I had Dad's apartment number, I filled out a change-of-address card at the school office, and from then on everything was sent to his place—referrals, report cards, sign-up sheets for parent-teacher conferences. Now my parents would get their information when, how, and if I chose to relay it to them, which was basically not at all.

Without being asked, Dad automatically handed over anything that arrived from the school, envelopes still sealed, which my mother never would've done, since she's intrigued by everyone else's mail (and phone conversations), describing herself as "naturally curious." Mom's autobiography will most likely be titled *Too Nosy to Die*.

Going forward, holidays meant half a day with my mom's family and half a day with Dad and his girlfriend, who eventually became my stepmother. There were good things about the arrangement: my step-mother has six terrific daughters, and we had lots of fun together. And there were bad things: someone had to drive me to my next gig, and if the meal was running late then that person either had to leave in the middle or else we'd be delayed, thus gumming things up at the other end. On Thanksgiving I had to eat twice to be polite, and when the matriarchs began plate-gazing they'd suspiciously inquire, "Why don't you like the stuffing? Why don't you want ice cream with your pie?" I wanted to say, "Because I'd just had stuffing, pie, and ice cream an hour ago."

In the weeks and months that followed Dad's departure, we realized he'd taken a few things in addition to his typewriters. It was like the story of Abiyoyo that Pete Seeger used to perform in the sixties, about a boy with a magician father (who was also a practical joker) who goes around town making things disappear exactly when people need them. For instance, a man would go to sit down after a hard day's work, and the chair would disappear. We went to plug in a radio and, zhoop! the extension cord was gone. We'd go for a hammer to pound a nail into the wall, and the toolbox was gone. We'd go to play a song on the record player, and the record was gone. At Thanksgiving dinner we went to carve the turkey, and there was no carving knife. It occurred to me to use a saw, but that was gone too.

It wasn't that my father didn't technically own most of these things. It's just that we didn't have two of everything. The only item that raised a question as to who actually bought it was the Neil Diamond album featuring a duet with Barbra Streisand titled "You Don't Bring Me Flowers," which even they had to admit contained a certain amount of irony.

In retrospect, my parents should have gone to a mediator. There were no villains, just victims. The lawyers' bills exceeded half the value of the house. What people often don't realize when it comes to divorce is that they can't make two out of one. It's just not possible to go and create two households that are similar to the one they shared before, unless they're extremely rich or else an amoeba.

❀ ❀ ❀

Our modest brick ranch house was never what one would describe as a showplace. Who could compete with Germans manicuring their lawns to putting-green perfection using nail scissors, Italians who draped everything in plastic, and Poles scrubbing out the stains on their garage floors with acid? Having grown up in this melting pot, I can't imagine where slurs about the sanitary habits of immigrants arose, because I've never seen anything so sparkling clean as the toolshed of a carpenter from Bavaria.

Even when Dad was home, we were the worst-looking lot on the block, with overgrown shrubbery, paint chipping off the trim, and rust-encrusted gutters. It didn't help that the Stankos across the street and the Zavarellas next door were compulsively mowing, weeding, watering, and pruning every day.

Actually, Jenny and Victor Zavarella, the neighbors to our left, were operating an Italian home and garden fit for royalty. Victor worked at the local Ford plant, and his wife was a freelance seamstress. Their place was beyond immaculate. One could have performed surgery in any room of the house, including the garage and basement. Even their two pet rabbits were pristine. When I went over there with my mother, she always warned me ahead of time not to touch anything—not the walls, statues, or even the floor if I could possibly help it. And under no circumstances was I to ask about using the bathroom or accept any food or beverage that may be offered.

But don't take my word for it. The Roman Catholic Church designated the Zavarellas' house as the cleanest and most free from sin in the New World, and thus Our Lady was kept in their basement, complete with paper money tacked all over her white silk gown. I'd never seen anything like Our Lady and thought it was the biggest Barbie doll that Mattel had ever made.

Meantime, our bushes covered much of the windows and a good half of the front porch. Roots from the willow tree were marching on our water system and began making cameo appearances in the sump pump and toilet. The subsistence vegetable garden in the backyard disintegrated into a Darwinian weed patch where only the most pugnacious tomatoes and zucchinis made it to the kitchen. Our roof was blowing off one shingle at a time, while the driveway sank like the *Titanic*.

Once the divorce proceedings were under way there was actually an incentive *not* to make any improvement to the house or grounds, as this could raise the appraised value, and why pour money into something they might lose, or lose half of. At the start of the divorce there was no way of knowing it would take almost four years, so in the meantime the house just collapsed around us.

When an assignment at school called for students to draw their dream homes, kids sketched Spanish haciendas, Italian villas, and palaces by the sea. I drew the Marriott hotel that had recently been built at the end of our street. It was truly my dream home: contractors to do maintenance and landscaping, food delivered to the room, housekeeping service, cable TV, and a pool. Home sweet heaven.

However, the fact that we were a commercial for Dogpatch, USA, didn't bother us. Mom and Dad and I were nocturnal typists and readers, not sun worshippers or members of any garden club. With everyone preoccupied by work, school, and divorce, we hardly noticed the state of our decaying homestead. The way to locate our house in August was to look for the one with the Christmas lights still strung up and the gutters hanging down. The cracks in the driveway, front porch, and garage were quickly becoming crevices, chasms, and then canyons. That didn't include the hole in the garage wall where Mom had created a low, oblong window onto the backyard with the ramming end of the Oldsmobile.

One task that Dad did undertake was to cover the mailbox with grease in an effort to keep away vandals. Blowing up and ripping down mailboxes was big back then—the suburban version of drive-by shootings. Ours was on a corner and made a good target, only it was usually the snowplow and not disaffected youth that destroyed it. Also, Dad finally had to give the heave-ho to the weeping willow tree, which had become a wandering willow, and then a full-out marauding willow. Despite its great shade and beauty, the tree had metamorphosed into something out of *The Little Shop of Horrors*, with paramilitary gangs of roots threatening to commandeer the pipes and water supply for the entire town.

After Dad left, Mom and I really skidded down the slippery slope of homeownership. With our fair skin, we simply chose to stay indoors rather than take notice of what needed to be done outside. And even if we had wanted to tackle the great outdoors, we didn't have the money to do so.

By this time our lives were completely jerry-rigged. One had to know exactly how to jiggle the doorknob to enter the house, push the oven door to close it all the way, and yank the fireplace screen to get it unstuck, and the sink taps required a surgical touch. The car door only closed with the correct velocity and style of swing, and to turn on the windshield wipers we dialed the radio knob. To go up, my window shade needed three tugs in quick succession, hard, but not hard enough to pull it down. The toilet only flushed with the correct lever pressure, and to get the hot and cold water running properly in the shower, we needed to be qualified mechanics. We knew exactly where to hit and kick everything, while visitors were flummoxed to so much as flush a toilet or close a door. Christmas ornaments were attached to the tree with paper clips, and I used masking tape to mend my clothes. Mom and I could both sew a hem easily enough, but when standards are dropping like the mercury in March, seeking shortcuts becomes habit forming.

The doorbell hadn't worked in over a decade, and since Mom had wallpapered over the chimes, it couldn't be fixed. But we didn't really care since we assumed that anyone who didn't know the bell was broken probably shouldn't be ringing it in the first place. On the plus side, it had put an end to being awakened by the Jehovah's Witnesses and their extensive presentation, complete with visual aids, on entering the kingdom of Jesus Christ. The downside was no Sunday morning doughnuts, sold door-to-door by high school sports teams to raise money for uniforms and equipment.

The good thing about a house going to hell is that it happens incrementally and doesn't hit all in one day. Sure, there are small things like the rusted wheelbarrow and pitchfork that could pass for yard art. But sometimes the compulsively tidy Italian neighbors couldn't stand looking at the lawn anymore and came over to mow, edge, and weed the entire property. Embarrassed by this charity and feeling contrite about our laziness, we'd sneak into the car through the garage or wait to leave until the Zavarellas were safely tucked inside their shipshape house. A suburban shame spiral.

In retrospect, our gardening policy was rather environmentally forward-looking. We were naturalists, not the kind who study nature so much as the ones who leave it alone, thus taking the "Don't mess with Mother Nature" adage literally. We didn't weed, prune, water, or use pesticides. We just grew what we needed with as little impact on the ecosystem as possible. We figured that tall grass did a nice job of hiding the dandelions, weeds died at the end of the growing season along with everything else, and dead leaves eventually turned to mulch.

Nor were we a great family of shovelers, like the folk in and around Buffalo who view snow as a personal challenge. The way that caring for grass is the Summer Olympics for many men, snow removal is Buffalo's competitive winter sport.

No, Mom and I took a much more holistic approach: that the sun would eventually melt the snow one flake at a time come spring. In the meantime we just had to back the Oldsmobile out of the driveway at about fifty miles an hour in order to pack down a good hard track. As for the sidewalks, we were on a grammar-school route, and the first hundred or so kids trampled that down just fine.

266

During the winter months we didn't bother with the front door at all, because this meant digging out the front stoop and the front walk. However, we did like to send the dog out through the front door rather than traipse through the cold garage on a winter night. So we'd put our aging poodle, Fifi, out into the snow on the porch, she'd go to the bathroom, and come back inside.

The problem with this scheme was that by April we had a lot of fertilizer on the front porch and front walk. It was actually a minefield of dog debris until the spring rains did their job, and by June or July we had a fully functioning front walk again. In the meantime, friends and family knew to go around to the back door. And the Jehovah's Witnesses skipped our house entirely.

The only person who braved the front walk every day was Mike, the paperboy. He was exceptionally bright and athletically talented, and we were in the same class at high school. After graduation, Mike would attend Princeton and land a tryout for the Washington Redskins.

Mike had an assistant named Jimmy who was slightly retarded and eventually took over the paper route. The first week that Jimmy did the route on his own, we didn't get a paper. My mother phoned and was told that we did receive a paper. It was the middle of winter, and she assumed it had blown away. However, the next day she found the paper tucked inside the back door that exited from the garage, which we never used in winter because it was more or less snowed and iced closed from October to June.

The following day, when we saw Jimmy approaching the house with his wagon of papers, my mother said, "Jimmy, would you please deliver the paper to the front door so I don't have to go through the cold garage?"

Jimmy shook his head and my mother assumed that his mental problems left him uncomprehending of her directive. She explained again, this time very slowly. Jimmy shook his head. He pointed at the front walk and said, "Dog shit!"

From that day forward we shoveled the front walk every day during the winter.

Twenty-Nine

Are Red and Green Making You Blue?

Catholic Charities posted the above title on a billboard along the expressway on the way into downtown Buffalo every December. To which my mother, who's been known to put the *dark* in *dark Irish* answered back, "Merry Fucking Christmas."

Christmas at our house had always been a subdued affair, even before my father moved out. We'd have a tree, real or plastic, depending on how much the cat had peed in the box while the latter was stored in the basement. And my mother would light Burberry candles and cook dinner for us and her two siblings.

However, the Christmas following my dad's departure was particularly bleak. Between the ever-present dismal economy and dividing the household, spending was drastically curtailed. If that wasn't bad enough, the hospital employing my mother was about to retrench and hundreds would be laid off.

Mom can sometimes be one of those glass-is-half-empty people. If we saw a person my age smoking, she offered to take me over to the nearby Roswell Cancer Institute and show me patients with emphysema puffing cigarettes through tracheotomy tubes. And whenever a motorcycle roared past she reminded me that this was a one-way ticket to a head injury and, most likely, permanent brain damage. The thinning of the herd, if you will. In her book, these foolhardy motorcycle enthusiasts represented a constant stream of organ donors to the more evolved of the species.

And she hasn't mellowed with age. A few winters ago, in subzero weather, Mom was at the public library when a flasher rapped on the window and, after getting her attention, exposed himself. She turned, looked him up and down, mouthed, "You're going to contract bronchial pneumonia," and went back to her book.

Anyway, two days before the dreaded Yuletide, Mom arrived home from work and unloaded a box of handmade drawings, paintings, and sculptures that her patients had presented as gifts—crazy-looking stuff, which would be added to a growing pile of psychiatric art projects.

And that's when she unveiled her Christmas austerity program, her subcontract with America. The red arrow on the thermostat was pushed down to fifty-eight, which she insisted would be good for our complexions.

The next morning, in the shadow of our two-foot-tall aluminum tree, absent of presents, Mom announced her Christmas wish: "To keep my job, buy a self-cleaning bathtub, and not have the crappiest car in the hospital parking lot." The pine aroma came from a ninety-nine-cent aerosol can, a lot cheaper than a genuine blue spruce. She wasn't in the best of spirits, having just trapped me drinking milk directly out of the carton and unmoved by my argument that I was saving wear and tear on the drinking glasses. After all, the whole point of being an only child is to be able to drink out of milk cartons. I couldn't resist asking, "So am I an only child due to an earlier budget cut?"

The night before, I'd parked a brownie for Santa next to the fireplace. When it wasn't there the next morning, I noticed a trail of crumbs leading to Fifi's bed. Of course, I had stopped believing in Santa around the age of eight, after I received a check from the tooth fairy. Still, I figured chances for receiving more presents were better by playing along. Was I ever wrong. I hadn't banked on the seriousness of our plight until I saw Mom crisping the free turkey she'd gotten from the hospital in a brown paper bag because aluminum roasting pans cost too much. Any gifts I might want, she told me, would have to wait until the after-Christmas sales.

We were expecting the usual crowd for dinner: Mom's sister and brother, his current girlfriend, and a string of people who were the parents of his former girlfriends, who had somehow settled in as regulars at our place despite their offspring having moved on.

I spent the morning making Lauralogs out of old newspapers and twine, in lieu of the more festive and costlier Duraflames with their artificial color crystals.

As I would first be visiting my father at his girlfriend's house for brunch on Christmas Day, Mom asked me whether I could cadge some leftovers to serve later, at our shindig.

When we finally sat down to dinner, I noticed, among other things, that Welch's strawberry jam was substituting for cranberries. And when I said, "Please pass the rolls," I was told there weren't any.

Defiantly, Mom looked around the table and asked, "Does anyone else want rolls?" She had the inflection of an interrogator trying to get the suspects to give up the location of HQ.

The guests vigorously shook their heads no while busily rearranging the turkey on their plates, and conversation fell into a coma. Aunt Sue finally broke the tension by saying, "I think I read somewhere that rolls are bad for you."

The next day, the *Buffalo News* carried a big article reporting that the art world was going gaga over sculpture and paintings produced by the mentally ill, dubbed "Art by the Insane" at the time. (Nowadays it is titled the politically correct catchall "Outsider Art.") And some of it was fetching prices that were utterly insane. Mom was ecstatic that something had finally gone her way. She even turned the heat back up.

We went to church the following Sunday, and perhaps it did some good because all Mom's New Year's resolutions eventually came true. She no longer has the worst car in the parking lot, she eventually retired without losing her job, and ever since I moved out of the house, the ring around the bathtub has gone for good.

Thirty

In All Probability

Although I didn't know exactly what a Wall Street trader did before visiting the stock exchange, in retrospect there were a number of clues that I'd become one. Dad started me collecting coins back when I was four or five. He elaborated on the art and science of being a numismatist—the various mint marks, design changes throughout the years, how pennies were made of silver during World War II, and why coins containing mistakes were especially valuable.

However, waiting fifty years while a 1945 Lincoln cent minted in San Francisco doubled in value was too long a timeline for me. Much more interesting was the stock market, where a new issue worth twenty-five cents might trade at five dollars a week later. I'd noticed the same thing could happen with metals. Gold was three hundred dollars per ounce, and I certainly couldn't afford that. Silver was only ten dollars an ounce, and so whenever I had some cash, I'd invest in a bar or two. Little did I know it was the start of the greatest silver boom since Mark Twain had moved west to seek his fortune as a miner back in the 1860s.

During the government gold auction of 1979, demand was greater than expected. The second energy crisis brought with it a new round of double-digit inflation, and bullion prices went through the roof. Silver rocketed from ten dollars an ounce to fifty, further fueled by Arabs purchasing silver in bulk with freshly minted petrodollars and an attempted takeover of the market by the Hunt brothers of Texas.

I sold some of my stockpile near the top, signaled by the immigrants in Buffalo delivering heirloom tea sets, the only thing they'd managed to bring from the Old Country, to the smelter, solely for the value of the metal. But I didn't sell all of it, and that was my first lesson in trading—what goes up can go down, and at a substantially faster rate than it went up. The market crashed within a few months. I also learned that when a market is plummeting, everyone is a seller.

Every summer, Dad and I left for our two-week Long Island pilgrimage to visit Grandpa Hjalmar, who was now in his eighties, though in excellent shape. He wore aviator sunglasses, still drove a bronze Camaro, swam in the ocean every morning from June until September, and juggled calls from women all day long.

Grandpa would drive an hour from his home in Huntington to meet us in Hampton Bays, where we'd rent a condo and spend most of our time at the beach, or shooting pool when it rained. In the evening, Dad and Grandpa barbecued, and between the smoke from their steaks, Dad's cigarettes, and Grandpa's cigars, it's amazing the fire department wasn't called out. At night, my objective was to fall asleep before the two smokers did, since they could take the roof off with their snoring.

The world was much more tolerant toward smokers back then, even if my mother was not. They could puff away in movie theaters, restaurants, malls, and on airplanes. Basically, the only place they couldn't smoke was in the rooms and corridors of a hospital, though the visitors' lounge was fine. The world was their ashtray.

In Hampton Bays we had a neighbor named Bill Reese who was in his seventies and comfortably retired. Most of his career had been spent working on the floor of the American Stock Exchange. Bill and I would sit on the veranda for hours and talk about the market. He explained how to determine where a stock was headed based on price movement and volume, rather than what was going on with the company. Bill also taught me how to dive off the end of the dock, not a bad thing to know if eventually heading for Wall Street.

One day when I was fourteen years old, I shared with Bill my plan to catch a train into Manhattan and head over to the visitors' gallery of the New York Stock Exchange. He suggested stopping at the American Stock Exchange and handed me a note with the names of some of his old cronies.

There were six people on the list that I presented to the guard. Two were dead, which should have been a clue right there that I was interested in a dangerous business. Three were retired. And the last one the guard wasn't able to find. Just as I was about to leave, the son of the man we couldn't find showed up at the door because he had heard a page and shared the name, Joe Petta, with his father. (Back then if someone yelled Joey, Louie, or Vinnie on the floor of the AMEX, twenty guys looked up.)

Anyway, Joe gave me an oversized broker's jacket to cover my shorts and escorted me down onto the trading floor. A huge, neon green ticker tape crawled across the walls high above us, and the latest business news scrolled down a large board next to it. People were shouting, arguing, signaling, and generally racing around like maniacs, a few taking large bites of sandwiches as they scurried past. Suddenly one would stop, look up toward the balcony, cup a hand to the side of his mouth, and let fly what must be akin to a wild-moose mating call. It was glorious! I wanted to return as soon as possible.

My school offered an elective class on economics, but it was very basic, along the lines of "What is a stock?" During sophomore year of high school, I rode my bike to the nearby University of Buffalo and asked the admissions office if I might take economics classes there. They said no because I didn't have a high school diploma, which was required for entrance.

However, I was determined to treat the word *no* as a request for more information. What did they have to lose, I politely asked the woman. I was willing to pay my way. If I flunked out then that was that. And no matter what happened, I wasn't a matriculated student and couldn't ruin any of their published statistics.

Eventually I was granted provisional acceptance and signed up for macroeconomics. The class was great, though the Indian teacher was a bit difficult to understand. He'd put scads of numbers on the board and then tell us to "dehttermine" the answer. I'd taken algebra and geometry, but this appeared to be some fancy logarithm he was after, one I hadn't yet been taught. When I glanced around the room, sixty other faces looked equally perplexed. After a few classes it hit us that he wanted us to "determine" the answer.

Oh, and he *loved* shoes. We're talking all-out fetishist. Every single supply-and-demand example involved thousands of shoes changing hands, or feet, as the case may be. Being from India, maybe he didn't approve of the traditional economics examples of guns and butter—perhaps guns were reminiscent of colonialism and butter off-limits as a by-product of the sacred cow.

Thirty-One

Home Alone

My parents seem to have borrowed most of their child-rearing procedures directly from nature—training the offspring to be independent and self-sufficient as early as possible. Mom and Dad wanted me capable of feeding, dressing, and transporting myself at an early age, not so much as a reprieve for themselves, but because this was in my own best interest. Same with personal safety.

Back when Dad was in basic training, before heading off to Korea, they taught him hand-to-hand combat, along with the art of digging foxholes. As I was an only child and Mom was going back to school to start a career, it became clear to Dad early on that I would be alone in our house more and more as the years passed. So he decided some self-defense classes were in order.

Though we lived in a sleepy suburb, strange things were known to happen. Occasionally there'd be a string of robberies, or kids playing in the nearby woods would stumble across a dead body. There were mental hospitals and prisons in the area, and patients and inmates would occasionally escape.

Dad's first piece of advice if I found myself in a dangerous situation was to simply get out of the house as fast as possible and run for help. We are not a family that goes looking for fights and danger in general, much preferring a quiet room, a good book, and a chocolate bar. In fact, young Pedersens are built for fleeing, with the long, lean bodies that track teams covet. We're built for speed, not comfort, as declared in the Pedersen family motto: This body may not be much to look at, but it sure does work. This is fine for a girl, so long as at age thirty-six you don't mind having lifeguards at water parks yelling, "Hey, mister, take off your shirt!"

So Dad made it clear that if I ever heard anyone entering the house, I should be in the business of exiting the house through a door or window, whatever was closest. Phone calls to the police could be made from the home of a neighbor. Don't hide under the bed or in a closet, don't try to prevent a crime, just get out!

However, there might be a time when I'd come face-to-face with a criminal and not be able to escape, such as if I was sleeping or doing something in the basement and the exit was blocked. Dad showed me three ways that a young girl could attack a large man with her bare hands. Thinking kickboxing and karate, I assumed Dad was going to take me out back and teach me chops and feints.

No chance, Grasshopper. Dad said the martial arts were fine as hobbies, but eight-year-old, eighty-pound me wasn't going to be giving any burglar a knockout back-fist blow.

The first move he taught me involved extending two fingers and driving them directly into an opponent's windpipe as hard as humanly possible. Without air and a way to breathe, criminals apparently lose their effectiveness. The next maneuver required making one's hand very flat and then smashing the butt of the palm up under the intruder's nose. This is rumored to be quite painful and inhibits further motion. It can also result in immediate death. The final self-defense tactic was taking two fingers and poking them directly into the maniac's eyeballs, creating a Greek tragedy right there in the comfort of your own living room.

Dad was a pacifist and not into guns, knives, and killing in general, but he was well aware of their usefulness in certain situations. We never kept a real gun or bowie knife in the house. He said that most of the time they ended up being used against you. But when I was eight, Dad did provide me with a life-size and properly weighted replica of a handgun. He pounded some fishing sinkers into the barrel so it appeared to be fully loaded. Even Uncle Jim, who worked as a police reporter, thought the replica was convincing.

Dad said the best use of the fake gun was to hit someone over the head with it as he walked through the door. But if that wasn't possible, I shouldn't pretend to be in a spaghetti Western and point it at the robber using one hand. Instead, Dad showed me how to firmly plant my feet, hold the gun out in front of me with two hands, aim it at the intruder (so he can be sure to see the "bullets"), and then start to shake my hands as if I was having a seizure. Dad says there is nothing more frightening to an adult than a scared kid with a handgun. And at this point, if the intruder has any regard at all for his own life, he will abandon the mission.

Even though Dad gave me this "gun" to keep in my night-table drawer, his weapon of choice was a wooden baseball bat, which I kept right next to my bed. (I eventually added a carving knife to my cache, thinking that after killing someone it might be necessary to draw and quarter him.)

Once again, we went out in the backyard, and Dad demonstrated how to conduct oneself when using a baseball bat for self-defense. In my eyes, the obvious move was to bonk someone over the head or let him have it across the chest, as if hitting a line drive, but once again Dad said no.

The best use of a bat, according to Dad, is to point it forward and drive it directly into the sternum of the opponent as hard as possible, thereby removing the person's air supply and hopefully sending him over backward and to the ground in the process. (I noticed some cross-over here with my mother's first-aid training, where one always checks the airway and breathing first.)

Speaking of the sternum, Dad explained that should any of the hand-to-hand combat or batting techniques result in a victim with a bit of fight left in him, once he is on the ground, simply place the heel of a foot on the sternum and step down hard. Dad put his hand on my sternum and pressed ever so slightly, and I could feel the discomfort. (Once again, I was very familiar with the sternum as a result of my mother's enduring devotion to the Heimlich maneuver.) Unwanted visitor still being pesky? Then place weight on the heel and snap the bone right off. If the person doesn't die, then at least he's been put out of the breaking-and-entering business for several weeks.

Dad reviewed these safety procedures fairly regularly. Occasionally he would decide on a slight modification. Overall, I felt confident that I could protect myself in most any situation. Dad maintained that it had been proven again and again that a small person could overtake a large person, even if the assailant was stronger and carrying a weapon. But the secret lay in not doing any of the things seen in the movies, because the real and most effective ways to kill a person do not make for interesting film footage, and thus are not regularly performed on the silver screen. I took him at his word. The only other defense I knew would have been to try to get the intruder to eat my mother's pork chops.

Finally, my skills were put to the test when I was fifteen, a five-foot-nine soccer player with stevedore shoulders and the night radar of a junkyard dog. My room was an armed camp, equipped with baseball bat, fake gun, knife, slingshot, and guard poodle. Dad was living in his apartment a few blocks away, and Mom was working the night shift. It was after midnight, and I'd just crawled into bed with Fifi.

Some people might think I'd want a rottweiler or a Doberman for protection. But ask any cat burglar who landed in prison and he'll say a yappy Yorkshire terrier or teacup poodle is basically a criminal's worst nightmare, barking away from under the couch or bed—can't get to them, can't shut them up, can't hit them, can't poison them. In fact, poodles are so smart some of them have gone for help. Small dogs are the smoke detectors of household burglary—they sound the first alert so that professional crime fighters can take over.

I heard the front door rattling, and Fifi and I both leapt up. Could Mom be coming home early from work? Sure, but she had the car and always came in through the garage. Could my friend Mary be coming to sleep over, borrow shampoo, or make a late-night snack? Entirely possible, but she knew where we hid the key and would have been inside by now, poking her head in my bedroom to wake me up.

The door continued to rattle, and the string of Tibetan bells that hung from the knob jingled as they smacked against it. Even when the door was nudged ever so slightly they tinkled. This was Mom's contribution to safety. Though I'm pretty sure their original purpose was to keep track of me.

Grabbing my trusty wooden baseball bat I ran toward the front door. The knob was obviously being jimmied, and as it wobbled, the bells continued to ring. Fifi came to assist, though more for moral support than anything else. At fourteen, her senses were okay but her teeth were a distant memory.

There was a chair next to the front door on which we kept the newspapers. I climbed on top of it and stood just opposite the door so that when and if it opened I had a clear shot at the intruder's skull.

Finally the door was unlocked. The knob turned freely. I went into my windup, took a deep breath, and raised the bat high above my head. The door inched open. A man's head appeared. I began to lower my bat.

"Gadzooks!" my father and I both yelled at the exact same moment, me just averting my swing to miss cracking his head wide open.

"What the heck are you doing?" he asked, more terrified than mad.

"What the heck are *you* doing?" I asked. "It's one o'clock in the morning, and I'm here alone."

"I'm stopping to pick up my mail. Is it that late?" he asked and glanced down at his watch. "Betty and I were playing Scrabble and must have lost track of the time."

I climbed down from the chair, and we walked into the kitchen where his mail was kept in a pile on the counter. Normally he picked it up after work.

"You almost killed me," he said, nerves not quite calmed after such a near miss.

"You got that right," I said. "Just like you taught me."

The following week I was on my own again when, around nine, the phone rang. It was Dad. He was leaving Betty's house and wanted to stop by to pick up his mail on the way home. Fifteen minutes later I heard something banging against the front window and thought maybe it was a broken tree branch. Then I heard a man's voice, "It's me! I'm coming for the mail!"

As I walked toward the window in the dining room there was a knock at the front door. Now the voice was coming from the front porch. "It's me, your father. I'm coming to get the mail!"

I headed toward the front door and shouted, "All clear!"

He knocked once more before opening the door and then carefully peered inside before entering.

Just like in the wild, if human parents do their job correctly, they train their young to displace their elders and become responsible for the future of the tribe.

Thirty-Two

It Could Be Worse

My parents may not have had much in common, but they did share an outlook typical of the era in which they were raised—a strong work ethic combined with low expectations and a sense of impending doom.

Like many immigrants from Northern Europe, Mom and Dad possessed a fatalistic attitude. My mother's Celtic ancestry combined with my dad's Nordic psyche didn't exactly suggest that the sun will come out tomorrow. They are not excitable people, and neither am I. We do not become enthusiastic over vacations, celebrations, or emergencies. Our internal mechanism automatically assumes that something will go wrong at any moment and we'll all die or cause the needless deaths of countless others. My mother can always be found locating the fire exits. Ask my dad how he's doing, and he'll say that he got up this morning.

Both of my parents grew up during hard times. The thirties were the years of breadlines, soup kitchens, and hoboes riding the rails, and the forties of food and gas rationing and victory gardens. Working-class people were conditioned by circumstances to gird themselves for the worst. When nothing terrible happened they seemed surprised, and when anything remotely good happened they were suspicious that the bad news was still lurking around the corner. Waiting for the other shoe to drop is the popular sport played by people of my parents' generation, who were raised with the mentality of trying to get by with the hope that their children would do a little bit better, God willing.

No one expected much from my parents professionally, and they didn't expect much from themselves, other than to make a living. Growing up, they were products of the nation's "proud poor"—a large percentage of Americans, many with immigrant roots, who made do with whatever was available and tried to be responsible citizens. In other words, they treated all comers politely whether anyone was watching or not. When people didn't have money, good jobs, education, or family ties, they could still take pride in their civility. Like good grammar and the air they breathed, it was free.

My parents didn't have any expectations for me either. After telling me to be a decent human being, they viewed my destiny as entirely out of their hands. I quickly realized that I wasn't the brightest or the prettiest. Not in the world, in the country, in my school, or even on my block. Many of the kids in my class were much smarter, and a few were even headed to Harvard, Princeton, and Dartmouth.

Yet there was still one road to success that was wide open: hard work. I'd have to start young, rise early, and stay up late. And even that might not be enough.

My parents' stressful jobs were constant reminders that money came the hard way. There would be no inheritance. When I graduated high school, both my parents were in debt, mostly from the divorce; they certainly weren't extravagant in their spending. If anything, it was the opposite. They drove old cars with lots of mechanical problems and wore the same clothes, coats, and shoes year in and year out.

In high school, my grades were mostly As, a surprise most of all to myself after a dismal elementary school performance. My friends and I felt as if we weren't pulling our weight around the house if we didn't do well in school. Our parents liked to remind us that going to work, keeping a roof over our heads, and putting food on the table was their job, and doing well in school was our job. And most of us saw our parents working very, very hard, coming home exhausted, and yet barely making ends meet. There were conversations about what to spend money on—if we cut down the dead tree (which is about to fall on the house) then we can't afford new tires for the car. Difficult choices constantly had to be made. Bills were occasionally left to mature as if they were bottles of wine.

There were numerous Norman Rockwell and *Leave It to Beaver* moments in our neighborhood—caroling, stringing popcorn for the tree, moms baking in kitchens, dads building go-carts in driveways— but we didn't grow up completely sheltered. Most of us had an older sibling or cousin who'd become involved with drugs or alcohol or who'd had an unwanted pregnancy to deal with. Some had returned from Vietnam with a lot of problems.

The city of Buffalo was rife with drugs, prostitution, racketeering, gambling, vandalism, and vagrancy. When I was growing up, almost one-third of the population received public assistance. And living only six miles from downtown, most of us saw bums, winos, and hookers as we were taken to department stores, government office buildings, and theaters.

If one didn't manage to see the crime-ridden East Side or the mafia-controlled West Side up close, we still heard stories; everyone had a relative who was a cop, a fireman, a social worker, or a lawyer working in the city. They told us about abandoned children, drug-addicted mothers, domestic violence, and the prostitutes down on Chippewa Street. We managed to put two and two together—if a person didn't go to school and didn't work hard, the concrete jungle was waiting for them.

My own small family provided an excellent window onto the wider world—Dad heard it all in the courtroom, Mom had patients living on the city streets and made home visits in the most blighted areas, Uncle Jim worked as a police reporter, and Aunt Sue was by then a schoolteacher at an alternative Buffalo high school (the last stop before reform school or jail).

Mom's coworker recounted the tale of two cops who took turns going up in the firefighters' cherry picker, trying to talk a suicide off a ledge on the coldest day of the year. After six hours of going up and down, one of the freezing cops muttered, "For Christ's sake, just jump already." The man did.

There was the woman picked up for prostitution who insisted she had to go to the hospital. (My uncle explained that everyone who is arrested attempts to be taken to the hospital rather than the jail because it is more comfortable.) The cops were understandably cynical about such requests. "Why do you need to go to the hospital?" asked one officer.

"Because I'm having flames in my eucharist," was the woman's reply.

Similarly, a drug dealer who demanded an emergency-room visit claimed that he was "suffering from multiple confusions of the upper body."

My favorite story was about a man who went to the police station to report being bitten by a dog. In the seventies, Buffalo was one of the few cities where dog bites still had to be reported. The man told the clerk at the police station that a neighbor's Dalmation had bitten him. The clerk on duty was not a strong speller, and so he began to write D-A-L-L. But he crossed that out and began again with D-A-H. That didn't look right either, so he scratched it out. After one more false start, the form was becoming messy, and so in big letters he wrote, "FIRE DOG" and that was the end of that.

Aunt Sue had summers off from teaching, and when she wasn't working at Bethlehem Steel, before it closed, or teaching summer school, she went court watching. Court watching was practiced by inner-city neighborhood organizations to ensure that when drug dealers and pimps were arrested, charges were actually pressed or the perpetrators were sent to treatment programs, and not simply released back onto the street, which happened to be the same street my aunt lived on.

Mary's dad, a detective for United States Customs, would show us the lockers containing all the drugs confiscated from people trying to smuggle them into the country over the Peace Bridge.

The bridge to Canada was only a few minutes from downtown Buffalo. Whereas we were only ninety minutes from Toronto by car, New York City was almost an eight-hour drive. We could ride or walk across the bridge whenever we wanted. The sidewalk was narrow, the bridge was steep, and there was usually some construction under way.

When I rode my bike over it to go to the racetrack on the Canadian side, the journey would become very surreal. On my left, huge trucks would quake and rumble past, spewing gravel at me and occasionally even touching my arm. On my right, far below, was the swirling water of the Niagara River. I accelerated toward Canada, since it was downhill and there was no way to brake without losing control, all the while considering whether I wanted to die under a Mack truck or by falling over the ledge and plunging several hundred feet into the mighty Niagara. It passed through my mind that it might be fun to have a place in the history books as the first person to go over the falls on a ten-speed bicycle.

Thirty-Three

The (Sweet) Home Stretch...Faking It

As it does with many students, senioritis hit hard. Junior year of high school I was busy. There were advanced placement classes and chemistry labs and college admissions tests—the SAT, the ACT, and achievement tests. There were college applications, that pesky driver's test, and a class ring to order. It was one thing after another. Most of them required money.

So I started a new business that year: writing term papers for cash. It was still a decade before the Internet, and thus impossible to patch something together using search engines and websites, or just outright purchase a paper online. In fact, only one boy even owned a computer back then. Arlan was head of the nerd herd, our *Hobbit*-carrying *Dungeons and Dragons* aficionado and connoisseur of *A Hitchhiker's Guide to the Galaxy*. Check under *Middle Earth* in the phone book, and he'll probably be there.

I'd write papers by hand, and the only job of the purchaser was to copy it over in his or her own writing. I charged twenty-five dollars for an A, twenty dollars for a B, and fifteen dollars for a C, and could almost always get within half a grade of what I'd promised. However, there were no refunds for half-grade differentials.

This enterprise had a unique set of challenges. First, there were the knuckle draggers who turned in the papers without rewriting them, as if the teacher wasn't going to pick up on a dramatic shift in penmanship. And though the customer was now screwed, my identity was safe because there were around two thousand kids in the school, far too many to undertake a handwriting analysis. Also, the teacher's first guess would have been that it was recycled from an older brother or sister. As for snitching and turning me in, forget it. The kids who bought term papers may not have been good students, but they never ratted anyone out. Still, they were slow to comprehend that after flunking a class all year it isn't realistic to suddenly turn in an A paper. They constantly wanted to pay top dollar for A papers, and I actually had to talk them into the more reasonable and lower-priced B and C models.

The business finally became too hellish. One of the English teachers, Don Rydell, assigned *The Caine Mutiny* by Herman Wouk to all five of his classes, at least a hundred kids. Forget writing about the 560-page tome; nobody would even read it. I realized too late that I could have easily doubled my prices on that fiction fiasco. As it was, I stayed up every night until 2:00 AM scribbling away about nasty old Captain Queeg, using every study guide available. By the fifth paper, I'd exhausted all the symbolism, having done everything with that quart of strawberries short of turning it into shortcake. Although it had been a profitable voyage, I never wanted to hear the name Willie Keith or the words *court martial* ever again.

Writing about *The Caine Mutiny* is the closest thing I've ever had to a religious experience. When, after handing in the last of the papers, I went to my Unitarian church, guess who was the visiting minister for the summer? None other than Don Rydell, the English teacher who'd assigned *The Caine Mutiny* in the first place. During every sermon I couldn't help but wonder if he was looking straight at me and contemplating a church martial.

My only total walk in the park during high school, aside from gym and health class, was French. My teacher, Mr. DePass, concentrated more on planning cheese parties, making a good *bouche de noel*, and playing Monopoly *en français* rather than teaching vocabulary and verb conjugation. Though I knew it was wrong, I rather appreciated this focus on our social lives during the midst of an otherwise full academic schedule, especially the trip to Quebec, weeks off for quiche-cooking competitions at area colleges, and the many, many fondue parties.

Unfortunately, after three years of recipes and reading about fashion and celebrities in his copies of *Paris Match* magazine, we were faced with the New York State Regents Exam in French. Fortunately the first part was oral and we had Monsieur DePass to guide us. He'd read some French gibberish that was supposedly a scene or dialogue. The only words I recognized were *s'il vous plaît*, and that was only from saying, "Pass the hors d'oeuvres, please" at parties. (Though with my pronunciation of *hors d'oeuvres* sounded more like "horses ovaries.")

Next, he read aloud the questions. For instance, he'd ask if Sylvia was at the movies, the school, or the pool. However, he would place an extreme emphasis on the correct choice. Also, prior to the exam, Mr. DePass kept stressing that we were allowed to ask for help during the exam if we didn't understand the question. He was, of course, not allowed to tell us the answer (*oh, mon dieu!*), but it said right in the proctor's guidebook that he could answer questions about the question if we didn't understand it. Though I don't know how the hell we were supposed to understand any of the questions since they were all in French!

Anyway, he basically went around the room pointing to the right answers. The essay was another matter. We had to memorize a few paragraphs of text word for word right before going in, immediately spew it onto the paper, and then find some way to make it fit by strategically plugging in the names we saw in the question. Most of us couldn't even figure out what the question was in the first place. But thanks to Mr. DePass's generous grading system, voilà, we all passed.

When senior year began, I had more free time. So I imagined myself a sort of Renaissance student and signed up for first-year Latin, with the notion that it would serve as a lifelong vocabulary aid and allow me to watch the original *Spartacus* starring Laurence Olivier. Almost any time a grown-up defined a word, they knowingly insisted that studying Latin had made this extraordinary feat possible.

However, it quickly became apparent that the only Latin teacher, a man, didn't appreciate the girls as much as he did the boys, and I feared a bad grade would ruin my high average, which was necessary to maintain for college scholarships. When it came time for the Latin award, there'd oftentimes be a girl practically jumping out of her seat right before the winner was announced because she maintained the best average, perfect attendance, and had flawlessly completed every homework assignment. Then, out of nowhere, a boy's name would be called and a strapping young athlete would stride to the stage and collect the certificate. The Latin teacher always made it very clear in his presentation that the award wasn't just for good grades, but also for participation.

I thought I'd also tackle physics, even though a fourth year of science wasn't required. There was all sorts of talk about the cosmos back then. Carl Sagan was riding high, and I wanted to be ready to live on Mars, especially as it didn't appear to receive any direct sunlight. However, my teacher turned out to fancy himself an upstate New York incarnation of the Dalai Lama. He took the liberty of writing the following memo to his students. (Spelling, punctuation, and grammar are in their original form.)

To My Students 9/21/82

I've been setting here working on communication with your for about two hours.

We have a problem where I see parts of our world very clearly and I am working to be your teacher.

My world view is in pictures. My average mind moves through the pictures of our physical and behavior world at about the speed that you leaf through a bunch of photographs.

For me as a high school physics teacher this is a beautiful but lonely world view. Other teachers and administrator have not learned this clarity of a physical world view (or behavioral world view).

As I was writing and listening to music, the song kodakrome was played on WBUF-FM. The words said "When I think of all the crap I learned in high school, it is a wonder I can think at all."

I wonder if you see the problem of our culture that the song is talking about?

Background

I grew up in a farm town. We had a two room school. My life was rich and exciting. We raised plants and animals. Every day we were in nature (out in the field). We played hunted, fished, ice scated, sledded, swam, trapped, hunted and built things.

School was a distraction from a very exciting life. I failed first and seventh grade. When I got through Jr. High I turned 16 and quit.

I went on the road till I turned seventeen and then jointed the Air Force.

They gave me tests that told them I was not a dumb as my teachers had led me to believe. Note that I did not need my teacher's approval to feel good about my self.

My life has continued to grow by just doing what was interesting to me.

At 43 my clarity on human behavior and the physical world are beyond what the people I'm in contact with understand.

I see how our culture disables people. Operationally by this I mean I see the attitudes and distractions that you use to disable your potential for growing and seeing clearly. I see your lack of confidence.

The problem of caring about you and trying to help you is almost more than I can deal with.

I have only one friend that sees the problem as clearly as I do. That is John Marvin III.

John and I talk about once a month. Without that sharing I would leave teaching.

If I am able to function this year some of you will be on your way to seeing clearly. (Maybe some of you are already)

I can see a world filled with people that see you clearly. If you want to you can learn physics from me. Your sincerity and honest feed back on where you are at will help me function and direct your attention.

Don't worry about me or my being heavy. I respect you as soverign beings and ask the same in return.

Please understand that you are not fully baked yet. You need to trust me to learn. You will only be able to evaluate me as your teacher after the fact of the experience.

If you think I'm "out to lunch" or not acting in your best interest, confront me. If I don't respect you or am insensitive demand these things.

I demand them of you.

> Please understand that clarity is threatening to damaged
> people. They are afraid that they will be seen to be as ugly
> by others as they see themselves. They will try to create
> turmoil.

> Don't miss understand my evaluation of other students,
> teachers and administrators. Many of them help as much
> as they are able. Many of them have good intentions.

This musing about being "not fully baked yet" led a few of us, myself included, to wonder if our science teacher had been baked too long, if his mind had been opened too wide. Prior to Memogate, he simply spent the class time rambling about life according to gestalt and how he'd spent the weekend stacking beer cans. I was pretty sure he was sanity challenged. On the other hand, I assumed the school would have twigged on by now and removed him from the classroom, at the very least. But who was I to be evaluating crazy people when my parents were both crazy and a court had recently declared me legally crazy?

The Manifesto arrived during the fifth week of senior year and ultimately answered the question of whether to drop his class for reasons of insanity. However, when I went down to the guidance office they wouldn't let me escape without issuing a permanent grade of F, because it was slightly past the deadline for dropping without penalty. This would mean good-bye scholarships, grade point average, class standing, and the chance of being accepted at a good college.

I argued that it took me six weeks to figure out that he was nuts. We were supposed to be studying physics, not psychosis. They suggested changing to the other physics teacher, but he was also well known for being nuttier than a squirrel's dowry.

The situation was a drag, particularly because it was the first time I had to bring my mother in to fight a battle for me. And it annoyed my mom that she had to waste time on such nonsense. She had to deal with enough crazies at work. Mom informed the principal that: (1) She was a psychiatric nurse; (2) The physics teacher was certifiable and shouldn't be near children; (3) She'd be happy to turn the Manifesto over to the editor of the local newspaper and see what he thought of it; and (4) How dare they waste her time with such nonsense?

The principal surely realized that if he wanted to take on this fight it would be necessary to do a lot more than just tighten his helmet and adjust his cup. Suddenly I was out. No penalty.

I left the class, but my teacher remained. He'd eventually be demoted to hall monitor before the mother ship finally came back for him and he was able to resume using his real name, Gordzikon 16. It was just about impossible to get rid of a public-school teacher in those days. The principal my mother reeducated would come out of the closet as a gay man on Rochester radio a few years later. How much of a surprise this was to his wife and kids, who lived in the district, I don't know. The other physics teacher, whose class I didn't switch to, was later dismissed and convicted of sexually harassing several of his students. Those were the days.

❋ ❋ ❋

After dropping Latin and physics, I no longer had enough classes to qualify as a student. However, by assisting the blind Spanish teacher, I was able to pick up the necessary credits. That was actually fun because she was chairperson of the Language Department, therefore I was able to see all faculty correspondence and even write evaluations of the teachers. Even better, she and her husband had two children with upcoming birthday parties and they needed a magician.

However, I never squealed on Mr. DePass for his party planning and being a full-service exam proctor. Sure, he should have been teaching us some French all those years. But we had fun and he was kind, told us about his personal life, treated us like adults, and took us on trips. Can anyone say café klatch? I had only one small problem with Mr. DePass over four years, and I handled that privately. Mr. DePass had a swimming pool that he was obsessed with and always talked about, even telling us the name of the company that had installed it.

One day he was extremely grumpy and passed a misogynistic remark that I didn't care for, and so that weekend I called his home pretending to be from the Beauty Pools Company, said there was a recall of his model under way, and asked what would be a good day for us to come with the backhoe and dig it out.

My senior year of high school was a grim time in my hometown. On September 19, 1982, the newspaper where my uncle Jim had worked his entire career printed the last issue. With the *Buffalo Courier-Express* out of business, a city that had once sold more than six daily newspapers was down to one.

Right before Christmas, Bethlehem Steel, up until then the largest manufacturer in Buffalo, announced that it would permanently shut down almost all steelmaking over the next six months. Not only was this bad news for steelworkers, but also for the local lawyers and merchants who counted on the steel operations for their businesses as well. More department stores closed. Teetering on the brink of bankruptcy were the Buffalo Philharmonic, the Albright-Knox Art Gallery, the Buffalo Museum of Science, and the Buffalo Historical Society. When the American Brass Company announced that it was hiring forty people, ten thousand hopefuls showed up.

The only bright spot was the release of the movie *Flashdance*, giving us all "the feeling" that we could somehow overcome the despair of an industrial town in decline. And of course we could, it was now made clear, by donning leg warmers and a sweatshirt with the neck and bottom cut off.

By the time spring arrived, I was restless and uninterested in academics. I was bored with myself. I'd planted marijuana seeds in the window boxes of the high school office as a small distraction. I had no intention of ever harvesting or smoking it, but simply enjoyed going to sleep at night knowing the school district was watering and caring for this contraband.

Otherwise, I was ditching school and riding my bike to the racetrack most days there wasn't a test, straining every muscle toward the future, just like the horses locked inside the starting gates. Since junior high school I'd always forged my own excuses for the attendance czars. It was just easier. When Dad lived at home, he left early in the morning and Mom slept late, especially if she'd worked all night. Only now I began to get creative: "Laura's ponytail got caught in the toaster," "The moral majority tried to burn down our home last night," "Laura was bitten by a tsetse fly." Sometimes I'd dash off a bad sonnet as an excuse.

While I was at it, I composed a poem for the school anthology that contained a hidden message. My parents weren't aware of my subversive activities, since referrals and notices about parent-teacher conferences still went directly from Dad's mailbox into my wastebasket.

This time the principal called my mother. He said he hoped that in the future I'd use my creativity in a more positive direction (perhaps the way he was planning to retire—by hooking up with a guy and opening a B&B in Vermont). The subtext was that he expected my parents to take his side and punish me.

I showed her the poem from the school anthology.

Impressions

Finally we understand the
Caring and kindness which
You generously offered to
Us.
And so now we appreciate
Each and every special
Teacher who helped cultivate
Our integrity, maturity, and
Excellence.
True, but the ultimate and
Real test now begins
Impressions of nostalgia shouldn't
Hinder every move.
Lovely memories last forever.

Take the first letter of every other word and it reads, "Fuck you, Sweet Home, burn in hell." The irony was that the secret message wouldn't have been discovered had the superintendent not decided to read the stupid thing at our commencement ceremony. Word got out. I was turned in.

My mother said, "I don't know what he thinks I'm supposed to do. You're just one of those kids who will either make a living or wind up in jail."

The principal charged me restitution for the cost of having the page cut out of the book, barred me from receiving a diploma at graduation (it arrived in the mail), and attempted to revoke one of my scholarships. He outlined this in a letter to my parents, but I, of course, intercepted it.

The year wound down and my boyfriend, Rick, took me to the senior prom. However, after going to school with the same crew for most of our lives, we all went together and hung out as a mob.

The most amazing thing about the senior prom was not anything that happened there or afterward, but beforehand. When I put on the dress (mail-ordered from the J. C. Penney catalog) my mother said, "Hell's bells! Aren't you even going to iron it?"

"I just spent an hour and a half at the ironing board," I moaned. I'd fought to the death down there with that miserable old steam iron, the cord eventually wound around my neck and all my fingers scorched.

"You put more wrinkles in than you took out!" declared Mom.

I checked the mirror. Indeed, I looked like a trampled drapery.

"Give it to me!" she barked.

I couldn't believe it. No one had ever seen Mom iron. There were rumors that she'd pressed dresses with accordion pleats back in the sixties, but at some point her motto had become, "If you can't dry it then don't buy it!"

In fifteen minutes the dress was prom-picture perfect. My T-shirt tan line and farmer shoulders lent the outfit a certain *je joue au football*.

I walked the stage at high school graduation in June 1983, on the same day that 3,900 employees were let go from Bethlehem Steel. Of those, 3,400 wouldn't be recalled.

For graduation, Mom gave me a photo album and a raincoat. The gifts suggested that I was embarking upon a life worthy of pictorial documentation if I didn't first die of pneumonia.

It was my dream to attend and study entrepreneurship at the Wharton School of Finance at the University of Pennsylvania. Unfortunately, it was not theirs. I received the thin envelope in the mail, not the fat one containing a catalog of classes and dorm assignment.

My good friend Debbie was heading to the University of Michigan. The application required a one-paragraph essay, as opposed to those of most Ivy League colleges, which demanded two or three full-page essays. So I'd filled it out as my backup. I was accepted, and her parents offered me a ride to Ann Arbor.

As we pulled out of the driveway, my mother warned us to watch out for rabid squirrels. The University of Michigan was well known for many things, but this one I hadn't heard about.

Thirty-Four

When the Chips Are Down, the Buffalo's Empty

In 1983, the Equal Rights Amendment was defeated following a ten-year struggle for ratification. After this Herculean effort failed, the Unitarians were left with thousands of clipboards that they'd find creative ways to recycle.

But there was a bright spot on the horizon. On June 18, 1983, Sally Ride became the first American woman to travel in space. Maybe women could succeed without an amendment, one at a time.

That August, a week before I left my hometown, a group of workers at Bethlehem Steel's Lackawanna plant raised an American flag upside-down—the international distress signal. Buffalo had finally hit rock bottom and would continue to rest there for some time. The city no longer brought to mind great industry or magnificent architecture. It was now a place regularly asking to be declared a federal disaster area in order to buy road salt. The Buffalo Philharmonic Orchestra, constantly teetering on the brink of bankruptcy, would advertise for another city to adopt it.

After arriving in Ann Arbor, it took me three full days to realize that college wasn't going to work out. It had nothing to do with the University of Michigan. Or the numerous squirrels, none of which appeared to be rabid so far. I wouldn't have been happy at any college. It seemed as if there were thousands of students just like me, many a lot smarter, all studying the same boring stuff and listening to the same lectures. It was pretty obvious that success didn't know where I lived and that I'd have to go out and find it.

Compounding the feelings of doubt were concerns about money. Dad was willing to spiral further into debt for me to attend college. However, I knew that he was paying alimony and engaged to be married. Meantime, my mother was finishing her master's degree and still in possession of some hefty unpaid legal bills.

I called around to brokerage firms in Ann Arbor to see about finding a job trading stocks. They all said the same thing: a person has to be twenty-one years old to work buying and selling securities. Recalling my first visit to the floor of the American Stock Exchange three years earlier, I phoned their personnel office from my dorm room. To get an entry-level gig there, all one needed was a high school diploma. And it just so happened that they were hiring!

I went to the guidance office at the University of Michigan and asked about taking a semester off to work on the floor of the stock exchange. They said no. I flew to Manhattan the following week and interviewed for a position on the trading floor. A few weeks later, the stock exchange phoned and offered me a job as a data clerk for $375 per week, which would put me near the poverty line at the time. But it didn't involve shoveling snow.

I rented a car for seventy-five dollars and posted a notice on the ride board to see if anyone needed to go from Ann Arbor to New York. Four people signed up and paid twenty-five dollars each, which left just enough for gas and tolls. Having been raised in a place with a high suicide rate, I eagerly headed for one with a high homicide rate.

When I started working on the trading floor, I had no way of knowing that it was the beginning of the biggest bull market in history, one that would see the Dow Jones rise more than tenfold. I also had no idea how to get to my new job. The third day it rained and I lost my way because the flag wasn't flying out front. After explaining my reason for being late to a supervisor, he said he'd never before heard anyone use the excuse of getting lost, and after being at the exchange for thirty years, he thought he'd heard everything. At the end of each workday, I'd scurry off to nearby New York University to earn my finance degree by taking night classes.

It transpired that my years of independent living, stock trading, and gambling had indeed been the perfect jumble to prepare me for life in the big city and success on the trading floor. The best traders were not Harvard MBAs, but championship bridge, backgammon, chess, and poker players. There were also a considerable number of track junkies and several racehorse owners. Not only that, but a handful of traders had actually been thrown out of casinos all over the world for counting cards in games of blackjack and winning big money off the house.

After working my way up from clerk to trader, combined with the advent of financial instruments known as index options, by age twenty-one, I was a millionaire—most of it made before I was legally old enough to buy, sell, or own a single share of stock. Or have a drink, for that matter. I was also ready for semiretirement, having lost a good chunk of my hearing and seared my throat and vocal cords by becoming one of those screaming lunatics I'd observed with such fascination during my first trip to the floor as a teenager.

Eventually, I had my medical moment in a crowded Manhattan movie theater when an older woman fainted. It was as if Nurse Ellen momentarily possessed my body. Without thinking, I ran over to see if the woman had any medical-alert bracelets or pill bottles, ordered the youthful and bewildered manager to call 9-1-1, and then checked to see if the woman was breathing. She was. By the time I began searching her bag for identification a large crowd had gathered around us. Contrary to popular belief, New Yorkers are not coldhearted pedestrians who casually step over dying moviegoers. All the people in that theater dug into their pockets and purses and helpfully offered all the prescription medications they had with them, which came to about two hundred bottles of beta-blockers, amyl nitrites, antidepressants, eyedrops, and asthma inhalers.

The manager returned and said that an ambulance was on the way. It was a large movie theater, and the rubberneckers were pressing in. The manager suddenly awoke from his trance and asked me if I was a medical professional. "No," I replied. And then I don't know what was going through my mind because I added, "My mother's a nurse."

The manager began pushing the crowd back and officiously shouting, "Stand back everyone! Her mother's a nurse!"

Epilogue

The People's Republic of Buffalo

The Republic Steel plant shut down for good five months after I left Buffalo. Throughout the eighties and nineties, the local population continued to decline, with the city sinking from eighth largest in the country at the beginning of the twentieth century to fifty-ninth at its close. From 1991 to 1994, the Buffalo Bills lost four straight Super Bowls. In June 2003, a control board was imposed by the governor and state legislature to investigate and reorganize the city's finances after an audit revealed a $24 million budget deficit, which ballooned to $100 million by 2005, and an advisory board was added.

In the last two decades, however, Buffalo's economy has been lifted from despair by an influx of high-tech companies and white-collar industries, such as healthcare and financial services. Perhaps as a result of decades of economic distress, the locals have become proficient at debt collection, with over one hundred such agencies now operating in the area. And what was just a small, local airport when I left in the early eighties is now the Buffalo International Airport, either as a result of offering regular flights to nearby Toronto, or because flocks of Canada geese fly overhead twice a year.

The city itself remains an ethnically rich community, with accompanying street festivals every weekend in the warm weather. It continues to be a melting pot of Irish, Italian, British, German, Greek, Slavic, Jewish, Native American, Polish, and dozens of other cultures. In fact, nearby Lackawanna was discovered to have its very own Yemeni American terrorist cell providing material support to al Qaeda in 2002.

"Like a dowager in decline, Buffalo still has good bone structure to remind people of her more prosperous and glamorous days," wrote R. W. Apple Jr. of *The New York Times*. "Buffalo has an even longer history of architectural distinction than Chicago; you could do worse than take it as a textbook for a course in modern American buildings." Indeed, it was home to some of the country's first skyscrapers and outstanding buildings, such as the Art Deco City Hall and Shea's Theater. Five local residences were designed by master architect Frank Lloyd Wright: Barton House, the Gardner's Cottage, Heath House, Davidson House, and the crown jewel, the prairie-style Darwin D. Martin House, with its wide terraces and overhanging roofs. In 1938, the famous father-son team Eliel and Eero Saarinen designed Kleinhans Music Hall, a major work of modern architecture still renowned for its acoustic excellence and home to the Buffalo Philharmonic Orchestra.

Buffalo is ranked among the top twenty-five arts and entertainment communities in the country by *Places Rated Almanac*. It has a vibrant and diverse music scene. Major concert venues routinely bring jazz, chamber music, rock, blues, folk, country, bluegrass, musical theater, and world music to town. Meantime, a homegrown alternative-rock scene has produced acts as varied as the Goo Goo Dolls, 10,000 Maniacs, and Ani DiFranco. DiFranco runs her music label, Righteous Babe, from Buffalo and is active in the preservation of local architecture.

Lake Erie is no longer a repository for industrial waste and sewage runoff. Fishermen, kayakers, and swimmers enjoy the clean water, which is once again home to walleye, bass, trout, lily pads, bald eagles, and great blue herons.

Despite being better known for having double the country's unemployment level and triple the snowfall, Buffalo has earned the designation The City of Good Neighbors, where small-town values prevail over city-slicker anonymity. Meet anyone from Buffalo at a party and within minutes you'll come up with a list of people you both know. Six degrees of separation can usually be pared down to one or two at the most. Many will say that describing the Buffalo area as "a big small town" isn't reduction enough, and that it's actually one big living room. People talk to strangers, and one can easily wake to find the front walk shoveled, no note. A four-way stop results in a massive round of waving—"No, you go!" Citizens keep an eye out for those who live alone, and a stranger is just a friend with jumper cables you haven't met yet. A wedding wouldn't be a wedding without the hokey pokey and the chicken dance. And the management at the Holiday Valley ski lodge doesn't frown upon people bringing along their own Crock-Pots for a home-cooked meal; they've installed extra outlets so that hungry skiers can enjoy their own three-alarm chili.

The locals, of course, remain loyal to their Buffalo Bills football team in victory and, more often, defeat. In subzero weather it's always possible to see middle-aged men cheering from ice-encrusted bleachers, their shirts off and "Steelers Suck" painted across their chests. To these enthusiasts, the four seasons aren't winter, spring, summer, and fall, but preseason, regular season, postseason, and off-season. When the Bills win, many people think it's quite acceptable to take the following Monday off work. In fact, Buffalonians are such colossal sports fans that they have not one, but two large sports stadiums in the heart of downtown.

Regardless of gray skies, it's a city of good cheer, where when it rains, people are likely to say, "It could be snow." When it snows, they say, "It could be a blizzard." And when it's a blizzard and the vast whiteness eventually covers the rooftops and thereby provides free insulation, they say, "Now we can turn down the thermostat and save some money on heat." Buffalonians are, by nature, optimists. How else could so many people install unheated outdoor swimming pools that remain covered with tarpaulin nine months of the year?

Canada is a short hop away on the Tim Hortons trail. Stratford and Niagara-on-the-Lake have theater that's as good if not better than Broadway or London's West End. The big difference between Canadians and Americans is that Canadians have a lot more guns, only they tend not to use them on one another. And perhaps the cuisine is not yet entirely fleshed out—the country being best known for Canadian bacon and Tylenol with codeine, at least back when I was growing up. No, you've never heard anyone say, "Hey, let's go out for Canadian food!"

Meantime, weather records continue to be broken. On October 2, 2003, Buffalo was on the national news for having the earliest snowfall. But because winters are a varsity sport, in this friendly city everyone's on the team. A freak blizzard struck in October 2006, while the leaves were still on the trees. It left the area without power for days and killed almost half the trees. Professionals and volunteers headed out with chain saws, and a massive replanting is under way.

Buffalo earned the nickname Barfalo because of its numerous bars, most with a last call of 4:00 AM. Such conviviality has resulted in one of the highest gonorrhea rates in the country. Though with a house of worship on almost every corner, generating a church-to-bar ratio of about one to one, it could be argued that they cancel each other out. Still, the area is a wholesome place to raise children. It's so cold outside that rather than open their trench coats, flashers just describe themselves. And people trying to smoke outdoors in wintertime can't tell when they're finished exhaling.

Since the invention of air-conditioning, the inspired citizenry has gone on to create the pacemaker, nondairy creamer, the Moog synthesizer, and, most importantly, the technology to put the *M* on M&Ms. Though the most celebrated development would have to be that of the buffalo wing, which everyone knows is the best part of a buffalo. According to local lore, these were invented at Frank and Teressa Bellissimo's Anchor Bar back in 1964. Mrs. Bellissimo made a late-night snack for her son and some friends with the ingredients on hand, which included chicken wings and hot sauce. When ordering the extra-hot variety I'd highly recommend keeping the toilet paper in the fridge.

Another Buffalo specialty is beef on weck—roast beef sandwiches slathered with horseradish and served on kummelweck. The distinguishing feature of these rolls is the caraway seeds and snowball-sized chunks of salt dotting the outside, which one assumes can be put to good use if a car gets stuck on the way home from a tailgate party.

I think what the city needs for completing its big comeback is to be the focus of one of these charming travel narratives like *My House in Umbria, A Year in Provence,* and *Under the Tuscan Sun,* so as to spark a flood of tourism. I've taken it upon myself to write one called *My Split-Level in Lackawanna.* I don't want to ruin it, but basically a single woman from a lovely and quaint Italian or French village sets about refurbishing a house just south of Buffalo, along the cheery shores of Lake Erie, in the dramatic shadow of the rusting Bethlehem Steel plant, aka The Buffalo Riviera. At the beginning, she argues with the man next door, a former union machinist who now runs a failing Sheetrock business. Then one night, she's frightened by the appearance of Good & Plenty–sized silverfish, and this outwardly gruff but secretly bighearted neighbor comes to the rescue with a barrel of strong pesticide he found buried at a construction site. The two end up falling in love. Only, they don't marry, because it would mean receiving less public-assistance money. Perhaps the obligatory quirky neighbor will be a Mafia don who loves gardening and bowls a perfect three hundred. Since Buffalo has no shortage of character and characters, the possibilities are endless. And as they say, the only difference between comedy and tragedy is where you end the story.

About the Author

© Denise Winters

Laura Pedersen was the youngest columnist for *The New York Times* and, prior to that, the youngest person to have a seat on the American Stock Exchange. She has a finance degree from New York University's Stern School of Business. Her nonfiction book *Play Money*, about working on Wall Street, became a best seller. In 1994, President Clinton honored Pedersen as one of Ten Outstanding Young Americans.

Pedersen's first novel, *Going Away Party*, won the Three Oaks Prize for Fiction. Her short stories and humorous essays have won numerous awards and have been published in literary journals and magazines. Her second novel, *Beginner's Luck*, was selected by Barnes & Noble for its Discover Great New Writers program, by Borders for its Original Voices program, and by the Literary Guild as an alternate selection.

She has appeared on CNN, *The Oprah Winfrey Show*, *Good Morning America*, *Primetime Live*, *The Today Show*, and *The Late Show with David Letterman*. She has also performed stand-up comedy at the Improv, among other clubs, and writes material for several well-known comedians. Pedersen lives in New York City and teaches at the Booker T. Washington Learning Center in East Harlem.

More information can be found at www.LauraPedersenBooks.com.

ENVIRONMENTAL BENEFITS STATEMENT

Fulcrum Publishing saved the following resources by printing the pages of this book on chlorine free paper made with 100% post-consumer waste.

TREES	WATER	ENERGY	SOLID WASTE	GREENHOUSE GASES
31	**11,367**	**22**	**1,460**	**2,738**
FULLY GROWN	GALLONS	MILLION BTUs	POUNDS	POUNDS

Calculations based on research by Environmental Defense and the Paper Task Force.
Manufactured at Friesens Corporation